The Holy City

Jerusalem in the Theology of the Old Testament

Leslie J. Hoppe, O.F.M.

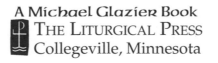

A Michael Glazier Book

THE LITURGICAL PRESS
Collegeville, Minnesota

A Michael Glazier book published by The Liturgical Press

Cover design by Ann Blattner. Detail of the city of Jerusalem and Temple area in A.D. 66, as shown in a model at the Holyland Hotel, Jerusalem. Photo by Robin Pierzina O.S.B.

1   2   3   4   5   6   7   8

Library of Congress Cataloging-in-Publication Data

Hoppe, Leslie J.
     The Holy City : Jerusalem in the theology of the Old Testament /
     Leslie J. Hoppe.
          p. cm.
     Includes bibliographical references and index.
     ISBN 0-8146-5081-3 (alk. paper)
     1. Jerusalem in the Bible. 2. Bible. O.T.—Theology. I. Title.

BS1199.J38 H67 2000
263'042569442—dc21

00-021486

Contents

1

Jerusalem, the Holy City

Jerusalem is unique among the world's "holy cities" because it is sacred to three major religions: Judaism, Christianity, and Islam. These religions have their shrines in this city. Their pilgrims come to pray at these shrines because many of their most sacred memories center on this one city. This has proven to be a heavy burden for the city to bear. Each of these religious traditions is an heir to the religion of ancient Israel. The Scriptures inspired by ancient Israel's priests, prophets, and sages provide the foundation for the status of Jerusalem in today's three monotheistic religions. A study of ancient Israel's sacred literature on the topic of Jerusalem, then, cannot be simply a speculative exercise. It is a subject of immediate relevance to millions of believers. A survey of what Judaism, Christianity, and Islam believe about Jerusalem is the way a study of the biblical traditions about the Holy City must begin.

Judaism

It is impossible to overestimate the significance of Jerusalem for Judaism. No matter where they live, Jews pray toward Jerusalem—a rabbinic tradition that has its inspiration in the Bible (see 1 Kgs 8:48; Dan 6:12). Three times a day religious Jews pray that God and they may dwell in Jerusalem (M. *Berakoth* 4:1). Jews in the Diaspora pray each year at the end of Yom Kippur and the Passover: "Next year in Jerusalem." Philo, a first-century Jewish philosopher who lived in Alexandria, called it the "holy city" for Jews of the whole world—not only for those living in Palestine (*Legatio ad Gaium,* 225, 281). Yearning for the restoration and the rebuilding of Jerusalem's Temple became the most common way religious

Jews have expressed their hope for future redemption. The attachment of Judaism to the land of Israel became concentrated on Jerusalem, as the liturgy of the synagogue makes clear in several of the *Eighteen Benedictions:*

Benediction 14

Be merciful, O Lord our God, in your great mercy, toward Israel your people, and toward Jerusalem your city, and toward Zion the abiding place of your glory, and toward your Temple and your dwelling, and toward the kingdom of the house of David, your righteous one. Blessed are you, O Lord God of David, the builder of Jerusalem.

Benediction 16

Accept (us), O Lord our God, and dwell in Zion; and may your servants serve you in Jerusalem. Blessed are you, O Lord, whom in reverent fear we worship.

Benediction 18

Bestow your peace upon Israel your people and upon your city (Jerusalem) and upon your inheritance, and bless us, all of us together. Blessed are you, O Lord, who makes peace.

While the centrality of Jerusalem and its Temple in early Judaism can explain this attachment to the city, two great disasters befell the Jewish people of Roman Palestine, which had the potential of ending the relationship between the Jews and Jerusalem. The first was the destruction of the Temple in A.D. 70 following an unsuccessful revolt against Rome. The loss of the Temple was a catastrophe for early Judaism, since temple worship was among its three fundamental expressions:

Simon the Just . . . used to say: By three things is the world sustained: by the Law, by the [temple-] service, and by deeds of loving-kindness (*Pirke Avot* 1:2).

Since the rituals of the Temple ensured the fertility of the land, some rabbis believed that the cessation of sacrifices meant the rains would cease and the land would be barren (*Avot of R. Nathan* 1:4). The Temple served not only as a setting for the collective worship that assured the fertility of the land; it also was essential for the religious life of the individual. The Temple of Jerusalem was the only place where the sacrifices necessary for the atonement of sin could be offered. Finally, the Temple was the setting for the annual pilgrimages mandated in the Torah (Deut 16:1-17). The pious believed that after the destruction of the Temple, all that remained for them was to live as mourners until Jerusalem's restoration. The hope of seeing the Temple rebuilt became a central component of Jewish religious consciousness.

Another disaster followed the unsuccessful conclusion to the second revolt against Rome in A.D. 135. When the revolt began three years earlier, Bar Kochba, its leader, expelled all Gentiles from Jerusalem. When the Romans regained control of the city, they returned the favor. Jerusalem now became a Roman colony with a new name, Aelia Capitolina. Jews were forbidden to live in or near it.[1] Jerusalem became a Roman city, its Jewish character suppressed. When the empire became Christian, the policy forbidding Jews to live in Jerusalem remained in force. An exception was made for the Ninth of Ab, the date on which Jews remembered the fall of Jerusalem and the destruction of its Temple.[2] For a fee, the Christians allowed Jews to assemble on the Mount of Olives and to look down onto the site of the Temple and lament its fate.[3] This act of cruelty was intended to reinforce Jewish acknowledgment of the empire's power. Constantine the Great changed Jerusalem's character again. It became a Christian city.

At the insistence of the empress Eudocia, the ban on Jewish presence in Jerusalem was lifted in 438.[4] One effect was a massive pilgrimage for Sukkot, the fall pilgrimage festival (see Lev 23:33-43; Deut 17:13-15).

1. This does not mean that Jewish presence in Jerusalem was totally eliminated. Michael Avi-Yonah provides evidence of Jewish presence in the city despite the Roman prohibition. See *Jews of Palestine,* 79–81. Still, many Jews left for Egypt and Syria after the second revolt failed. The result was that, for the first time, Jews were a minority in Palestine, comprising just one-third of the population. By the third century, the Jews comprised only one-fifth of the population. Jews continued to leave Palestine because of political and economic problems. The decline continued until Jewish population in Palestine leveled off at 9 percent. See Avi-Yonah, *Jews of Palestine,* 132–3, 241. The precise population of Palestine in the second century can only be estimated. John Wilkinson suggests about two million. See his "Jerusalem under Rome and Byzantium 63 BC–637 AD," *Jerusalem in History,* ed. K. J. Asali (Brooklyn: Olive Branch Press, 1990) 96.

2. Ab is the fifth month of the Jewish calendar. It can begin as early as July 8 and end as late as September 5. The Ninth of Ab became a day of fasting when Jews annually recalled the destruction of Jerusalem.

3. Eusebius, *The Life of Constantine,* 591.5.

4. Eudocia was the wife of Emperor Theodosius. In 438 she made a pilgrimage to Jerusalem in fulfillment of a vow. Her love for the city led to a spate of building projects in the city under her patronage. She had a falling out with her husband and returned to Jerusalem in 443. She continued to live there in exile from the court at Constantinople until her death in 460.

Thousands of Jews from both Palestine and the Diaspora came, hoping to witness Jerusalem's redemption. Enraged by the large number of Jews who came to the city, Christian monks stoned them as they were processing in the temple area, killing several. Though Eudocia wanted those guilty of this crime punished, even her influence was not enough to ensure justice. A trial before the imperial legate concluded that the murdered Jews died of "natural causes," since witnesses testified that the stones that killed them fell from the heavens. The pilgrimage of Jews from both Palestine and the Diaspora, which so angered the Christians, shows the strong Jewish attachment to Jerusalem despite an almost three-hundred-year forced absence from the city.

Though Jews were once again forbidden access to Jerusalem, they found other ways to express their devotion to it. For example, the rabbis studied laws that applied to Jerusalem with special attention. Because Jerusalem was the site of the Temple, early rabbinic law treated Jerusalem differently from other cities.[5] The rabbis instructed their people not to forget Jerusalem or its sad state. For example, one practice required by the rabbis was to leave a small area unfinished when whitewashing a house—in remembrance of Jerusalem (*Tosefta Sotah* 15:12-14).

Another tack taken in the rabbinic tradition to express continuing devotion to this city in which Jews were forbidden to live was to be extravagant in praising Jerusalem. According to the rabbis no city could be as beautiful as Jerusalem (*Avot R. Nathan* 28, 85), so a person who has never seen Jerusalem has never seen a beautiful city (*Sukkah* 51b). The often-quoted Talmudic dictum asserts that God gave ten measures of beauty to the world: nine were taken by Jerusalem and one was left for the rest of the world (*Kiddushin* 49b). The rabbinic tradition bestows seventy names on Jerusalem, illustrating its perfection.[6] The rabbis looked back to the days when Jerusalem was a Jewish city and lionized its citizens. Jerusalemites had such wisdom that even the Athenians were impressed (*Lam. R.* 1:1, nos. 4–14). God blessed the people from Jerusalem with physical beauty, which made them sought after as marriage partners (*Lam R.* 1:2, no. 2). Also, they were skilled at interpreting the Torah and reliable in business affairs (*Shabbat* 120a).

The rabbis also began to mythologize the city beyond its biblical portrait. For example, the foundation stone on the Temple Mount was the place where the creation of the world began:

---

5. The special status of Jerusalem according to the rabbis of the second century A.D. has been preserved in four different versions: *Baba Kama* 82b; *Tosefta Negai'im* 6:2; *Avot R. Nathan* A35 and B39.

6. Finkel, "Jerusalem in Biblical and Theological Tradition," 141, no. 6.

And it (the stone) was called *shethiyah* (foundation): A Tanna taught: (It was so called) because from it the world was founded (*Yoma* 54a).

At the beginning of time God created a shrine in Jerusalem in which God prayed: "May my children do my will that I shall not destroy my house and my sanctuary" (*Midrash Psalm* 76:3). Adam offered sacrifice on the great altar of Jerusalem (*Genesis Rabbah* 34:9). Jerusalem became the site of Adam's creation, the place where Cain and Abel offered their sacrifices, where Noah thanked God after the flood, the site where Abraham offered a tithe to Melchizedek, and where the sacrifice of Isaac was to take place (*Genesis Rabbah* 22:7; Maimonides, *Mishnah Torah,* Bet Haberhirah 2:2). One rabbi compared the world to the human eye: "The white of the eye is the ocean which surrounds the whole world; the iris is the inhabited land; the pupil is Jerusalem."[7]

Nowhere is Jewish devotion to Jerusalem clearer than in prayer. Prayers for the restoration of Jerusalem and its Temple are an essential component of Jewish worship. On Friday evening as the sun is setting, the synagogue welcomes the Sabbath with the hymn *Lekhah Dodi.* Six of the song's nine stanzas speak of a longing for Jerusalem. The religious Jew remembers Jerusalem and prays for its restoration at every meal. Part of that grace specifically prays for the city's redemption:

> O Lord our God, have pity on your people Israel, on your city Jerusalem, on Zion the place of your glory. . . . Rebuild Jerusalem, the holy city, speedily in our day. Blessed are you, Lord, who in mercy will rebuild Jerusalem.

The Jewish wedding service concludes with a prayer for Jerusalem:

> May she who was barren (Jerusalem) be exceeding glad and exult, when her children are gathered within her in joy. Blessed are you, O Lord, who makes Zion joyful through her children.

In Jerusalem today there are not many monuments to ancient Judaism. The obvious exception is the Western Wall. While the pious come to lament the destruction of the Temple, they also pray for the city's redemption. Jerusalem, then, is not so much a city of the past for contemporary Judaism as it is a city of promise. Jerusalem directs believers toward the future. One early rabbinic tradition held that earthly Jerusalem would rise upward until it reached the place of God's throne. Another envisioned God as commanding Mount Sinai, Mount Tabor, and Mount Carmel to come

7. Michael Higger, ed. and trans., *Masekhot Derekh Eretz,* (New York: Hotsaat, 1935) 7:38.

to Jerusalem and rest on Mount Zion. The new temple would rise on their combined summit. The ancient rabbis associated the manifestation of God's rule in this world with the coming of the Messiah and the redemption of Jerusalem, when Zion would be the center of God's rule on earth, as envisioned by the prophets.[8]

Jerusalem has existed for five thousand years. It was destroyed and rebuilt seventeen times. The city, however, has a significance that the historian and archaeologist cannot describe, given the limitations of their disciplines. The centrality of Jerusalem to Judaism is so strong that even secular Jews express their devotion and attachment to the city and cannot conceive of the modern State of Israel without it. Outside of the Western Wall, Judaism boasts of no great shrines in the city. Jerusalem is not sacred to Judaism because of shrines celebrating Judaism's past. For Jews Jerusalem is sacred simply because it exists. The Jewish shrines and monuments in the city are its streets and lanes, its walls and gates, its synagogues, homes, and schools, its theaters, museums, and shops—and above all, its people. Though Jerusalem's sacred character goes back three millennia, its sacred character in Judaism today depends on the promise that it holds for the future of the Jewish people.

Christianity

The place of Jerusalem in Christian thought and piety reflects the pattern of continuity and discontinuity that characterizes the whole of Christianity's relationship with early Judaism. The recognition of Jerusalem as a holy city is part of Christianity's heritage from the religion of ancient Israel, whose Scriptures it accepts as normative for its life and faith. The New Testament, Christianity's distinctive Scriptures, offers still another basis for the city's holiness: Jerusalem is the place where Jesus lived, died, rose from the dead, and ascended into heaven. Believers in Jesus Christ have lived in Jerusalem from the very beginnings of the Christian movement. They have built shrines over the places in the city that have a special connection with Jesus, but they have found it difficult to live in peace with the others who consider Jerusalem holy—Jews and Muslims. Sometimes Christians have been the perpetrators of intolerance, and other times they have been the victims. Of the three Abrahamic faiths, Christianity is the only one that does not mandate some form of pilgrimage; yet since the

8. Though some scholars hold that the early rabbis believed Galilee to be the place of eschatological events, W. D. Davies holds that careful consideration of the data leads to the conclusion that the rabbis believed that only Jerusalem could be the place of God's final manifestation in Israel's life. See his *Gospel and the Land*, 233–5, 426.

fourth century Christians have been frequent, devout, and enthusiastic pilgrims to Jerusalem and the rest of the Holy Land. The significance of Jerusalem for the Christian faith is complex. Jerusalem is where Christianity's theology, piety, and history mix, creating something that has proven to be vital, inspiring, and sometimes dangerous.

The Gospels agree that Jesus was a Galilean, as were most of his followers. The Synoptic Gospels locate the bulk of Jesus' activity in Galilee and have him make just one trip to Jerusalem as an adult. He spends only five days in the city before he is arrested, tried, and executed. In the Fourth Gospel, Galilee and Jerusalem are both hubs for Jesus' activity. He makes several trips from Galilee to Jerusalem (John 2:13; 5:1; 7:10; 12:12). Still, Jerusalem does not have a significant place in the preaching of Jesus in any of the Gospels. Apart from the predictions of his death, Jesus rarely mentions Jerusalem when he speaks to the people. In the Sermon on the Mount Jesus forbids the taking of oaths "by Jerusalem" (Matt 5:35). The parable of the Good Samaritan begins with the note that a man was attacked by robbers "as he went down from Jerusalem to Jericho" (Luke 10:30). Though Jesus does not mention Jerusalem explicitly when referring to the accident that killed eighteen people when "the tower at Siloam" fell on them, the location of this tower was in Jerusalem (Luke 13:4).

When Mark has Jesus predict his passion, Jesus does not mention Jerusalem as the setting for the fulfillment of his prophecy (see 8:31; 9:31; 10:33-34). The literary context of the third prediction, however, makes it clear that Jesus' passion was to take place in Jerusalem (10:32). Luke too does not have Jesus mention that place of his suffering and death except in the final prediction (9:22, 44-45; 18:31). Matthew does mention the name of the city in two predictions, in 16:21 and 20:18. The sayings in Matt 23:37-39 and Luke 13:33-34 in which Jesus laments over Jerusalem and asserts that "it is impossible that a prophet should die outside of Jerusalem" are variations of the passion-prediction motif. Jesus implies that he is going to accept the prophet's death himself and that the city will bear the guilt of having rejected another prophet sent to it.

Mark's attitude toward Jerusalem is ambiguous. He gives no significant role to the city except for the passion story. The people of Jerusalem respond to the preaching of the Baptist and Jesus (1:5; 3:8), yet the city is the home of Jesus' critics (3:22; 7:1-23). Matthew's narrative is less ambiguous. The reaction of Jerusalem to the appearance of the Magi inquiring about "the newborn king of the Jews" (2:1-4) is a harbinger of the city's reaction when the adult Jesus entered its gates to the acclamations of his followers. Matthew comments that after witnessing Jesus' entry, "the whole city was shaken" (21:10). A few days later the Jerusalemites called for Jesus' execution.

Except for the note in 4:25, Matthew portrays the response of Jerusalem to Jesus as negative. Jesus returns the favor by condemning the city implicitly in 22:7 and explicitly in 23:37-38. It will not be until the Second Coming that Jerusalem will greet Jesus appropriately (23:39).

It is a commonplace of New Testament interpretation that Luke gives Jerusalem a pivotal theological role in both his Gospel and the Acts of the Apostles.[9] Jerusalem sets the scene for the beginning (1:9) and the end (24:53) of the Third Gospel. Like the other Synoptics, Luke has Jesus make only one journey to Jerusalem, but the travel account that narrates Jesus' journey from Galilee to Jerusalem (9:51–19:27) contains most of the material unique to Luke. Among this material, however, is Jesus' prophecy concerning the destruction of Jerusalem (19:43-44), which is reminiscent of the prophetic critique of the city (see Isa 29:3; Jer 6:6; Ezek 4:2).[10] Finally, Luke places all of Jesus' post-resurrection appearances to the disciples in Jerusalem, while Matthew (28:16) and Mark (16:7) have the risen Jesus return to Galilee.

Jerusalem links Luke's Gospel to the Acts of the Apostles (Luke 24:47; Acts 1:8). The disciples received the Spirit in Jerusalem during Pentecost (2:1-47), and from the city they go to the ends of the earth to proclaim the gospel. While Luke gives Jerusalem great significance for the early Church (8:14-16; 11:1-18; 15:1-35), Stephen's speech in Acts 7 is among the most negative biblical passages condemning the worship that took place in Jerusalem's Temple (6:11-15; 7:48). Luke's attitude toward Jerusalem, like that of Mark, is ambiguous. Jesus comes to the city to complete his work, and from the city the gospel goes to the rest of the world. Still, Jerusalem is the setting for what Luke regards as worship that is displeasing to God. For Luke the new Israel has its beginnings in Jerusalem but then moves beyond it. The old Israel continues to abide in the city and offer its worship in its Temple, while the new Israel has taken the gospel from Jerusalem to "the ends of the earth" (see Acts 1:8; 13:47).

Jerusalem is important for the Fourth Gospel because it is the place where Jesus manifests his glory in his passion and resurrection. Still, it remains only the setting for Jesus' glorification. The city as such plays no significant role in John. In the conversation with the woman at the well Jesus asserts that in the future Jerusalem would be stripped of any special status as a place of worship (4:20-21). Various places in the city provide the setting for Jesus' activity. He heals a lame man at the pool of Bethesda (5:2). Another healing takes place at the pool of Siloam (9:7). Jesus preaches

---

9. Joseph A. Fitzmyer, *Luke 1–9*, AB, 28 (New York: Doubleday, 1981) 163–9.
10. King, "Jerusalem" *ABD* 3:764.

in the Temple (7:14), and he finds shelter in the homes of friends in nearby Bethany (11:18). Though John describes Jesus' triumphal entry into Jerusalem a few days before his execution (12:12-13), he does not have Jesus speak to the people of Jerusalem during those final days. Jesus' final discourses are for the disciples alone (13–17). The author of the Fourth Gospel does not even mention Jerusalem during the passion story, though it is obvious that the last days of Jesus' life take place in the city.

The first Christians believed that Jesus of Nazareth was the Messiah and that his life, ministry, and death fulfilled the prophecies about the messianic age. Though early Judaism showed a marked diversity in its messianic and eschatological speculations, there was one element that was common to most, if not all, of the Jewish visions of the future: the land. Jewish hopes for the future centered around something concrete and tangible: the reconstitution of Israel in its land, the return of the exiles, the reestablishment of Jewish rule over the land, and peace and prosperity in that land. Of course, Jerusalem as the site of the Temple and the capital of the former Judahite kingdom was an essential component of Jewish hopes for the future.

Christians had to justify their belief that Jesus was the Messiah, though he did not fulfill the expectations about the Jewish people in their land. The New Testament does not ignore this failure; it calls attention to it explicitly. Luke has the disciples ask Jesus after the resurrection: "Lord, are you at this time going to restore the kingdom to Israel?" (Acts 1:6). Jesus asserts that the time for the restoration is still in the future: "It is not for you to know the times or seasons that the Father has established by his own authority" (Acts 1:7). Another tack taken by the New Testament in dealing with the dilemma caused by its faith in Jesus as the Messiah is to abandon expectations for a messianic fulfillment in this world in favor of a fulfillment that can be a reality only in the "world to come." Focusing on a this-worldly Messiah ignores the spiritual reality of Jesus as the fulfillment of messianic prophecies.

Early Christian theologians and apologists found several New Testament texts helpful as they tried to redirect messianic expectations to a spiritual level:

> Hagar represents Sinai, a mountain in Arabia; it corresponds to the present Jerusalem, for she is in slavery along with her children. But the Jerusalem above is freeborn, and she is our mother (Gal 4:25-26).

Paul takes the image of "Jerusalem above" from the apocalyptic strain of early Judaism. Apocalyptic visionaries had little confidence in human potential and little hope for a better future in this world. They were looking for a new world and a new age. These would witness the final triumph of divine justice. Paul compares those who expect salvation to come through the Torah to the "present Jerusalem." Those who have been saved through faith in Jesus Christ are children of the "Jerusalem above." The point of Paul's argument is that God's final saving act in Israel's life is not something that is coming in an indefinite future. It has come already through Jesus. One effect of Paul's metaphors is to devalue the city of Jerusalem in the eyes of some readers.

Like Paul, the author of Hebrews contrasts the justification that comes through Jesus with those described in the Hebrew Bible:

> [Y]ou have approached Mount Zion and the city of the living God, the heavenly Jerusalem, and countless angels in festal gathering, and the assembly of the firstborn enrolled in heaven, and God the judge of all, and the spirits of the just made perfect, and Jesus, the mediator of a new covenant, and the sprinkled blood that speaks more eloquently than that of Abel (Heb 12:22-24).

In 13:14 the author affirms that Christians have no lasting city on earth, but the heavenly Jerusalem is not just the goal of Christian pilgrims on the way to the world to come. Believers have already arrived at the heavenly Jerusalem. It is significant that this heavenly city bears the name Jerusalem.

The book of Revelation presents a portrait of the new Jerusalem coming down to earth from heaven at the end of this age:

> The victor I will make into a pillar in the temple of my God, and he will never leave it again. On him I will inscribe the name of my God and the name of the city of my God, the new Jerusalem, which comes down out of heaven from my God, as well as my new name (Rev 3:12).

Those who are faithful to their Christian commitment will be citizens of the new Jerusalem, which will appear as a bride arrayed for her husband (Rev 21:2). Life in that city, which has come down from God, will mean the restoration of paradise (Rev 22:1-5). In the new Jerusalem, there will be no need for a temple, since God and the Lamb will be immediately accessible (Rev 21:22). The rabbis, too, envisioned a new Jerusalem, which they called "Jerusalem which is above" to distinguish it from "Jerusalem which is below." According to rabbinic tradition, there is a temple in the Jerusalem above. Every time the high priest enters the temple in "Jerusalem below" to offer sacrifice, the archangel Michael does the same in the temple above. Still, for the rabbis, the way to enter the temple above is through the temple below.[11]

---

11. *Taanith* 5a. Early Syriac Christians believed that the earthly Jerusalem was an

While both Jewish and Christian traditions envisioned a new or heavenly Jerusalem along with the Jerusalem of this world, they differed on the relationship between the two. Rabbi Yohanan represents the Jewish view, which saw an intimate connection between the two. One could arrive at the Jerusalem above only by passing through the Jerusalem below. Christian theologians began to allegorize and spiritualize biblical references to Jerusalem. Impetus for this spiritualization came, in part, from several New Testament texts that speak of a "Jerusalem above," a "heavenly Jerusalem," and a "new Jerusalem." When biblical texts that mention Jerusalem are allegorized, the city comes to represent a spiritual reality that has little to do with the historical, political, and social reality that is the city of Jerusalem.

These differences in theological perspective had significant effects in the political sphere. Since the allegorizing stripped the city of its significance, Jewish claims on that city became irrelevant. It became so much easier for Christians to countenance the imperial policy that did not allow Jews to live in the city. From a Christian perspective, Jewish claims to Jerusalem were based on biblical references that were not properly understood. The Old Testament texts that mention Jerusalem were actually speaking of a spiritual reality, not the city of Jerusalem, which the Jews were trying to reclaim for themselves. Eusebius went so far as to claim that the purpose of Christian pilgrimage to Jerusalem was to see firsthand the devastation that he believed was foretold by the prophets (*Demonsratio evangelica* 6.18; 288d). The devastation of the city pointed to the futility of Jewish claims on the city and the significance of the new and heavenly Jerusalem.

This negative attitude of Christians toward Jerusalem changed abruptly when the tomb of Christ was discovered in the city.[12] This discovery gave new value to Jerusalem in the eyes of many Christians. It became a "holy place" for believers. The tomb of Jesus was a visible, tangible connection with the events of Jesus' life and death. It was inevitable that a faith founded on the belief that God became flesh would sanctify the places where God in human flesh lived, died, and rose. Also, the tomb of Christ became a witness to the truth of the Christian proclamation. Though there were some pilgrims who came to Jerusalem before Constantine,[13] the finding of

---

image of the heavenly Jerusalem and therefore encouraged pilgrimages to Jerusalem. See Fiey, "Le pèlerinage des Nestoriens et Jacobites à Jérusalem," 113–26.

12. Eusebius describes the discovery of Christ's tomb and the building of the Church of the Anastasis (Resurrection) to honor this holy place in his *Life of Constantine* 3:28.

13. Both Eusebius and Jerome speak about pre-Constantinian pilgrims to Jerusalem. See Wilken, *The Land Called Holy,* 84.

Christ's tomb and the building of the Church of the Resurrection over it brought in a flood of Christian pilgrims to Jerusalem. These pilgrims—not the Church's theologians—gave Jerusalem the status it has come to have among Christian people through the ages. Pilgrims turned Jerusalem into a "holy city" for Christianity.

In just a few years after the discovery of Jesus' tomb Gregory of Nyssa thought it necessary to remind Christians that pilgrimage to Jerusalem was *not* a requirement for salvation (*Epistle* 2). Pilgrimage was a significant part of Greco-Roman religion, from which Christianity received most of its converts, so it was almost inevitable that Christians too would adopt the practice of pilgrimage, since it provided believers with a tangible experience of holiness. It offered them the opportunity to touch the holy. The lure of such a prospect was too great and could not be replaced by a spiritual concept of a heavenly Jerusalem, especially when one could actually walk down the streets of the earthly Jerusalem and pray at the tomb that sheltered Christ's body before his resurrection.

It is not necessary to speculate about the effects of visits to the Holy Places on the lives of believers. Several early pilgrims left behind diaries containing not only their itineraries but also their emotions on seeing the Holy Places. The oldest diary is the work of an anonymous pilgrim from Bordeaux who traveled from Gaul to Palestine by land in 333. His diary contains little more than terse notions about sites he visited. It is clear that the pilgrim valued the opportunity to visit places associated not only with Jesus but also with events narrated in the Old Testament. The late fourth century witnessed the visit of a Spanish woman named Egeria, who left a remarkably full account of her pilgrimage.[14] It is clear that Egeria wanted to see with her own eyes the places where the events narrated in the Bible took place. She wrote that whenever she visited a site she read the biblical passages associated with that site. The longest section of her diary deals with Jerusalem. When writing about her experiences in the city, Egeria does more than describe the Holy Places but writes extensively about the liturgy celebrated in the churches of Jerusalem. She notes that the liturgy celebrated at the shrine-churches was always relevant to the event commemorated there. Egeria and the other pilgrims testify to the Christianization of Jerusalem.

Christian pilgrimage to the Holy Land and Jerusalem did not wane even after the Arabs took control of Palestine. They allowed Christians to come on pilgrimage, but they had to pay a special tax for the privilege.

---

14. The text of the Bordeaux pilgrim's diary and that of Egeria are found in Wilkinson, *Egeria's Travels to the Holy Land.*

That changed abruptly during the reign of Hakim (985–1021), an eccentric and cruel ruler. He decided that all his Christian, Jewish, and Sunni Muslim subjects were to convert to Shiʾite Islam. In 1009 he ended all pilgrimages to the Holy Land and ordered the destruction of all synagogues and churches in his domain. The sole exception was the Church of the Nativity in Bethlehem, since Muslims used its southern transept as a mosque. The Church of the Holy Sepulchre was torn down, and the tomb of Jesus was demolished. This led the Christians of Europe to embark on the Crusades, a series of military adventures in Palestine whose stated goal was to end Muslim control of Palestine in order to make Christian pilgrimage to the Holy Land safe. After Hakim's death his successors allowed the Church of the Holy Sepulchre to be rebuilt and pilgrimage to resume, but the Turks captured Jerusalem in 1071 and renewed the prohibition of Christian pilgrimage. The Arabs retook Jerusalem in 1098, but their conflict with the Turks exhausted their resources, and they were unable to repulse the Crusaders when they arrived in Jerusalem a year later.

The early Crusader victories allowed pilgrimages to resume, but the Muslim victory at Galilee's Horns of Hattin in 1187 returned Jerusalem to Arab control. The Arabs monitored Christian pilgrimage with great caution. Pilgrims like Jacques of Verona, Ludoph of Suchem, and Felix Fabri left diaries that describe the way the Muslims allowed but carefully supervised pilgrim activity. In 1342 Pope Clement VI entrusted the guardianship of the Holy Places in Jerusalem and the Holy Land to the Franciscans, who had been in Palestine for more than one hundred years because of Francis' dream of converting the Muslims to Christianity. Of course, the Franciscans were not the only Christians who believed it was their responsibility to look after the Holy Places. There were the Greek, Syrian, Coptic, Ethiopian, and Armenian Orthodox.[15] To say that relationships between these Christian churches were not cordial is an understatement. Their rivalry was passionate and extreme, especially at Jerusalem's Church of the Holy Sepulchre. The effects of this rivalry were so serious that in 1757 the Ottoman Turks issued a ruling called *The Status Quo in the Holy Places*. This document lists with minute specificity the rights of possession and worship that each Christian group has at shrines that are jointly administered. The *Status Quo* remains in effect today.

---

15. Protestant Christians did not come to the Holy Land in great numbers until the eighteenth century, but they did not seek to control any of the shrines. Evangelical Christians do, however, locate Calvary and the tomb of Jesus outside the Old City at a site they administer called "the Garden Tomb." For a description of the site and evaluation of its claims to authenticity see Murphy-O'Connor, *The Holy Land,* 146–8.

The local Christian church in the modern State of Israel and the Palestinian Authority is small. Christians make up only 2.3 percent of the population. Also, Christian presence in Jerusalem suffers from the lack of unity that characterizes Christianity today. While the two largest Christian communities are the Greek Orthodox and Roman Catholic churches, many other Christian churches—Orthodox, Catholic, and Protestant—have a presence in the Holy Land. While some serve pilgrims primarily, most have local congregations with local leadership. Their small numbers, lack of unity, and a difficult political situation make living the gospel in Jerusalem particularly challenging today. A relatively new phenomenon is the activity of Evangelical and Fundamentalist Christians, who believe that the rise of the modern State of Israel is a harbinger of the imminent return of Christ. They visit Israel in growing numbers and have become ardent supporters of the territorial claims made by Israeli religious nationalists.

The New Testament does not afford Jerusalem a place in Christianity that is in any way comparable to its place in Judaism. The discovery of Jesus' tomb in Jerusalem, however, set off a wave of Christian pilgrimage to Jerusalem that continues to the present. It was the presence of Christ's tomb in the city that drew pilgrims, who then invested Jerusalem with the status it has come to have in Christianity. Still, the most genuine source of Jerusalem's holiness for Christians is the living community of faith trying to live the gospel of Jesus in the land that he called home.

Islam

Jerusalem has always enjoyed a prominent place in Islam. Frequently Jerusalem is spoken of as the *third* holiest city in Islam, though an early Muslim tradition has the Prophet suggesting that the faithful could make pilgrimage to three places of equal merit: "You shall only set out for three mosques: the Sacred Mosque (in Mecca), my mosque (in Medina) and the al-Aqsa mosque (in Jerusalem)."[16] A saying attributed to Muhammad suggests that Jerusalem's holiness surpasses even that of Mecca and Medina:

> A prayer in the mosque of Mecca—says the Prophet—is worth a thousand prayers, a prayer in my mosque (i.e., Medina) is worth a thousand prayers, and a prayer in al-Aqsa (i.e., Jerusalem) is worth ten thousand prayers.[17]

16. Kister, "'You Shall Only Set Out,'" 173; Tibawi, *Jerusalem*, 9.
17. Attributed to Muhammad by Ibn 'Abbas, quoted in C. D. Matthews, "The Kit. Baᶜitu-n-nufus," *Journal of the Palestine Oriental Society* 15 (1935) 54.

One reason for the privileged place of Jerusalem in Islam was its absorption into the Islamic political system just a few years after Muhammad's death in 632: "(To us belong) two Houses: the House of God of which we are the governors and the revered House in the upper (part) of Iliya'a (i.e., Jerusalem).[18] Caliph ʿUmar Ibn Al-Khattab took possession of the city from the Byzantines in February of 638. From that moment on a cultural transformation began in Jerusalem. What had been a Christian city gradually became a Muslim city.[19] To the credit of the new masters of the city, they allowed Christians to remain in the city and Jews to return. But Muslims were devoted to Jerusalem before their conquest of the city, since many of Islam's religious traditions focus on Jerusalem. For example, Muslims honor David, Solomon, and Jesus as prophets, though the great connection is with Abraham, whom the Arabs consider their ancestor and the first Muslim. It is this connection with Islam's traditions about Abraham that led the Arab armies to the Holy Land and to Jerusalem. They wanted to bring the land of their ancestor's migrations under Islamic control.

Upon entering Jerusalem, ʿUmar Ibn Al-Khattab asked to see the Holy Places. Sophronius, the Christian patriarch of Jerusalem, escorted the caliph, who was shocked by the condition of the area where the Temple had stood. Christians had used it as a dumping ground for the city's refuse, believing this to be a fulfillment of Jesus' prophecies about the destruction of Jerusalem (see Matt 24:1-2; Mark 13:1-2; Luke 19:43-44). The caliph ordered an immediate cleanup, in which the patriarch himself was to participate. Once the area was cleared, a wooden mosque was built. This was the first step in transforming the Temple Mount into a Muslim Holy Place.

In A.D. 691 Caliph ʿAdb al-Malik commissioned Byzantine architects to build a shrine known as the Dome of the Rock over the large outcropping of bedrock on the Temple Mount. The function of the building and the caliph's motives for having it built are still controverted points, but its role in solidifying Muslim attachment to Jerusalem is beyond question. The Dome of the Rock has become a symbol of Muslim Jerusalem.

18. Al-Fazardaq, cited in Kister, "You Shall Only Set Out," 182.

19. The transformation was not immediate. For a long time Jerusalem remained a Christian city whose rhythms were regulated by Christian holy days. The Judean hills to the east of the city remained the abode of thousands of Christian hermits. To help maintain the city's Christian character, Patriarch Sophronius asked that the Muslims retain the law that prohibited Jews from living in Jerusalem. At first the Muslims granted this request, but eventually they did allow Jews to resettle in the city. According to the Muslim geographer Muqaddasi, Jerusalem retained its Christian character into the tenth century. See Busse, "Sanctity of Jerusalem in Islam," 426. Today, the western part of Jerusalem is a Jewish city. The Old City and the eastern part of the area outside the Old City's wall is predominantly Arab, with most being Muslims.

Some suggest that ʿAdb al-Malik wanted to divert pilgrims from Mecca to Jerusalem, since a political rival ruled there. It is highly unlikely that the caliph would have challenged what was one of Islam's most funda-mental practices: the pilgrimage to Mecca, a duty of every Muslim. Such an innovation would have been unthinkable less than sixty years after Muhammad's death.[20] This does not mean that no political motives lay behind the caliph's building project. Surely those Muslims who saw the Dome of the Rock must have concluded that ʿAdb al-Malik was the real power in the Muslim world. No rival built anything comparable.

A second explanation for the building of the Dome of the Rock re-flects Muslim piety, which has interpreted a passage from the Koran as re-ferring to Jerusalem, although the text does not name the city explicitly:

> Glorified be He who carried His servant [Muhammad] by night from the Masjid al-Haram [the mosque in Mecca] to the Masjid al-Aqsa [the farthest mosque] (*Sura* 17:1).

Later biographers developed the details of the night journey during which Muhammad, escorted by the angel Gabriel, came to Jerusalem on a magi-cal horse named Buraq to join earlier prophets, including Jesus, for prayer. Also associated with this night journey was Muhammad's ascension, dur-ing which the Prophet went to heaven from the rock over which the Dome of the Rock now stands.

Did ʿAdb al-Malik build the Dome of the Rock to immortalize Muhammad's night journey and ascension? *Sura* 17 does not make an ex-plicit reference to Jerusalem as site of "the farthest mosque." It is likely that the cryptic reference to "the farthest mosque" in *Sura* 17 refers to a mosque in the neighborhood of Mecca rather than to Jerusalem. Some Muslim theologians hold that the "farthest mosque" refers to a heavenly place of prayer located directly above Mecca or Jerusalem.[21] There is no evidence that Muslims located "the farthest mosque" in Jerusalem during the seventh century when the Dome of the Rock was built. The associa-

20. While both a Muslim historian, Yaʿqubi, who wrote around 874, and a Christian historian, Eutychius (d. 940), suggest that ʿAdb al-Malik sought to have Jerusalem take Mecca's place as the religious center of Islam, both opposed the rule of ʿAdb al-Malik's dynasty and so had political motives for making their assertions. The notion that ʿAbd al-Malik built the Dome of the Rock to replace Mecca as a pilgrimage site came into scholarly circles through Goldziher, who argued it extensively in his *Muhammeda-nische Studien II.* It has been repeated in many popular and scholarly studies of Islamic Jerusalem since Goldziher, for example, Vincent, *Jérusalem,* 933b.

21. Gaudefroy-Demombynes, *Mahomet,* 93.

tion came three hundred years later. Even when Muslims began identifying Jerusalem as the place of "the farthest mosque," they did not consider the Dome of the Rock as the place from which the Prophet ascended into heaven. About 1200, Muslims built a smaller structure called the Dome of the Ascension next to the Dome of the Rock. Obviously, its builders did not consider the Dome of the Rock as built over the place of Muhammad's ascension.

It is necessary to look into the building itself to find the reason for its existence. One lament of archaeologists who work in Israel is that they find little textual material to help them clarify the material remains they find. There is, however, an inscription in the Dome of the Rock that can help explain the building. There is a six-hundred-foot inscription in the Dome that dates from the building's origins, while other inscriptions were added at later times. This original inscription has six parts. Each part contains a text from the Koran, except for the part that gives the date and builder of the building.[22] It is the final inscription that may clarify the building's purpose. It is made up of several passages from the Koran that challenge the Christian belief in the Trinity and the divinity of Christ:

> People of the Book (the Bible), overstep not bounds in your religion and of God speak only truth. The Messiah, Jesus, son of Mary, is only an apostle of God and His word which He conveyed to Mary and a Spirit proceeding from Him. Believe therefore in God and his apostles and say not "Three." It will be better for you. God is only one God. Far be it from His glory that He should have a son. His is whatever is in the heavens and whatever is on the earth. And God is a sufficient Guardian. The Messiah does not disdain being a servant of God nor do the angels who are near Him. And all who disdain His service are filled with pride. God will gather them all to Himself (*Sura* 64:1; 33:54; 4:169-71).

The inscription continues with a call to prayer: "Pray for your Prophet and your servant, Jesus, son of Mary." This is followed by two more long citations from the Koran:

> And the peace of God was on me (Mary) the day I was born and will be the day I shall die and the day I shall be raised to live. This is Jesus, the son of Mary. This is a statement of the truth concerning which they doubt. It beseems not God to beget a son. Glory be to Him. When he decrees a thing,

---

22. The inscription credits the building's construction to al-Mamun, a caliph from the Abbasid dynasty. It dates the building to A.D. 691. Al-Mamun, however, reigned from 813 to 833. Evidently, he wanted to take credit for the Dome of the Rock. While he substituted his name for that of ʿAdb al-Malik, he failed to change the date, making it possible for historians to recognize his attempted fraud.

He only says to it "Be" and it is. And truly God is my Lord and your Lord. Adore Him then. This is the right way" (*Sura* 19:34-37).

God witnesses that there is no God but He. And the angels and men endured with knowledge, established in righteousness, proclaim there is no God but He, the Mighty, the Wise. The true religion with God is Islam. They to whom the Scriptures had been given differed not until after the knowledge had come to them, and through mutual jealousy. As for him who shall not believe in the signs of God, God will be prompt to reckon with him (*Sura* 3:16-17).

The Dome of the Rock, then, calls Christians to accept Islam and to recognize the true place of Jesus in the plan of God.[23] Because the structure was built on a site that Jews associated with Abraham's sacrifice of Isaac, it also serves to co-opt the patriarch for the new faith. Apparently the original purpose of this Islamic shrine was to emphasize the superiority of Islam over Judaism and Christianity. In one sense, the prophecy of Jesus about the fate of the temple area has been voided and the shrine rehabilitated. It will no longer serve as a garbage dump for Christian Jerusalem. Neither will it serve Judaism, which Islam has superceded. It is a shrine that proclaims the central tenets of Islam: the unity of God and the finality of Muhammad's role as God's prophet. The Dome of the Rock, then, is a statement, in most tangible form, that the Arab conquest of Jerusalem had more than political consequences. ʿAdb al-Malik directed his statement primarily at Christians who controlled Jerusalem in the seventh century: the Arabs have initiated a third and final era of the city's life and have endowed it with the greatest significance. It is a holy city of the true faith: Islam. In time, the Dome of the Rock became a purely Islamic shrine whose purpose was to strengthen Muslims in their belief.

In the early years of the Muslim presence in Jerusalem, believers were satisfied with the simple wooden mosque that the Arab conquerors built on Haram es-Sharif ("The Noble Sanctuary"), the Arabic name for the Temple Mount. As the Arab desert dwellers became more accustomed to city life in Jerusalem and other Christian centers of Palestine and Syria, the magnificent Christian shrines of these cities began to reshape their aesthetic sense. Building a resplendent Muslim shrine in an area significant to both Judaism and Christianity was a natural reaction of nomads with simple tastes expressing their newly acquired refined tastes in art and architecture. The building of the Dome of the Rock is a striking example of acculturation: the Arabs adapted themselves to an environment

23. The inscriptions reject Christianity's claims about Jesus but support Muslim beliefs that Jesus was a true prophet.

where great shrines witness to the triumph of the Christian religion and the Christian Empire. The Dome of the Rock is an effective assertion that Islam has replaced Christianity and Muslim caliphs have replaced Christian emperors. The Dome of the Rock was a taller and more imposing building than the Holy Sepulchre. Every Christian who saw the building was to draw one conclusion: the day of Christianity has passed and the day of Islam has dawned.

The location of this shrine on the Temple Mount may give another clue to the motivation that led to the construction of the Dome of the Rock. Since the association of the rock with the ascension of Muhammad came after ʿAdb al-Malik built the shrine, it is necessary to consider another religious motivation. It may be that the caliph believed he had found the place where Solomon's Temple stood. The rock on the Temple Mount was similar to the Black Stone that is in the Ka'ba in Mecca.[24] Since Muslims regarded Solomon as a prophet and the Temple as a holy place, the building of a Muslim shrine over the site of Solomon's Temple was another coup for the new religion. The Dome of the Rock was the successor to Solomon's Temple just as Islam was the successor of Judaism.

There is a second Islamic shrine on the Temple Mount: the al-Aqsa mosque, which serves as the principal Muslim place of prayer in Jerusalem. Unlike the Dome of the Rock, which is a shrine, al-Aqsa always has been a mosque. It attracted Islamic theologians and ascetics who settled in Jerusalem to be close to this building. Soon the mosque became an important seat of learning for Muslims. By the eleventh century Jerusalem was home to 630 Islamic scholars, the most famous of whom was the philosopher and theologian Hujjat al-Islam Abu Hamid al-Ghazali, who came to Jerusalem in 1095.[25] In his day Jerusalem was home to these Islamic scholars, who produced several works describing the attributes that made the city especially sacred to Muslims. Jerusalem also attracted Muslim ascetics and mystics who came on pilgrimage to the city. Some stayed and settled in the Judean desert, which was once home to Christian monks.

There is an Arabic saying that "the multitude of names proves the excellence of the bearer." Among Islam's seventeen names for Jerusalem, several directly emphasize its holiness. The first of these is *Iliya.* Though this name probably derives from *Aelia Capitolina,* the name Hadrian gave the city in A.D. 135, Muslim soldiers who first heard the name *Aelia* were

24. Busse, "Sanctity of Jerusalem, in Islam," 442.

25. One hundred and fifty years before Aquinas, al-Ghazali used Aristotelian philosophy as a framework for expounding Islamic beliefs. No doubt Aquinas modeled his use of Aristotle on that of al-Ghazali.

unaware of its origin and invented several popular etymologies, each of which spoke of Jerusalem's sacred character. Another Muslim name for the city is *al-Bait al-Muqaddas,* "the holy house." This name likely derives from the Hebrew *bayit hammiqdosh,* a popular rabbinic name for the Temple. Arabic poetry sometimes refers to Jerusalem as *al-Balat,* that is, "the palace" or "the royal court," from the Latin *palatium.*[26] By far the most common Muslim name for Jerusalem is simply *al-Quds,* "the holy (city)."

The holiness of Jerusalem in Islam is the basis for the pilgrimages believers make to the city. There are many accounts of pious Muslims who came to Jerusalem on pilgrimage from the very beginning of Islam.[27] By the eleventh century pilgrimage to the city becomes recommended as a means toward perfection in the fulfillment of divine law.[28] Pilgrims are to visit fifteen sites on the Haram es-Sharif in a specific sequence that requires them to make several circuits of the site, just as pilgrims to Mecca circumambulate the Ka'ba. Still, pilgrimage to Jerusalem is not required, while one to Mecca is an obligation for every adult Muslim. For some Muslims pilgrimage to Jerusalem complements pilgrimage to Mecca. One may begin the pilgrimage to Mecca in Jerusalem or complete it there. The desire to make pilgrimages to Jerusalem waned by the fifteenth century, although the rise of Arab nationalism in this century has brought Jerusalem back into prominence as a goal of pilgrimage. However, some Muslims hold that the city must return to Arab control before religious journeys to its shrines can begin again.

There is an also eschatological flavor to some Islamic traditions about Jerusalem. The city will be the scene of the day of judgment.[29] All believers will be raised from the dead in Jerusalem. Even the Black Stone of the Ka'ba will be brought from Mecca to Jerusalem for that day. In the courtyard outside the Dome of the Rock there are open-air stone arches. Popular piety terms these *mawazeen* (scales), because on the Day of Judgment scales will hang from the arches to weigh the good and evil deeds of every person. Among the Muslim eschatological traditions associated with Jerusalem is one that sees the conquest of Jerusalem as a harbinger of the

26. Le Strange, *Palestine Under the Moslems,* 84. There is no "p" sound in Arabic so "b," another labial, is substituted. Excavations at the southern wall of the temple area have revealed a palace from the Muslim period. See Meir Ben-Dov, "Jerusalem: Early Arab to Ayyubid Periods," *NEAEHL* 2:973–5.

27. Goitein, "Sanctity of Palestine in Moslem Piety," 120–6.

28. Busse, "Sanctity of Jerusalem in Islam," 465.

29. This association began with Mu'awiya b. Abi Sufyan (661–80), who proclaimed Jerusalem as "the land where the people will gather and arise from the dead on Judgment Day." See Hasson, "Muslim Literature," 170.

Day of Judgment. When Jerusalem will be rebuilt following its conquest, this will mean the eclipse of Medina, making it necessary to bring Muhammad's bones to Jerusalem.

Early Muslims produced an impressive amount of literature on the topic they call *fada'il al-Bayt al-Maqdis,* that is, the "merits," or religious importance, of Jerusalem.[30] According to these traditions the value of acts of piety such as fasting, prayer, and almsgiving is enhanced when the pious do them in Jerusalem. Many of these traditions reflect the incorporation of Jewish and Christian traditions about Jerusalem into Islam. Muslim theologians have a name for these traditions: *isra'iliyyat.* Converts from Judaism and Christianity undoubtedly had a role to play in adapting traditions of their former faith to their new faith.[31]

Despite the city's importance in Islam, Muslims never bestowed any political status on the city. It never served as a capital for any Muslim dynasty.[32] It did not even serve as the regional capital of Palestine. The Arabs built the town of Ramla for this purpose. Perhaps the city's continuing Christian character led the Muslims to locate their capital elsewhere. For Muslims Jerusalem had no significance beyond the sphere of religion. There are practically no non-theological works about Jerusalem in Muslim literature through the Middle Ages. Today Jerusalem has become a symbol of Palestinian nationalism. A consistent policy of the Palestinian Authority is that Jerusalem must be the capital of the Palestinian state. This, of course, runs in direct conflict to the Israeli position that Jerusalem is the eternal capital of the Jewish people. Certainly, the status of Jerusalem will be the most difficult question to settle in the negotiations between Israel and the Palestinians.

30. Examples of this literature may be found in al-Muqaddasi, *Description of Syria, including Palestine,* trans. and annotated by Guy Le Strange. London: Palestine Pilgrims Text Society, 1896 (reprinted New York: AMS Press, 1971).

For detailed interpretation of the *fada'il form,* see Hasson, "Muslim Literature," 168–89. This literature emerged at the end of the seventh century and has not diminished in popularity. See Kister, "Antiquity of Traditions Praising Jerusalem," 186.

31. There was a comparable Christian literary form, the *Laudes Hierosolomytana,* which Eliyahu Ashtor considers superior from a literary perspective to the *fada'il.* See his "Muslim and Christian Literature in Praise of Jerusalem," *The Jerusalem Cathedra I,* 187.

32. The caliph Mu'awiya b. Abi Sufyan (661–80), founder of the Ummayyad dynasty, broke with the tradition that saw his predecessors take their oath as caliphs in Medina and took his oath in Jerusalem. Still, he chose Damascus as his capital.

Conclusion

That Jerusalem is sacred to the major world religions is both its glory and its curse. Millions of people revere Jerusalem as a "holy city," maintain their shrines there, and assert their right to make the city an object of religious pilgrimage. For Judaism, the city's holiness derives from the Temple that once stood in the midst of the city. Since the Temple's destruction and the dispersion of the Jews, Jerusalem has become a symbol of the return of the Jews to Zion. With the establishment of the State of Israel in 1948, that return has become a possibility. Religious Jews still look for the redemption of the Jewish people, which they believe will be the work of the Messiah. This Messiah will make his appearance in Jerusalem. The city, then, is sacred to both religious and secular Jews alike. Jerusalem is the greatest symbol of Jewish survival and triumph.

Christianity's relationship with Jerusalem is more ambiguous. In the Gospels, Jerusalem is the scene of Jesus' rejection as Messiah and his execution by the Romans. The first Christian community did not limit its preaching to the people of Judea and Jerusalem. The gospel was proclaimed to all nations. The New Testament spiritualizes Jerusalem as it looks to a "new and heavenly" Jerusalem. Once the Roman Empire became Christian, it was not long before Jerusalem became a Christian city—the object of pilgrimage because of the tomb of Christ that was venerated in it. In the Middle Ages European Christians fought the Arab rulers of Palestine to ensure access to Christian shrines. The divisions within Christianity are made no more apparent than in Jerusalem, where Christian churches jealously guard their rights at various shrines. The indigenous Christian community of Palestine is small, so the churches are concerned that the access of their pilgrims be maintained in any final political settlement between the State of Israel and the Palestinians.

For Muslims, Jerusalem is holy because its Dome of the Rock represents the triumph of Islam over both Judaism and Christianity. This city's holiness was mythologized by making it the locus of Muhammad's night journey to the "farthest mosque." The almost total identification of Arab culture and Islam guarantees that Jerusalem is a central concern for all Arabs, who find Jerusalem under Israeli rule a religious anomaly as well as a political problem. The question of Jerusalem's status will be a most difficult negotiating point between the Israelis and the Palestinians. Of course, Christians will be most anxious observers of these negotiations.

2

Zion, the City of God:
Jerusalem in the Book of Psalms

The book of Psalms is a compendium of ancient Israelite religious beliefs. After all, this book served as the hymnbook of the Temple, where those religious beliefs were celebrated in ritual. Since Jerusalem was the site of the Temple, it is not surprising that Zion is a major motif in this book. The psalms glorify Jerusalem by using both common ancient Near Eastern religious themes and those distinctive to ancient Israel. They celebrate the election of the Davidic dynasty, which rules from Jerusalem. Pilgrims to Zion sang psalms as they approached the city. The psalms also give voice to those Judahites who lamented the fall of Jerusalem and the destruction of the Temple. They also express the hope for the city's restoration. The obvious place to begin examining the religious significance of Jerusalem for the faith of ancient Israel is the book of Psalms.

God's Kingship

The peoples of the ancient Near East thought of their patron deities as their kings, while human monarchs served merely as viceroys of the gods. Similarly, the temples of these gods were their earthly palaces from which the gods ruled and at which received the homage of their people. The temple-cities were specially chosen by the gods to serve as their dwelling places on earth. Thus the real king enthroned in Jerusalem was not David but God, and Jerusalem was not really the city of David. Jerusalem was the city of God.

The book of Psalms, which served as the hymnbook of Jerusalem's Temple, celebrates God's kingship and God's choice of Jerusalem. The sheer number of references to Jerusalem (seventeen) and Zion (thirty-nine) in the Psalter testifies to the importance the city came to have in the religion of Judah.[1] Except for Psalm 132, the Psalter underplays David's initiative in taking Jerusalem and does not even mention Solomon, the builder of the Temple, except in the titles of Psalms 72 and 127. The Psalter's hymns prefer to use ancient Near Eastern mythological motifs in speaking of Jerusalem and its Temple. According to that mythology the gods that were worshiped by the peoples of the ancient Near East achieved their status as kings by defeating the powers of chaos in great primordial battles.[2] Usually this triumph led to the creation of the world and the building of the gods' earthly dwelling places: their temples. The rituals of those temples celebrated the victory of the gods over chaos. It is important to note that the peoples of the ancient Near East—Israel included—made no hard distinction between their gods' heavenly palaces and their earthly dwelling places. The earthly sovereignty of the gods, centered in their temples, reflects their heavenly sovereignty. Temples are places where earth and heaven meet. The book of Psalms calls this place "Zion."

Among the motifs related to Zion the most significant is the kingship of God. When Israel acclaimed Yahweh as king (Pss 93:1; 96:10; 97:1; 99:1), it did just what the Babylonians did when they proclaimed "Marduk is king" (*Enuma Elish* 4:28; see *ANET,* 66) and what the people of Ugarit did when they cried out "Aliyan Baal is our king" (*CTA,* 3.D.40). What made the Israelite acclamations different is their assertion that Yahweh, the God of Israel, rules from Zion:

> The LORD is king, the peoples tremble;
>> God is enthroned on the cherubim, the earth quakes.
> The LORD is great on Zion,
>> exalted above all the peoples (Ps 99:1-2).

Israel then identified Zion as the place from which Yahweh exercises sovereignty over heaven and earth. In using Zion to acclaim Yahweh's kingship, Israel's poets used motifs derived from ancient Near Eastern religious

---

1. While in the psalms Jerusalem and Zion are often equivalent terms referring to the place where God reigns on earth, the two words do have distinct but complementary connotations. Jerusalem is the more comprehensive of the two. It refers to the royal city of the Judahite monarchy, which includes the Temple. Zion is the mountain of God's temple. Together they delineate the city's role as the political and religious center of Judah.

2. The Bible preserves remnants of such myths, for example, Pss 74:12-15; 89:9-10; Isa 52:9, and has them refer to Yahweh's action of creation. The narratives in Genesis 1–2 avoid personifying the chaotic forces that God brings into order.

traditions. Edzard Rohland has identified four such motifs: Zion's identification with Mount Zaphon, the river that flows through Zion, God's victory over chaos, and God's victory over the nations.[3]

Mount Zion and Mount Zaphon

Mount Zaphon was the sacred mountain of the storm god Baal in ancient Canaanite mythology. It was the site of Baal's royal palace. The Psalter, however, claims Mount Zaphon for Yahweh. Psalm 89:13 asserts that God created this mountain along with three others: Yamin, Tabor, and Hermon.[4] Psalm 48:1-2 speaks of Mount Zion as the sacred mountain of Yahweh, though Zion is not much of a mountain. It is not even the highest mountain in Jerusalem, rising just 2,460 feet above sea level. The Mount of Olives across the Kidron Valley to the east is 217 feet higher, and the hill across the Tyropaean Valley to the west is 108 feet higher. Still, for most of the Old Testament period the people of Jerusalem lived on the Ophel hill just to the south of the hill on which the Temple was built. The Ophel was lower in elevation. There was a difference of 328 feet from the south end of the Ophel to the top of Mount Zion. Walking up the steep incline to the Temple from the Ophel may have led the people of Jerusalem to consider Zion a mountain.

A most curious phrase, as rendered in modern English translations of the psalm, occurs in the last part of v. 2:

Mount Zion, in the far north, the city of the great King. *(NRSV)*	Mount Zion, "the recesses of the North," is the city of the great King. *(NAB)*	Mount Zion in the heart of the North, the settlement of the great king. *(NJB)*

The word "north" appears in each of these translations because *sāpōn* came to mean "north" in Hebrew, although originally it was a proper geographical name. Clearly the word "north" makes no sense here. It should be rendered as a proper name: Zaphon.[5] Dahood translates this verse as

3. "Die Bedeutung der Erwählungstraditionen Israels für die Eschatologie der alttestamentlichen Propheten," 142. J. J. M. Roberts lists these in "The Davidic Origin of the Zion Tradition," *JBL* (1973) 329–44. See also Ollenburger, *Zion,* 15–6.

4. Mount Zaphon today is known as Jebelᵓel-Aqraᶜ in northern Syria. Mount Tabor is located in Israel's Jezreel Valley, and Mount Hermon is the southern spur of the anti-Lebanon range. No Mount Yamin is known, although it may be a poetic name for Mount Sinai.

5. The etymology and usage of Zaphon is still debated. There appears to be a consensus that "Zaphon" was applied to the mountain before it was applied to the point on

"Mount Zion is the heart of Zaphon, the city of the Great King."[6] Psalm 48 then transforms a Canaanite mythological motif by identifying Mount Zion with Mount Zaphon. For the psalmist Zaphon is no longer the residence of Baal but is identified with Zion, the residence of Yahweh. Contemporary readers of this psalm may not catch the important assertion this verse is making: Baal is not king of the gods. It is Yahweh who is supreme over all. By appropriating the cosmic-mountain motif from its ancient Near Eastern religious milieu, the psalmist underscores the greatness of God—a greatness that transcends the experience of ancient Israel.[7]

Though Psalm 48 uses mythological imagery, it ventures beyond the mythological and speaks about the threat to Zion posed by kings that ally themselves against it.[8] The impression left is that Zion is invulnerable. After all, it is the residence of the "great King" (v. 2), and Yahweh is its defense (v. 3). The attack made by hostile kings is short-lived. They reel back in panic (vv. 4–7). While the kings retreat in panic, pilgrims to the Temple rejoice when they catch sight of the impregnable city (vv. 8-11). A procession around the city is the most appropriate way to celebrate the victory God's protection has given Zion (vv. 12-14). Though the psalm does not identify "the great king" explicitly, it is clear that this king is Yahweh—not a human monarch—not even David, God's regent and adopted son. God's claim to sovereignty rests here on God's victory over a coalition of kings who threaten Zion.

It is important to note that the psalm calls Zion "[God's] holy mountain" (v. 1).[9] Psalm 68:16-17 describes a controversy between Mount Zion and the mountains that are rejected as the place for God's abode:

---

the compass. See Hector Avalos, "Zaphon, Mount," *ABD* 6:1040. There are three other biblical texts in which *sāpōn* should be considered a proper geographical name: Ps 89:12, Job 26:7, and Isa 14:13.

6. Mitchell Dahood, *Psalms I.* AB 16 (Garden City, N.Y.: Doubleday, 1963) 288. Dahood suggests that the expression he renders as the "heart of Zaphon" may be an allusion to the "navel of the earth" motif that appears in Ps 22:28. Later rabbinic literature did describe Jerusalem as on the highest mountain and at the center of the world.

7. For a complete discussion of this motif see Clifford, *Cosmic Mountain in Canaan and the Old Testament.*

8. Krinetzki, "Zur Poetik und Exegese von Ps. 48," 82, suggests that this psalm refers to the Assyrian invasion of Judah in 701 B.C. under Sennacherib. It is probably a mistake to look for an exact historical referent here. The kings of v. 4 are literary creations to speak about the security God provides for Zion. See Artur Weiser, *Psalms,* 381–3, which notes that the psalm makes no allusions to a thanksgiving service and there is no evidence of any alliance of kings against Jerusalem in 701 B.C. He concludes that attempts to relate this psalm to the events of 701 are misguided.

9. The phrase "holy mountain" also occurs in Pss 2:6; 3:5; 15:1; 43:3; 99:9. Psalm 24:3 speaks of "the mountain of the Lord."

High the mountains of Bashan;
    rugged the mountains of Bashan.
Why look you jealously, you rugged mountains,
    at the mountain God has chosen for his throne,
    where the LORD himself will dwell forever?

The next verse asserts that God "advances from Sinai" (Ps 68:18). She-maryahu Talmon suggests that this implies that even Mount Sinai is among those supplanted by Mount Zion.[10] Because God chose Zion over all other places on earth for God's residence, Zion shares in the very holiness of God. Zion is set apart as the setting for God's earthly palace. As such it is the object of pilgrimage and is defended by God against all enemies. The protection God affords Zion leads to a confession of God's supremacy (v. 14). The mythological motifs used by the psalmist have as their purpose underscoring the divine choice of Zion, which makes that city impregnable. While no enemy will be able to breach it, pilgrims enter it with joy.

Another significant development in this psalm in praise of Zion is the reference to God's justice and judgments in vv. 11-12. These make Zion "glad." These verses allude to the forgiving of debts and the release of prisoners that accompanied the accession of the king.[11] The triumph of God and God's enthronement as king has its effects in the social and economic order. It is the kindness of the king that makes it possible for his subjects to make a new start unencumbered by debts, which makes joy the most appropriate response of the king's subjects. The psalmists do not hesitate to adapt the religious language and imagery of their culture in praising Zion, but they also make certain they see that Israel needs to celebrate God's choice of Zion in ways beyond the rituals of the Temple. The election of Zion must touch the people's social and economic lives.

The River Running Through Zion

As was the case with Psalm 48, the imagery of the stream running through the city of God in Ps 46:5 is controlled by the ancient Near Eastern religious motif adopted by psalmist more than by the geography of Jerusalem. There is no river in Jerusalem. In antiquity a single spring, the Gihon, provided the city's supply of water, but the spring's output was inadequate and had to be supplemented with rainwater saved in cisterns.

---

10. "The Biblical Concept of Jerusalem," *JES* 8 (1971) 308.

11. Jon Levenson, *Creation and the Persistence of Evil* (San Francisco: Harper & Row, 1988) 100–6. This practice was universalized in Israel through the institutions of the sabbatical and jubilee years. See his "Zion Traditions," *ABD* 6:1099.

Still, ancient Israel's writers use this motif to emphasize the theological importance of Jerusalem. Genesis 2:13 mentions the Gihon as one of the four rivers that watered Eden. Ezekiel describes his vision of a spring gushing forth from under the Temple and becoming a river of universal significance (Ezekiel 47). Sirach also includes the Gihon among the rivers of paradise (Sir 48:17). The inclusion of the river-of-paradise motif in Ps 46:5 serves to underscore the importance of Jerusalem, not only as the place of Yahweh's throne but as the very center of the world.

Psalm 46 contains two other motifs that are usually associated with the Zion tradition: Yahweh's battle with chaotic powers (vv. 2-3) and the defeat of the nations (vv. 6, 9-10). The psalm offers a striking contrast between the uproar caused by unruly natural forces and rebellious nations and the peaceful city of God. Verses 2-4 assume the resurgence of chaotic powers. Though subdued by God in the distant past, they will once again try to disrupt the divinely created order. God will be victorious a second time over the powers that try to have the world revert to chaos.[12] Verses 4–7 describe how peaceful is "the city of God" amid political turmoil caused by the nations. The psalm concludes by describing the end of warfare and the triumph of God (vv. 8-11). The refrain ("The LORD of hosts is with us; our stronghold is the God of Jacob" [vv. 8 and 12]) makes it clear that God is responsible for the city's peace.

Psalm 46 begins with mythological imagery (the outbreak of chaotic powers) but then shifts to more concrete imagery (political turmoil). The psalm portrays Yahweh as the battling storm god who subdues the powers of chaos (vv. 1-3) and grants fertility to the earth (v. 5). The inclusion of God's power over Israel's political enemies (v. 7) is an example of the demythologizing tendency in some of the psalms. Still, the psalm concludes with a typically Israelite eschatological image: the end of wars and the destruction of weapons (v. 10, see also Ps 76:4; Hos 2:20; Zech 9:10). God's victories over chaotic powers at the beginning of time portend God's victory over every destructive human power in the future, just as the raging waters of v. 4 become the life-giving waters of v. 5. The primeval waters, which Yahweh subdued, serve to make the earth fertile. Still, the force of v. 5 focuses on the present—not on the future. While some texts envision a stream that will issue from the temple in the *future* (Ezek 47:1; Joel 3:18; Zech 14:8), Ps 46:5 speaks of the river that gladdens the "city of God" in the *present.*

The contrast drawn between the roaring waters with the gently flowing waters evident in vv. 4-5 is reminiscent of a similar contrast in Isa

12. Joel 4:16 is a variant on the same theme.

8:6-7. In trying to encourage the people of Jerusalem to be calm in the midst of the grave political crisis caused by the Assyrians, the prophet specifically identifies the gentle waters as those of Shiloah, a conduit of Jerusalem's Gihon spring. Because the Judahites refused to believe the prophet's assurances, they were going to experience a mighty flood—the Assyrian onslaught. Though both the prophet and the psalmist rely on mythological imagery, they recognize that it is not floods that threaten Jerusalem but the nations. Isaiah specifically names Assyria.

Though Psalm 46 does not mention Zion explicitly, the word "refuge" *(RSV)* or "stronghold" *(NAB)* in vv. 4, 8, and 12 point clearly to the Jerusalem Temple.[13] The Temple stood on the acropolis of Jerusalem. This location alone made people look upon it as a fortress. While few temples were designed to serve as military fortifications, the features of their construction led people to use them as places of refuge when under military threat. The inspiration for the metaphor in vv. 8 and 12 may have been the huge temple building in Jerusalem. Usually when the psalms speak of God in this way, some natural feature of the landscape is the inspiration, for example, Pss 18:2; 31:3; 42:9; 71:3. The assertion that God is in the midst of the city (v. 6) points to the Temple as providing the impetus for speaking of God as a "fortress."

What is particularly significant for this study is that the entire city—not just the temple area—is the "holy dwelling of the Most High" (v. 5). God is in the midst of the city (v. 6). This contrasts with the Sinai tradition. That tradition underscores the inaccessibility of God (Exod 19:12, 23). God's dwelling place on Sinai is inapproachable, while God's dwelling in Zion makes it possible for God to be present to Israel. It is God's presence in Zion that makes the city a place of refuge, since God is Israel's defender against chaotic powers that threaten to engulf it. Just as God's victory over the primordial chaotic powers was complete, the victory over historical powers will be complete. The sign of God's victory is that Zion, God's dwelling place on earth, is secure. The response of Israel is to recognize that Yahweh is God.

God's Victory over Chaotic Powers

Canaanite and Babylonian creation accounts describe the creation of the world as the consequence of a god's struggle with chaotic forces,

---

13. Dieter Eichhorn has studied the metaphor of God as "Rock, Fortress, and Refuge." He concluded that the origin of this metaphor also belongs to Canaanite mythology. See his *Gott als Fels, Burg und Zuflucht: Eine Untersuchung zum Gebet des Mittlers in den Psalmen* (Bern: Herbert Lang, 1972) 42–54.

symbolized by primordial waters that the god's power is able to contain. That ancient Israel was familiar with these motifs and applied them to Yahweh is clear from the many allusions to them found primarily in biblical poetry (cf. Psalms 18, 19, 24, 29, 33, 46, 93, 95, 104; Job 38–41; Isaiah 40–42). The analysis of Psalm 46 above has already examined this motif as it relates to the Zion tradition. Ancient Israel's poets did not merely adopt this motif from the wider ancient Near Eastern culture. They adopted it in accord with their own religious beliefs. Psalm 98 shows how ancient Israel's poets and theologians adapted this motif.

While both the sea and rivers appear in Ps 98:7-8, both have been thoroughly demythologized. The sea and rivers are no longer chaotic powers that threaten the world. They are simply bodies of water and nothing more. Far from being threats to God's hegemony and human security, they are to join in praising God. Related to the demythologizing of ancient Near Eastern religious language is the psalm's focus on the effects of divine rule in the human realm. The psalm does not describe the effects of God's victory (v. 1) in mythological terms. God's victory brings justice and equity (vv. 2, 9). Rather than having God subdue the chaotic waters, this psalm has God bringing the order of justice to the chaos caused by exploitation and injustice in human affairs.

The psalm begins with a call to praise Yahweh for the divine help shown to Israel (vv. 1-3). Verse 3 uses traditional covenantal language in speaking about what God has done for Israel. The psalm describes it as "kindness and faithfulness."[14] Since "the ends of the earth" have seen what God did for Israel (v.3), the next section of the psalm (vv. 4-6) calls all peoples to join Israel in the praise of Yahweh, its king.[15] The musical instruments mentioned in vv. 5-6 suggest the setting of formal worship in the Temple. The final section of the psalm calls all nature to join in the praise of Israel's God. The use of words for watery places and dry land in vv. 7-8 is a merism that implies that all creation is to join in praising God.[16]

Psalm 98 contains no explicit mention of Zion or its Temple. Still, vv. 4-6 envision a solemn liturgical assembly in which congregational singing is supported by several musical instruments. The psalmist no doubt imag-

---

14. The Hebrew words translated by the *NAB* as "kindness" and "faithfulness" are *hesed* and *ʾemunah* respectively. They are technical terms that refer to the qualities shown by those who keep their covenantal responsibilities.

15. The expression "all the ends of the earth" reflects ancient Israel's belief that it occupied the center of the world and other peoples lived at the earth's edges beyond which no habitable land existed. The Egyptians, Babylonians, and the other peoples of the ancient Near East believed it was they who lived in the center of the world.

16. John S. Kselmann and Michael L. Barré, "The Psalms" *NJBC* 34:115.

ines this worship taking place in the Temple on Mount Zion, the place from which Yahweh rules Israel, the nations, and all creation as king.

God's Victory over the Nations

Psalm 76:3 asserts that God dwells "in Zion." Immediately following this is the claim that God has destroyed the weapons of war. This assertion is hardly a pacifist manifesto; rather, it follows from the total defeat God has inflicted on Zion's enemies. The psalm celebrates God's defense of Jerusalem, which has rendered ineffective all military threats against the city. Mythological imagery lies just below the surface here. The Canaanite god associated with war was Reshef. The "arrows" of (v. 4) are literally "Reshefs of the bow" in the Hebrew text. This expression asserts God's supremacy over all military powers. The next section of the psalm (vv. 5-7) develops the theme of God's victory over Jerusalem's enemies by describing the enemies' immobility in the face of God and the consequent defeat of their chariot forces. The word "rebuke" (v. 7) also carries mythological connotations. According to Pss 18:16 and 104:7, the chaotic waters responded to God's rebuke. Here God rebukes military forces. The final section (vv. 8-13) asserts the supremacy of God over all other powers.

There is one notable translation problem in v. 11 that calls for some attention. The *NAB* and the *NRSV* render this verse very differently:

For wrathful Edom shall glorify you, and the survivors of Hamath shall keep your festivals. *(NAB)*	Human wrath serves only to praise you, when you bind the last bit of your wrath around you. *(NRSV)*

While both translations are possible, the rendering of the *NAB* makes better sense given the context, which speaks about God's victory over nations threatening Zion. At one time Edom was in Judah's sphere of influence (see 2 Sam 8:12-14), but the Edomites proved to be particularly restive subjects. At times they were able to assert their independence, although the Judahites managed to reclaim their territory until the time of Ahaz (ca. 742–745 B.C.), when Edom became completely independent again (see 1 Kgs 22:47; 2 Kgs 8:20-22; 14:7; 22; 2 Chr 28:17). Hamath was a district of the Aramean kingdom to the north of Israel. Its border was the traditional northern limit of Israelite territory (see Num 34:8; Ezek 47:15). The region's ruler paid tribute to David (2 Sam 8:9), although Hamath was able to reassert its independence following the death of Solomon. In Psalm 76 Edom and Hamath represent all those who threatened Jerusalem. The psalm asserts that God's power inspires fear in the hearts of all kings who are enemies of Zion.

Like the other motifs that make up the Zion tradition, the one that describes Yahweh as defeating the nations that threaten Zion and the Temple mirrors the religious culture of the ancient Near East. Certainly no patron deity could stand by as foreigners attacked his temple and city. Though some have described the Zion tradition as a development of the Davidic tradition, that is unlikely.[17] Another suggestion derives the Zion tradition from Deuteronomy's law of cult centralization (Deut 12).[18] The relative lateness of this requirement seems to make this impossible. Most likely the Zion tradition developed from the motif of the patron deity defeating the enemies of the place where his temple is located.

Pilgrimage to Zion

Hans Wildberger added a fifth motif to those of Rohland: the pilgrimage of the nations.[19] Pilgrimage, a journey to a shrine for a religious reason, is a feature common to many religious traditions. According to the traditions of ancient Near Eastern religion, shrines were built at sites connected with some sort of divine activity—especially a theophany. These shrines became the goal of pilgrimages. Pilgrims brought offerings to the shrines to accompany their petitions or thanksgiving to the gods. Such shrines, which the Bible usually calls "high places," existed throughout Israel, although both Hezekiah (ca. 705 B.C.) and Josiah (ca. 622 B.C.) tried to close all those except Jerusalem (see 2 Kgs 18:4; 23:4-20). The book of Deuteronomy asserted that there was to be only one shrine for Israel's one God (Deuteronomy 12). The Deuteronomistic tradition explicitly identifies that one shrine as Jerusalem.

Pilgrimage to Zion is the focus of Psalm 84. The psalm begins by attesting to the longing for the Temple that motivated pilgrimage to Jerusalem (vv. 2-4). Verses 5-8 describe the happiness of the pilgrims who have arrived at their goal. Following the prayer for the king (vv. 9-10) is the assertion that God and the Temple bring blessing to Israel. Three verses (5, 6, and 13) begin with the word "happy." The recurrence of this word underscores the elation that accompanied pilgrims on their way to the Temple. The psalm testifies that pilgrimage was not merely a religious obligation but a source of joy.

17. At one time J. J. M. Roberts held that the Zion tradition was a development of the Davidic tradition. See his "Davidic Origin of the Zion Tradition," *JBL* 92 (1973) 329–44. He has since departed from this position. See his "Zion in the Theology of the Davidic-Solomonic Empire," in *Studies in the Period of David and Solomon,* ed. T. Ishida (Winona Lake, Ind.: Eisenbrauns, 1982) 102–3.

18. Ollenburger, *Zion,* 61.

19. "Die Völkerwallfahrt zum Zion," *VT* 7 (1957) 62–81.

Verse 10 speaks of the Davidic monarch by using a Judahite royal title: "messiah," that is, "the anointed one." Here the term "messiah" refers to the reigning Davidide rather than the ideal king of the future.[20] In ancient Near Eastern religious thought the king was *the* priest—the intermediary between the gods and human beings. Israelite religious practice came to separate the royal and priestly offices, although the close relationship between the king and the temple remained, as is clear from 2 Sam 7:1-13 and Psalm 132. Psalm 110:4 has God award the king the priestly office. That the Zion psalms do not mention the king more often probably reflects the intention of these psalms to present Yahweh as Judah's king reigning in Jerusalem, but the precise relationship of the Zion tradition with Davidic theology is not clear. While Ps 132:13 also associates the election of Zion with the election of David, most other psalms that reflect the Zion tradition do not make this connection.

The Lord's Anointed

Though the foundational image behind the Zion tradition is that of Yahweh's kingship, this tradition does not entirely ignore the place of the human being acting as God's viceroy on earth: the Davidic king. The figure of David is central to Psalm 132, as it celebrates the election of both David and Zion, also linked by both 2 Samuel 7 and Psalm 78. This psalm bears several similarities to Psalm 89, which celebrates God's covenant with David and the Davidic dynasty—with one significant difference. While Psalm 89 promises that God will never abandon the dynasty despite the failings of individual kings (see vv. 31-34), Psalm 132 ties the future of the dynasty with obedience to the Torah:

I will make his posterity endure
  forever
  and his throne as the days of
    heaven.
If his sons forsake my law . . .
  I will punish their crime . . .
Yet my kindness I will not take
  from him,
  nor will I belie my faithfulness
  (Ps 89:30-34).
	If your sons keep my covenant
	  and the decrees which I
	    shall teach them,
	Their sons, too, forever
	  shall sit upon your throne
	  (Ps 132:12).

20. This title took on an eschatological connotation in the late post-exilic period when it became clear that Judah's native dynasty was not going to be restored. Its restoration came to be seen as a sign of God's final and decisive movement in Judah's life.

The connection with Zion comes at the very beginning of Psalm 132 and highlights David's piety in building the Temple. The first five verses form a poetic version of the story found in 2 Sam 7:1-6, in which David tells Nathan of his intention to build a temple to house the ark. Acting like any other ancient Near Eastern king, David wished to show his devotion to the patron deity of his kingdom by building a temple for that God in the capital of his kingdom. Ancient Mesopotamian iconography portrayed the king as a temple builder—even portraying the king as hauling mortar for the building's construction.[21] The temple-building hymn of King Gudea of Lagash reads:

> To build the house for his king (God)
> he does not sleep by night,
> he does not slumber at midday.[22]

This suggests that the psalmist was using conventional language and imagery in speaking of David's piety in Ps 132:3-4.

The "resting place" of v. 8 must be Zion, as v. 13 confirms. This psalm does not explicitly relate Jerusalem's security to God's dwelling in Zion but to the eternity of the Davidic dynasty, a motif that v. 10 makes explicit. This is a poetic version of Nathan's oracle (2 Sam 7:8-17). Verses 14-18 recapitulate the subject of Psalm 132: God's presence in Zion brings blessings. While the psalm focuses on the blessing that will come to the Davidic dynasty, blessing will also come upon the land, the poor, the priests, and the faithful. The enemies of Zion, however, will experience something quite different: shame (v. 18).

While David is the focus of this psalm,[23] it is important to note that Zion enjoys a theological priority over the monarchy. The dynasty's future is secure because God has chosen Zion as God's "resting place" (v. 14). David receives divine approval because he relocated the ark from Kireath-jearim, the "fields of Jaar" (v. 6), to Zion, the place God has chosen. Jerusalem is holy not because it was David's capital but because God chose to dwell there. The dynasty is blessed because of David's bringing of the ark to the place God chose. However, the continuation of this blessing depends upon the fidelity of David's descendants to the Torah (Ps 132:12).

---

21. Keel, *Symbolism of the Biblical World,* 269.

22. A. Falkenstein and W. von Soden, *Sumerische und akkadische Hymnen und Gebete.* (Zurich-Stuttgart, 1953) 154.

23. Notice how the name of David appears at the beginning and end of the major divisions of this psalm: vv. 1 and 10; vv. 11 and 17.

The significance of the divine title "Mighty One of Jacob" in vv. 2 and 5 is a mystery. The Psalter mentions Jacob more than any other figure of ancient Israel's distant past. The thirty-four occurrences of his name is more than double the total for Abraham, Isaac, and Moses. Psalm 132 is the only psalm in which this title appears. Other psalms use the expression "the God of Jacob" (Ps 20:2; 24:8; 46:8, 12; 75:10; 76:7; 81:2, 5; 84:9; 94:7; 114:7). Weiser believes the use of this expression was an attempt to link the traditions of northern Israel with those of the south.[24] Dahood finds in it an indication of an eleventh-century date for this psalm.[25] The phrase occurs for the first time in Gen 49:24. The only five occurrences of the phrase "Mighty One of Jacob" outside Genesis are in texts related to the Zion tradition: Ps 132:2, 5; Isa 49:26; 60:16. A variant, the "Mighty One of Israel," also occurs in a Zion text: Isa 1:24. Ollenburger argues that this phrase must have a particular connection with the Zion tradition and locates its origins in the ark tradition of Shiloh.[26] While his suggestion about the origins of this epithet may be hypothetical, it is clear that the phrase "Mighty One of Jacob" became associated with the Temple at Jerusalem. This title never occurs with El or Baal, so its origins are probably Israelite and probably before the rise of the Davidic dynasty, since there seem to be no other links between Jacob and Judah's monarchy.

Psalm 132 exemplifies the relationship between the monarchy and the temple in ancient Near Eastern religious traditions. The king builds a temple for the patron deity of his nation and then receives his crown from that deity (vv. 5, 18). The psalm develops that theme along Israelite lines in several ways. The epithet chosen for God is the "Mighty One of Jacob" (vv. 2, 5)—a title that comes from earlier tribal traditions and is reapplied to the Zion tradition. The psalm underscores the role of the Davidic dynasty in Israel's life. It traces divine support for that dynasty to David's relocation of the ark in Jerusalem (vv. 6-10) and his determination to have a temple built to house the ark (vv. 1-5). To secure their future the kings of David's dynasty must be faithful to the Torah (v. 12). God will defeat David's enemies (v. 18) and bless the entire nation from Zion (vv. 14-16).

Mother Zion

Another aspect of the Zion tradition that calls for comment is its universalism. Psalm 87 is a good example of the inclusion of the nations in the worship of Yahweh. This short psalm contains several obscure

24. Weiser, *Psalms,* 780.
25. Dahood, *Psalms III,* 243.
26. Ollenburger, *Zion,* 41–2.

phrases.[27] Still, its basic thrust is clear: it is a psalm that glorifies Zion as a city founded by God and in which all peoples of the world will find their home. The psalm thus combines a common ancient Near Eastern mythological motif and a distinctively Israelite eschatological hope. It looks back to the distant past when God established order in the world, and it looks to the future when God will reassert control over this world and its peoples.

The psalm begins in an unusual way. It addresses Zion directly—something that is not clear from modern English translations, although Dahood tries to convey this sense.[28] An alternative translation of vv. 1-3 is

> O (city) founded by (God) on the holy mountain
> the LORD loves you, O gates of Zion.
> Wonderful things are said about you,
> city of God.

While these verses may be difficult to translate into idiomatic English, what they try to communicate is clear enough. Their imagery is clearly mythological. In ancient Near Eastern thought the gods founded major cities. Each of these was home to a temple. The god that resided in that temple was the founder, defender, and king of that city. Though the Deuteronomic tradition speaks about the place God will *choose* to make the Divine Name dwell (Deut 12:11 and passim), some of the psalms prefer to use mythological imagery that has God *building* the Temple, or Zion (Pss 78:69; 102:17; 147:2). Still, both the mythological imagery of the psalms and the demythologized version in Deuteronomy reflect the belief that the decision to locate the Temple in Jerusalem was God's choice—this despite the tradition that credited David with locating the ark in Jerusalem and Solomon with building the Temple there (2 Samuel 6; 1 Kings 5–8).

Psalm 87:4-7 also have their obscure phrases, but the threefold repetition of the phrase "This one was born there/in it" (vv. 4d, 5b, 6b) implies that whatever a person's national origin, that person can claim Zion as home. The psalm pushes the religion of ancient Israel toward a universalism that is not characteristic of ancient Near Eastern religious thought. Each nation had its patron deity. It was this god who protected the interests of that nation. Assyria had Asshur; Moab had Chemosh; Babylon had

---

27. See E. Beaucamp, "Le problème du Psaume 87," *LA* 13 (1962–3) 53–75, who describes in detail the textual problems of this psalm. Dahood saw the problems not with the original Hebrew of the text, which contained only consonants, but with the later vocalization of the psalm by the Masoretes. See his *Psalms II*, 298–9.

28. Dahood, *Psalms II*, 298.

Marduk; Philistia had Dagon; but Yahweh, Israel's national God, was to embrace all peoples. It is remarkable that pilgrims to Zion sang this song in spite of their experience with the other peoples of the eastern Mediterranean. Other Zion songs (Psalms 46–48) also have a universalist scope, but they tend to see the nations as enemies to be subdued by the God of Israel, for example, Pss 46:7-8; 47:4; 48:5-8. Here the nations are children of "Mother Zion."[29] Of course, the Isaianic tradition, especially Isaiah 40–55, is known for its universalism (Isa 2:2-4; 49:6; 54:1; 55:5, 11). That ancient Israel's cultic traditions affirm that Jerusalem will embrace all the nations one day is astonishing. The singing of this psalm by Judahite pilgrims was their assent to a vision of the future that embraced all peoples as one family of God. The psalm begins with a most particularist assertion: God founded Zion. Still, within the space of a few verses an extraordinary universalism springs forth.

The Inviolability of Zion

A serious problem arose because of Jerusalem's designation as "the city of God." Some people began to see the city as inviolable.[30] The city's religious significance affected judgments about its political and military status. Again, the psalms offer the clearest expression of this view, as they praise God who is Jerusalem's source of safety and strength (Pss 46:2-4; 76:2-3). The nations surrounding Israel are hostile to Jerusalem (Pss 46:7; 48:5), but God acts to protect the city because it is God's own (Pss 46:9-10; 48:6-9; 76:4-10). The Temple's hymns sing of Jerusalem as divinely guarded. This makes it impossible for any enemy to conquer it. Such an attitude is understandable given the mythological origin of much of the Zion tradition. From a historical perspective, it was very dangerous.

From the rise of the kingdom of Judah and through most of its history, the state, which Jerusalem served as the capital, was a satellite of more powerful nations in the region. It was subject first to the kingdom of Israel, then to Assyria, Egypt, and finally Babylon. There was very little opportunity for Judah to chart an independent course. Its destiny was guided by others. Of course, there were Judahites who resented this and called for political and military action that would free Judah from foreign domination. The Zion tradition offered them religious support for their revolutionary plans. These never succeeded and usually led to more firm foreign control, until Babylon besieged Jerusalem, destroyed its Temple, and ended

29. The Septuagint adds "mother" to Zion in Ps 87:5.
30. See John H. Hayes, "The Tradition of Zion's Inviolability," *JBL* 82 (1963) 419–26.

even the semblance of Judahite independence by incorporating Judah into the Babylonian provincial system in 587 B.C.

Exile and Restoration

Several psalms reflect on the fall of Jerusalem and the destruction of its Temple in 587 B.C. These psalms testify to the central role Zion came to have in ancient Israelite religious thought and life. Of course, the disaster of 587 B.C. led the Judahites to pray for the restoration of their city and its Temple. The restoration following the decree of Cyrus in 539 B.C. (see 2 Chr 36:22-23) prompted prayers of thanksgiving.

This is a communal lament over the destruction of the Temple. Judah came under Babylonian hegemony in March 597 B.C., when Nabuchadnezzar's siege of Jerusalem led to the surrender of King Jehoiachin, whom the Babylonians exiled along with many leading citizens of Judah (2 Kgs 24:8-16; see also the account in "The Babylonian Chronicles," *ANET,* 564, and "The Weidner Tablets," *ANET,* 308). Nabuchadnezzar allowed the Judahite state to continue to exist, although it had to pay tribute to Babylon. He also installed a member of the Davidic house to rule as king: Jehoiachin's uncle Mattaniah, who received the throne-name, was Zedekiah (2 Kgs 24:17). During his ten-year reign he was subject to great internal and external pressure to reassert Judah's independence from Babylon. With the assurance of help from Egypt, Zedekiah revolted against Nabuchadnezzar in 589. Egyptian help was too halfhearted to save Judah (see Jeremiah 37). Jerusalem fell again in 587 and was systematically destroyed by order of Nabuchadnezzar. The fall of the city and the destruction of its Temple inspired laments like Psalm 74.

The psalmist asks God to "remember" Mount Zion, God's dwelling place (v. 2). In developing this motif, the psalm begins by reversing the "defeat of the nations" motif from the Zion tradition. Verses 4-11 give a concrete description of the actions the Babylonians took in destroying the Temple. These verses describe the victory of Zion's enemies and ask how long God will be inactive as the enemy continues to subject Zion. To stimulate God to act the psalm uses another motif from the Zion tradition: God as the conqueror of chaotic powers, personified here as the mythological sea creature Leviathan (vv. 12-17). The psalm ends with a reprise of the "remember" motif (v. 18) and adds a variant, "do not forget" (vv. 19 and 23).

Zion, God's dwelling place on earth, was a symbol of Judah's security. Its fall meant that the very foundation of the people's future was gone. But the use of the motif connected with the destruction of Leviathan implies that the destruction of Zion was not merely a national tragedy for Judah but an event of cosmic significance. Jeremiah does the same when he portrays Nabuchadnezzar as a dragon that consumes Jerusalem (Jer 51:34). Still, the psalm implies that what Yahweh did to defeat Leviathan in the distant past, Yahweh can do again to Judah's enemies, which the psalm characterizes as God's enemies (v. 23). This lament is a prayer that God show supremacy over Judah's enemies just as God did in the primeval age. God ought not to allow the Babylonians to take away the fruits of victory.

Psalm 137 is a reaction to the request made by the Babylonians that the exiles of Judah sing "the songs of Zion" for them (v. 3). Singing such songs celebrating Yahweh's kingship and Zion's election would have been too painful given the fall of the city and the exile of its citizens. This psalm exposes the painful separation experienced by those exiled from Zion. The psalm begins with a poignant image: exiles longing for Jerusalem— their pain multiplied by the insensitive requests of their captors to sing about their homeland (vv. 1-3). The centerpiece of the psalm (vv. 4-6) makes clear the position Jerusalem came to have among the Judahites. The singers of this psalm promise that if they forget Jerusalem, God should make it impossible for them ever again to play a stringed instrument (v. 5) or sing (v. 6). The passionate intensity of the psalm's final strophe (vv. 7-9) is difficult for some modern readers to appreciate. The horrifying sentiments of these final verses, which call for vengeance against those people who left Zion in ruins, are a testimony to the significance that Zion came to have.

Babylon eventually fell. Cyrus the Persian added Babylon to his empire in 539 B.C. Cyrus allowed all captive peoples to return to their native lands and restored the worship of their national deities. The Persians believed that there were two conflicting divine principles in the world: a benevolent one, Ahura Mazda, and the malevolent one, Ahriman. Cyrus believed that the gods worshiped by other peoples were simply manifestations of Ahura Mazda rather than deities competing for supremacy in the heavens. Of course, the Judahites still regarded their national deity, Yahweh, as guiding their destiny. They ascribed the restoration of Judah to their God, who chose Cyrus for the task of liberating the Judahites (see Isa 45:1-4).

Psalm 147 celebrates Yahweh as the restorer of Jerusalem (vv. 1-6). The second part of the psalm (vv. 7-11) does not mention the city as it calls worshipers to praise God, who restores creation by the gift of rain.[31]

---

31. Because Israel had no river system that could make large-scale irrigation possible, its agricultural enterprises were completely dependent on rain. In such circumstances, having enough rainfall was a continuing source of anxiety, and religious rituals served to relieve that anxiety by assuring worshipers that God would provide sufficient rain to ensure an adequate supply of food.

The final strophe (vv. 12-20) calls worshipers to praise God, whose power and presence are clear from the created world and the word revealed to Israel. Verse 12 begins the final call to praise by inviting Jerusalem/Zion to praise the God who strengthens the city's defenses and blesses its citizens.[32]

Throughout Psalm 147 God alone is active. Thus the restoration of Zion is just as much the result of God's power alone as are the creation and sustenance of the world. Human beings do nothing more than stand in awe of the divine deeds—an awe that leads to praise. By implication, then, the restoration of Zion is a confirmation of the city's status in Judah's religion, since it was chosen by God and then rebuilt by God. The appropriate response is to praise the Lord, who has rebuilt the city and granted peace and prosperity to its people (vv. 2a, 12-14).

Conclusion

Although it was originally a name for a portion of the city, Zion came to be a synonym for the whole of Jerusalem, then for the entire land of Israel, and eventually for the people of Israel as well. The etymology of this name and its exact meaning are uncertain, although similar Arabic forms suggest the term originally referred to a fortress located on a ridge.[33] Zion's fame, however, derived from its identification as the place where the Temple stood:

> God chose the tribe of Judah,
>   Mount Zion which he favored.
> He built his shrine like the heavens,
>   like the earth which he founded forever (Ps. 78:68-69).

Once this identification was made, it was not long before Zion became a synonym for all of Jerusalem. The book of Lamentations, for example, uses Zion and Jerusalem interchangeably:

> To what can I liken or compare you,
>   O daughter Jerusalem?
> What example can I show you for your comfort,
>   virgin daughter Zion? (Lam 2:13a).

Finally, Zion became a metaphor for the people of Israel, since the fate of the Temple, city, and people were woven together:

32. In Egypt, a pharaoh who ruled for thirty years participated in a ritual called the Sed festival, which served to renew his strength. During a part of that ritual the pharaoh walked around his capital city striking each gate with a mace. This was to reestablish the gate's defensive strength and to protect the sphere of blessing around the city. Verse 13 attributes this to Yahweh, who restored Zion. Keel, *Symbolism of the Biblical World,* 122.

33. W. Harold Mare, "Zion," *ABD* 6:1096.

I have put my words into your mouth
   and shielded you in the shadow of my hand,
I, who stretched out the heavens,
   who laid the foundations of the earth,
   who say to Zion: You are my people (Isa 51:16).

Ancient Israel's psalmists use the word "Zion" to speak of Jerusalem more often than any other. In praising Zion, the site of Jerusalem's Temple, the psalmists adopt imagery from the religious culture of the ancient Near East. They wish to portray Jerusalem in terms of God's kingship. God defeated the powers of chaos to become king and chose Zion as the place from which God would rule. Zion, then, is God's holy mountain, which God will protect from all threats. The presence of God in Zion attracts pilgrims to this city of God, which is also the place where David and his descendants rule. One day, however, all nations will find a home in Jerusalem.

The psalmists' dreams of Zion as a mother to the nations have come true beyond the psalmists' wildest expectations. Not only Judaism but Christianity and Islam consider Jerusalem to be a "holy city." The fallout from the competing religious and political claims has served only to obscure the city's sacred character. Both the modern State of Israel and the Palestinian Authority claim Jerusalem as their capital. The Vatican wants guarantees that whatever political solution is reached on the status of the city, unhindered access to shrines will be maintained. Such guarantees will not mean an end of disputes, since the Orthodox religious establishment in Israel prevents Reform and Conservative Jews from praying at the Western Wall according to their traditions and beliefs. The tensions among various Christian churches at shrines like the Holy Sepulchre are well known.

The psalmists describe Zion as the place where heaven and earth meet. It is the "city of God." This vision of the city has been its greatest blessing and greatest burden. The place of Jerusalem in the hearts of so many believers has helped the city survive from the Bronze Age to the present. Unfortunately, the city has become the scene of intense political and religious struggles. The city's future will depend upon the triumph of God's justice:

As your name, O God, so also your praise
   Reaches to the ends of the earth.
Of justice your right hand is full;
   let Mount Zion be glad,
Let the cities of Judah rejoice,
   because of your judgments (Ps 48:11-12).

3

A Place for God's Name:
Jerusalem in the Deuteronomic Tradition

The book of Psalms does not hesitate to use motifs derived from ancient Near Eastern culture to express its belief that Jerusalem was the "city of God," the place that God chose to dwell on earth. Psalm 132 expressly declares that "the LORD has chosen Zion, desired it for his dwelling" (v. 13), and Psalm 76 asserts that "God's abode has been established in Salem (i.e., Jerusalem), his dwelling is in Zion" (v. 3). Using motifs drawn from this tradition, Isaiah tells of a vision he had of God sitting on a throne in the Temple (Isaiah 6), which the prophet calls "the place of Mount Zion" (Isa 4:5). Indeed, the prophet explicitly states that God dwelt on Mount Zion (Isa 8:18). The people of Jerusalem had good reason to believe their city and its Temple were, in fact, chosen by God as God's dwelling place. The Deuteronomic tradition expresses its attitude toward Jerusalem in a mode quite different from the poetry and mythology of the psalms. While still affirming that the city was chosen by God for a unique role, the Deuteronomic tradition is more restrained in its language about Jerusalem.

The Book of Deuteronomy

A principal aim of the book of Deuteronomy was to centralize all sacrificial worship at Jerusalem's Temple. The book wanted to eliminate all other sanctuaries from the land. Although Deuteronomy aimed to curtail the sacrificial cult of ancient Israel, it enhanced the status of Jerusalem by making its Temple the only place where legitimate worship of Israel's God was permitted (see Deuteronomy 12). Still, what Deuteronomy gave to Jerusalem with one hand it took away with the other. The book did indeed elevate Jerusalem to a unique status within Israel, but it also divested the city of its claim to be God's chosen dwelling place. Jerusalem's Temple was not the place where God dwelt but merely the place where God's name dwelt. It is God's name rather than the Deity itself that was to be found in Jerusalem. The repeated use of the Deuteronomic phrase "to cause (God's) name to dwell there" (see 12:11; 13:12; 14:23; 16:2, 11; 26:2) was likely intended to undercut the anthropomorphic belief that the Deity actually dwelt in the Temple.[1] There is not a single example of a text in the book of Deuteronomy asserting that God dwells in the Temple.

Deuteronomy, then, introduced Israel to the transcendence of the Deity. The existence of a temple, its rituals, and its theology complicated Deuteronomy's task. The very idea of a temple leads to the conception that God has need of a house or at least dwells in a building constructed by human beings. Within Jerusalem's Temple, although removed from the human eye, God sits between the two cherubim, and God's feet rest upon the ark, God's throne (1 Sam 4:4; 1 Chr 13:6) or footstool (1 Chr 28:6; Ps 99:5). Priests attend to God's every need. They place loaves of bread on a table that also supports the vessels with drink (Exod 25:29; 37:16). They light the lamps that furnish light and burn incense for God's pleasure. In contrast to all this, Deuteronomy's God has no need for food or shelter. In fact, Deuteronomic phraseology does not have God dwelling in the Temple. In Deuteronomy the ark is not God's footstool or throne. It is simply a receptacle for the tablets of the covenant (Deut 10:1-5). The ark, then, does not mediate or represent the divine presence in the Temple. It is made of acacia wood (Deut 10:3), but nothing is said about the wood being gold-plated (cf. Exod 37:2). Deuteronomy appears to downplay the importance of both the Temple and the ark. The Temple is the place where God's name dwells, and the ark is a box beside which the covenant documents are placed (Deut 31:26).

Deuteronomy does affirm that Jerusalem is God's city, but it chooses to do so without recourse to anthropomorphic motifs. More than any other book of the Bible, Deuteronomy implies that Jerusalem has a status unique

---

1. This was the thesis of Gerhard von Rad. See his "Deuteronomy's 'Name' Theology," 37–46. Roland de Vaux rejected von Rad's hypothesis because he claimed that analysis of similar phraseology in Egyptian literature leads to the conclusion that the Deuteronomic phrase simply means that God is the owner of the sanctuary. See de Vaux, "Le lieu que Yahvé a choisi pour y établir son nom," *Das Ferne und nahe Wort,* Fest. L. Rost. BZAW 105 (Berlin: Töpelmann, 1967) 219–28. Even if de Vaux's reading of the Egyptian literature is correct, this does not preclude a Deuteronomic reinterpretation of the Egyptian formula.

among ancient Israel's cities. At the same time, however, it does not allow the reader to conclude that Jerusalem or its Temple could be God's dwelling place. For Deuteronomy, God's dwelling place can only be in the heavens. This is clear from a prayer the book has the Israelite farmers say when they give the triennial tithe to the poor: "Look down from your holy dwelling, from heaven" (Deut 26:15). The Deuteronomists introduce the phrase "from heaven" into their prayer so that no one could misconstrue "your holy dwelling" as referring to Jerusalem or its Temple.

Deuteronomy presents itself as Moses' final testament to Israel, given just before he dies. It cannot, therefore, explicitly name Jerusalem as the "place that God will choose to make (God's) name dwell there." The book purposely avoids mentioning any proper names that might sound anachronistic.[2] The books of Kings, which derive their theology from Deuteronomy, do make it clear that this place was, in fact, Jerusalem.[3] This is especially clear in Solomon's prayer at the dedication of the Temple:

> Since the day that I [God] brought my people Israel out of Egypt, I have not chosen a city out of any of the tribes of Israel for the building of a temple to my honor. . . . I [Solomon] . . . have built this temple to honor the LORD the God of Israel (1 Kgs 8:16, 20).

Jerusalem, of course, was the city in which Solomon built the Temple. The Deuteronomistic designation of Jerusalem as "the place God chose" is another moment in the process that led to the city's sanctification. Like the psalms, the Deuteronomic tradition believes Jerusalem is "the city of God," yet its expression of that belief is entirely devoid of the mythological motifs the psalmists did not hesitate to use.

What led the Deuteronomist to raise Jerusalem to a unique status among ancient Israel's cities while divesting it of the honor of being God's dwelling place on earth? The origins of Deuteronomy have been associated with the so-called reform of Josiah (see 2 Kings 22–23) for almost two hundred years. Wilhelm de Wette's study of the Josianic reform, in which he identifies the book that inspired the reform with Deuteronomy, has proven to be a most durable hypothesis.[4] Still, it is likely that the story of the finding

2. Weinfeld, *Deuteronomy,* 6.
3. See 1 Kgs 8:26, 44, 48; 11:13, 32, 36; 14:21; 2 Kgs 21:7; 23:27.
4. W. M. L. de Wette, *Dissertatio critica, qua Deuteronomium a prioribus Pentateuchi libris diversum, alius cuiusdam recentioris opus esse monstratur* (Jena: 1805). Reprinted in *Opuscula Theologica* (Berlin: 1839). De Wette was not the first to identify the law book of 2 Kings 22 with Deuteronomy. Jerome, Chrysostom, and Athanasius made the same identification. See Nestle, "Das Deuteronomium und II Könige xxii," 170–1, 312–3.

of the law book (2 Kgs 22:8) was an attempt by the Deuteronomist to de-scribe Josiah's attempt at cult centralization in terms of obedience to the Torah when Josiah's motives were more political than religious. Weinfeld has noted the similarity between Josiah's attempt to centralize Judahite sacrificial worship in Jerusalem and a similar action taken by Nabonidus in Babylon about eighty years later.[5]

Anticipating an invasion by the Persians, Nabonidus brought the images of Babylonian gods honored in various cities of his empire to the city of Babylon. Apparently he hoped that this move would cement the loyalty of his subjects to him and his royal city. This action had the very opposite effect. The Babylonians welcomed Cyrus as a liberator and opened the city gates for him. It is possible to understand Josiah's attempt to central-ize sacrificial worship in Jerusalem as a move designed to unite Judah be-hind him as the king began his political and military moves and the Assyrian Empire was disintegrating. Josiah's untimely death (2 Kgs 23:29) brought an end to the political ambitions of the Judahite state and the Davidic dy-nasty and ushered in a period of vassalage to Egypt (2 Kgs 23:31-35). Josiah's "reforms" died with him, and each of his successors is con-demned for doing "evil in the sight of the LORD, just as his forebears had done" (see 2 Kgs 23:32, 37; 24:9, 19). This "evil" likely included permit-ting worship at the "high places" Josiah had removed (2 Kgs 22:8, 19).

The incorporation of Judah into the Babylonian provincial system fol-lowing Zedekiah's revolt devastated Judah and Jerusalem. What shape the Judahite cult took following the destruction of the Temple (2 Kgs 25:9) can only be surmised. With the restoration following the victory of Cyrus over Babylon, the Temple continued to lie in ruins, although the Persians encouraged its rebuilding and supported the project financially. The eco-nomic problems during the early part of the restoration period (see Hag 1:5-6) meant that the people of Judah could not support sacrificial wor-ship at local shrines. Limiting sacrificial worship to Jerusalem was a prac-tical solution given Judah's limited territory and economic resources. In other words, Deuteronomy's program of cult centralization was a matter of making virtue out of necessity.

Deuteronomy was less concerned about the Temple and its ritual than it was about the future of Israel. This book assumes that Israel's future was dependent not on the presence of God in the Temple but on Israel's obedience to the written authoritative law found within it. After all, the presence of God in Jerusalem's Temple did not prevent disaster from be-falling Israel. The people's failure to observe the stipulations of the covenant

5. Weinfeld, "Cult Centralization," 202–12.

brought a curse upon them, Jerusalem, and the Temple (Deut 28:15-68). It follows, then, that if Israel were to have any future at all, that future was dependent upon the blessing that comes through obedience (Deut 28:1-14). Of course, worship was an element of Israel's obedience to the Lord, but it was only one element. Deuteronomy plays down the role of the liturgy and the priesthood so central in Exodus and Leviticus in favor of a more comprehensive understanding of obedience. The Deuteronomists agree that Jerusalem has a significant role in Israel's life. Still, one can overplay its importance. More important than any city or Temple is the obedience that brings life (Deut 30:15-20).

The Deuteronomistic History of Israel

Far more theologically significant than cult centralization is the Deuteronomic tradition's understanding of the Temple. This understanding is clearest in the Deuteronomistic History of Israel, the story of Israel's life in its land (Joshua—2 Kings)—a story whose theological assumptions derive from the book of Deuteronomy. The last event narrated in Second Kings: the parole of Jehoiachin by the Babylonian king Amel-marduk (the Bible calls him Evil-merodach) can be dated with some certainty to the years 561/560 B.C. (see 2 Kgs 25:27-30). This means that the work modern scholarship has termed the "Deuteronomistic History of Israel" took the shape it now has some time after Jehoiachin's parole— almost thirty years after the fall of Jerusalem. It is likely, then, that one purpose of this "history" was to explain that disaster to a people whose religious beliefs included the conviction that Jerusalem was inviolable since it was the city of God. The characterization of this work as Deuteronomistic reflects the conviction that its ideological principles derive from the book of Deuteronomy. The "history" is a long negative example story with two foci. First, it looks to the past as it makes the fall of Jerusalem comprehensive from a moral point of view. Second, it looks to the future as it describes the kind of behavior the Judahites would have to avoid were there to be a restoration of the city. In other words, the Deuteronomistic History turns the past into a sermon—a sermon about infidelity and its consequences. It serves as a warning to the Judahites that they must pattern their lives according to the moral principles found in the book of Deuteronomy were they to have any hope for the future.

What does the Deuteronomistic History say about Jerusalem? At first the picture is confused. The book of Joshua describes a miraculous Israelite victory over a five-king coalition led by Adoni-zedek of Jerusalem (10:1, 5, 23; 12:10). The irony here is that, in the end, it was not a Canaanite king the God of Israel fought against and defeated. Jerusalem fell because God fought against a Davidic king and used the Babylonian armies to execute judgment upon Jerusalem for the infidelity of its people. Joshua also assigns the city of Jerusalem to the tribe of Judah (15:8) but notes that the Judahites were not able to completely dispossess the indigenous people, so the city had a mixed population (15:63). The naming of Jerusalem as one of the cities assigned to Judah is part of a long list of such cities that take up the entire fifteenth chapter of Joshua. This list reflects the continuing claim of the exiles to the land that belonged to their ancestors. By the middle of the sixth century most of these cities were either incorporated into the Babylonian provincial system or had fallen into Edomite hands. Joshua 15 is an expression of the exiles' hope that they will be able to reclaim the land that God gave their ancestors. The book of Joshua also assigns Jerusalem to the tribe of Benjamin (Josh 18:28), but Judg 1:21 asserts that the Benjaminites were not able to drive out the Jebusites completely. Contradicting both these traditions, Judg 1:7-8 maintains that Judahites indeed did take Jerusalem, killing its inhabitants and setting the city afire. Later the same book speaks of Jerusalem as a Jebusite town that Israelites avoid (19:10). All these details underscore the sad past of Jerusalem. Its fall in 587 B.C. was its latest and most unexpected defeat. The Deuteronomists want to make it clear that Jerusalem enjoyed no special privileges as "the city of God." Its inhabitants had to live according to the divine will or face divine judgment.

The confusion in Joshua and Judges ends with the story of David's rise to power. Immediately following Saul's death the members of David's own tribe, Judah, acclaimed him as their king. David ruled over Judah from the city of Hebron (2 Sam 2:1-11). It was not until seven years later that representatives from the other tribes offered to accept him as their king as well (2 Sam 5:1-5). David then moved to eliminate the one remaining Canaanite enclave that separated Judah from the rest of the tribes: the "stronghold of Zion." He took the city and made it his capital, renaming it "the city of David" (2 Sam 5:6-10). Jerusalem then became the principal city of Judah and Israel, united under the rule of David. It is necessary to note that the Deuteronomistic History never calls Jerusalem "the city of God." It is merely "the city of David" and, as such, is subject to divine judgment.

What gave Jerusalem its significance in the Deuteronomistic History was the Temple. Deuteronomy's program of centralizing Israel's sacrificial worship in the one place designated by God is developed in Deuteronomistic literature by explicit reference to Jerusalem and its Temple. Though David had planned to build a temple in his city, a prophetic oracle advised him against it:

[T]he Lord spoke to Nathan and said: "Go, tell my servant David, 'Thus says the LORD: Should you build me a house to dwell in? I have not dwelt in a house from the day on which I led the Israelites out of Egypt to the present, but I have been going about in a tent under cloth. In all my wanderings everywhere among the Israelites, did I ever utter a word to any one of the judges whom I charged to tend my people Israel, to ask: Why have you not built me a house of cedar?'" (2 Sam 7:4-7).

David's intention to build a temple for the patron deity of his kingdom was one way for him to assert his legitimacy as Israel's king, since temple building was a royal prerogative.[6] A preliminary step was his bringing the ark of the covenant to Jerusalem (2 Samuel 6). The ark of the covenant, which represented the divine presence among the tribes, moved to the different shrines maintained in the areas where the Israelites settled. Among the shrines where the ark was rested were Shechem (Josh 8:33); Mizpah (Judg 20:1); Bethel (Judg 20:27); and Shiloh (1 Sam 4:4). Centuries later Jeremiah recalled this and announced that as God abandoned Shiloh so God would abandon Jerusalem (Jer 26:9). The building of Jerusalem's Temple as a permanent location for the ark (2 Sam 7:1-3) was a genuine innovation because, until the Temple was built, the ark of God had no fixed location. The earliest Israelite tradition is that God wandered among the people of Israel. Perhaps this was a deliberate decision of the tribes to avoid the possibility that one tribe would feel superior to the others.[7]

Although the prophet Nathan informed David that God did not want a temple (2 Sam 7:5), the Deuteronomists, of course, note that Solomon, David's son and successor, was designated by God to build a house for God's name (see 2 Sam 7:13). The Deuteronomists felt they had to justify this departure from tradition by noting that under Solomon the Israelites finally had "rest" from all their enemies. They were enjoying their full inheritance as promised by God to their ancestors. God, too, deserved a "resting-place," which Solomon provided in the form of Jerusalem's Temple (1 Kgs 5:17-19). Though Solomon built the Temple, the Deuteronomists made it clear that Jerusalem was the city that God chose as the dwelling-place for God's name (see 1 Kgs 11:36), not for God. In speaking of the Temple, the characters in 2 Samuel and the books of Kings always use the formula typical of Deuteronomy, that is, the Temple is the place where God's name dwells (1 Kgs 5:17, 19, and passim).

Another Deuteronomic concern that gets a prominent place is the centralization of sacrificial worship in the place God will choose (see

6. Kapelrud, "Temple Building," 56–62.
7. Weinfeld, "Zion and Jerusalem," 89.

Deuteronomy 12). While Deuteronomy cannot name the place as Jerusalem, since that would have been patently anachronistic, 1 and 2 Kings do identify the place of God's choosing as Jerusalem (1 Kgs 8:44; 11:13; 14:21; 2 Kgs 21:4, 7). Because the kingdom of Israel had temples for sacrificial worship at Dan and Bethel, the Deuteronomists condemn every one of its kings. First Kings 12:26-30 blames Jeroboam I for what it considers a violation of the explicit command of God to offer sacrificial worship only at the place of God's choosing, that is, Jerusalem. The Deuteronomists call this violation "the sin of Jeroboam." Most of the kings of Judah were also condemned because they either instigated or tolerated sacrificial worship at "the high places," local shrines in addition to the official national cult at Jerusalem (e.g., 1 Kgs 14:23). Though kings like Hezekiah and Josiah attempted to centralize sacrificial worship in Jerusalem for political reasons, in all likelihood (2 Kgs 18:4; 23:5, 8-9, 12-15) centralization of worship was an innovation of the Deuteronomic tradition. A staunch Yahwist like Elijah repaired an altar to Yahweh on Mount Carmel. Fire from heaven came down to consume the sacrifice offered on it, demonstrating God's acceptance of the sacrifice (1 Kgs 18:30-38).

The Deuteronomists make explicit what they thought of the Temple and, therefore, of Jerusalem in their account of the Temple's dedication (1 Kgs 8:14-66). In typical Deuteronomistic fashion they take the opportunity of a momentous event to have someone in the story relate the significance of that event to the reader.[8] Solomon begins by reminding the people that God chose David with the added suggestion that God did not chose a city:

> Since the day I brought my people Israel out of Egypt, I have not chosen a city out of any tribe of Israel for the building of a temple to my honor; but I choose David to rule my people Israel (1 Kgs 8:16).[9]

Still, the magnificent building for God's name is spectacular testimony to God's choice of Jerusalem. Although Solomon's prayer begins by charac-

8. Other examples include Joshua's address to Israel just before his death (Josh 24:1-25) and Huldah's speech to Josiah's emissaries authenticating the law book found in the Temple (2 Kgs 22:15-20). After the fall of the kingdom of Israel there was no one to make the speech, so the Deuteronomists simply offer an extended editorial comment (2 Kgs 17:7-23).

9. The Septuagint adds "and I chose Jerusalem that my name may abide there" to 1 Kgs 8:16. See also 2 Chr 6:6. Both couple God's choice of David with God's choice of Jerusalem. In the tradition about David's election in 2 Sam 7:5-16 there is no mention of Jerusalem, and here Solomon follows suit. That is why commentators suggest that the Septuagint text and 2 Chr 6:6 are the result of a secondary addition. Even if that is true, it shows that it was difficult to treat of David's election without soon getting into God's choice of Jerusalem.

terizing the Temple as "a dwelling where [God] may abide forever" (1 Kgs 8:13), the rest of the prayer uses the more explicitly Deuteronomic phraseology that describes the Temple as built "to the honor of the LORD" (1 Kgs 8:17-20).[10] Solomon's prayer insists that God's dwelling is in heaven (see 1 Kgs 8:30, 39, 43, 49). The Deuteronomic description of the Temple as a place for God's name underscores this tradition's idea of the Temple's significance. Deuteronomy's notion of the Deity excludes the anthropomorphic and corporeal, and therefore it cannot describe God as dwelling in a temple. While God caused the divine name to dwell in the Temple, the Deity itself does not dwell in any building.

Solomon's prayer sees the Temple not as a place where God dwells but as a place of worship where all people may come to offer their prayers to God. Among the occasions most appropriate for prayer in the Temple is a time of national crisis (1 Kgs 8:33-34). The Deuteronomists believed that such crises were the result of Israel's sin, so if people offer prayers of repentance, then God will hear and forgive. The phase "bring them back to the land you gave their fathers" (v. 34) is an oblique reference to the Exile, which was a principal impetus for the composition of the Deuteronomistic History in its final form. For the Deuteronomists the Exile happened because of the people's infidelity. Repentance and prayer are the ways to deal with that problem.

A surprising component of Solomon's prayer is his inclusion of foreigners who come to the Temple attracted by the religious values of ancient Israel. This motif will be developed by the prophets of the exilic and post-exilic era, though this is a very ancient motif in Semitic literature. Two thousand years before Solomon, the Sumerians dedicated their temples with the expectations that nations from all over the earth would bring offerings to the gods for which the temples were built.[11] Usually the Deuteronomic tradition is not very positive toward the nations (see Deut 23). This likely reflects the experience of the people of Judah and Jerusalem who experienced the nations primarily as threats to their continued existence. Perhaps the significance of this motif in ancient Near Eastern temple-dedication ceremonies was too great to omit in Solomon's prayer of dedication.

Verses 46–51 speak unmistakably about the Exile, blaming this disaster on the people's sin. Solomon prays that God will forgive the people if they turn to God "with all their heart and soul" (v. 48; cf. Deut 6:5) and

10. The *NAB* chooses to translate the Hebrew expression as "in honor of the Lord." Still, a more literal rendering is "for the name of the Lord."

11. Weinfeld, "Zion and Jerusalem," 104–5.

pray in the land of their exile, facing Judah, Jerusalem, and the Temple. This underscores the Deuteronomic view of the Temple as a place for prayer. Sacrificial worship may be implied, but it is not mentioned. While sacrificial worship may be offered only in Jerusalem, those devoted to Yahweh can offer prayers anywhere. In the Deuteronomistic perspective, Jerusalem and its Temple become simply the means for believers to orient themselves for prayer. It is ironic that the Deuteronomic tradition, whose program of centralization exalts the place of Jerusalem's Temple, at the same time undercuts it. If the Temple is a place of prayer and prayer can be offered anywhere, how central is the Temple in the religion of Yahweh?

Another way the Deuteronomic tradition undercuts the centrality of the Temple is its approach to the role of the priesthood and sacrifice. Deuteronomy underplays both—especially when compared to the priestly tradition found in Exodus, Leviticus, and Numbers. Except for Deut 18:1-8, the book never mentions priests unless some layperson has a reason to deal with one. Also, the book does not go into detail about the different types of sacrifices, the furnishings of the tabernacle, priestly vestments and rights, and feast days, as does the priestly tradition. The Deuteronomic tradition, then, effectively diminishes the importance of the Temple. The principal activity in the Temple is prayer—principally the prayer of repentance and supplication. Indeed, the Temple is even dispensable. All that is necessary is that one prays in the direction of the Temple—in the direction of Jerusalem:

> Whatever the direction in which you may send your people forth to war against their enemies, if they pray to you, O LORD, *toward* the city you have chosen and the temple I have built in your honor, listen in heaven to their prayer and petition, and defend their cause (1 Kgs 8:44-45).

If the Deuteronomic tradition reduces the significance of the Temple, why does Jerusalem have such significance in this tradition and in the early Jewish and rabbinic traditions so influenced by it? Deuteronomy, in the form we now have it, presents itself as a "constitution" for Judah restored to its land. The restoration the Persians not only allowed but encouraged was limited to the city of Jerusalem and a few square miles surrounding the city. In a sense the Deuteronomists were making virtue out of necessity, although the reason they gave was that Jerusalem was the city chosen by God. How did the Deuteronomists envision the shape of the restoration following the end of exile? Here is the most frustrating element in appreciating the work of the Deuteronomists: their work ends so abruptly. In 2 Kgs 25:27-30 they note the parole of the exiled King Jehoiachin. This should have provided the Deuteronomists with another occasion for a speech or an editorial comment on the significance of Jehoiachin's parole for the future of Judah, but they passed up the opportunity. This has prompted several attempts at identifying the purpose of the Deuteronomistic History.[12] Certainly one purpose of the work is to trace the tragic story of Israel in its land from the time the Israelites entered it under Joshua until the Judahites left it in exile under the Babylonians. Of course, the Deuteronomists were not writing a history in the modern sense of the term. They turned Israel's past into a succession of example stories. They reported Isaiah's words that spoke about a remnant from Jerusalem:

> The remaining survivors of the house of Judah
> shall again strike root below
> and bear fruit above.
> For out of Jerusalem shall come a remnant,
> and from Mount Zion, survivors.
> The zeal of the LORD of hosts shall do this (2 Kgs 19:30-31).

They believed that the people of Judah would survive and have a future and that Jerusalem would have a central place in that future. Still, the surviving remnant could not afford to make the kind of mistakes that provoked divine judgment upon the city, so they turn the past into a sermon.

The Influence of the Deuteronomic Tradition

Later generations followed the lead of the Deuteronomic tradition as they tried to understand their experience of God's judgment in their lives. The explanation that recurs is the same one offered first by the Deuteronomist: Jerusalem fell because of the moral failures of its kings and people (2 Kgs 21:10-15; 22:16-17). Texts written almost five hundred years after the Deuteronomistic History offer that same explanation for the evil that befell Jerusalem and its people. The Song of Azariah acknowledges that God's judgment on Jerusalem was just:

> You have executed proper judgments
>   in all that you have brought upon us
>   and upon Jerusalem, the holy city of our fathers.
> By a proper judgment you have done all this
>   because of our sins (Dan 3:28).

---

12. See Walter Brueggemann, "The Kerygma of the Dueteronomistic Historian," *Int* 22 (1968) 387–402; Hans W. Wolff, "The Kerygma of the Deuteronomic Historian," *The Vitality of Old Testament Traditions,* ed. W. Brueggemann and H. W. Wolff (Atlanta: John Knox Press, 1975) 83–100.

The same sentiments recur later in Daniel's prayer of confession (Dan 9:4-19), which contains a petition for God's mercy:

> O Lord, in keeping with all your just deeds, let your anger and your wrath be turned away from your city Jerusalem, your holy mountain. On account of our sins and the crimes of our fathers, Jerusalem and your people have become the reproach of all our neighbors (Dan 9:16).

Similar words occur in Bar 1:15 and 2:1-2. While these texts put the prayers of confession on figures associated with the Babylonian exile, they actually come from the second century B.C., when Jerusalem and its people had to endure the persecution of Antiochus IV, who desecrated the Temple and proscribed the practice of Judaism. Given this perspective, the key to Jerusalem's future is repentance. If Zion's children choose to keep their covenant with God, then God may relent and prevent their sins from destroying them and their city. Both Tob 13:9 and 2 Macc 5:19-20 expect that God will restore Jerusalem but confess that it has experienced God's judgment because of its sins. These sentiments derive directly from the Deuteronomic tradition, which sees Israel's future as a consequence of its repentance and obedience. While Jerusalem and its Temple have a role to play in Israel's religious life, they are not as central to that life as is a life of obedience to the Torah.

The book of Tobit combines the love of and loyalty to Jerusalem with the example of a life of obedience to traditional Israelite morality. John F. Craghan characterized the book of Tobit as "Deuteronomy Revisited."[13] Irene Nowell shows that Deuteronomy's notion of the virtuous life was a strong influence on Tobit.[14] Both Carey Moore and Alexander DiLella find Deuteronomic influence particularly strong in Tobit 14.[15] An important component of the Deuteronomic perspectives that Tobit reflects is the significance of Jerusalem.

Tobit introduces its protagonist as an exile not from Judah but from Naphtali—from the northern kingdom. Uncharacteristically for a northerner, Tobit worships in Jerusalem rather than in the temples build by Jeroboam (Tob 1:4-8). Tobit's concern for Jerusalem serves to frame the story of his life, as is evident in the hymn he sings shortly before his death in

---

13. *Esther, Judith, Tobit, Jonah, Ruth.* OTM 16. (Wilmington, Del.: Michael Glazier, Inc, 1982) 132.

14. Irene Nowell, "The Book of Tobit: Narrative Technique and Theology" (Ph.D. diss., The Catholic University of America, 1983) 259–71.

15. See Carey A. Moore, *Tobit,* AB 40A (New York: Doubleday, 1996) 284–5; Alexander A. DiLella, "The Deuteronomic Background of the Farewell Discourse in Tob 14:3-11," *CBQ* 41, 380-9.

chapter 13. In this hymn Tobit praises God in view of Jerusalem's pending deliverance and exaltation. After an opening call to praise (vv. 1-3), Tobit addresses the people of Jerusalem, whom God has punished for just cause. Then Tobit speaks to the city directly (vv. 9-18). His topic is the new status of its citizens, for they were no longer sinners but "children of the upright" (vv. 9, 13). The climax of his address to Jerusalem comes as he praises God for the city's restoration:

> My spirit blesses, the Lord, the great King;
>> Jerusalem shall be rebuilt as his home forever (vv. 15, 16a).

That Tobit fully expects Jerusalem's deliverance is evident from his repeated references to gladness and joy (vv. 7, 11, 13, 17). Given the literary setting of this prayer in the Diaspora, Tobit expresses hope for the return of the exiles to Jerusalem—a common motif in early Jewish literature (v. 12; see also 2 Macc 2:18; 1 *Enoch* 90:35; 4 *Esdr* 13:39-40). Tobit's description of Jerusalem's beauty reflects the pious exaggeration sometimes characteristic of liturgical expression of hope for the future:

> The gates of Jerusalem shall be built with sapphire and emerald,
>> and all your walls with precious stones.
> The towers of Jerusalem shall be built with gold,
>> and their battlements with pure gold,
> The streets of Jerusalem shall be paved
>> with rubies and stones of Ophir (Tob 13:16-17; see also Isa 54:11-14;
>>> Rev 21:10-21).

Tobit believes that the prophets foretold Jerusalem's restoration (14:5), so it is natural that he would look to one of them for inspiration. The principal source of his hymnic expressions of hope in the city's eventual restoration can be found in the book of Isaiah (see especially Isa 54:11-14 and 60:4-14). The book of Tobit is a testimony to the power of both the Deuteronomic and Isaianic traditions in sustaining people's hope in a glorious future for Jerusalem:

> Alleluia!
> Blessed be God who has raised you [Jerusalem] up!
>> may he be blessed for all ages.
> For in you they shall praise his holy name forever (Tob 13:18).

Conclusion

The principal concern of the Deuteronomic tradition is to motivate Israel to obey the Torah. Obedience offers the only hope for Israel's future.

Matters of worship have a place in Israel's life of obedience but only a limited place. The tradition may be reacting to a type of confidence in ancient Israel's cult that was unrealistic. Still, Jerusalem has a prominent place in the Deuteronomic tradition because it was the city that housed the Temple, the place where God's name dwelt. Jerusalem's significance in the Deuteronomic tradition derived from that tradition's concern for the centralization of sacrificial worship in the city "that God chose" as the dwelling place of the divine name. That divine choice, however, did not exempt Jerusalem from experiencing the consequences of its people's disobedience. The restoration of Jerusalem depended on its people's commitment to the Torah. While the Deuteronomistic History did not speak of Jerusalem's restoration, the book of Tobit, which was shaped by Deuteronomic perspectives, does. The city will have a future, because in it God's holy name will be praised forever.

4

Ariel: Jerusalem in Isaiah 1–39

While the basic contours of the Jerusalem tradition in the books of Psalms and Deuteronomy are clear, the relation of Isaiah to that tradition is more complex. Gerhard von Rad asserted that the Zion tradition formed the entire basis of the prophet's message.[1] Until recently von Rad's view of the prophet's theology has guided the majority of interpreters in their analysis of the book. In contrast, Sheldon Blank held that Isaiah predicted the fall of Jerusalem and that texts asserting God's continuing protection of Zion were secondary glosses and expansions.[2] Less confident about this issue, James Ward noted that there "is nothing more difficult to evaluate in the prophecy of Isaiah that the Zion motif which runs through it."[3] Christopher Seitz characterized Isaiah's Zion theology as "supple and ambiguous."[4] Still, it is clear that the Zion tradition is especially prominent in the book of Isaiah. The prophet did proclaim that Zion was founded by God:

> The LORD has established Zion,
> and in her the afflicted of his people find refuge (Isa 14:32).

This verse, which is part of an oracle against Philistia, alludes to the Zion tradition in claiming that Yahweh founded the city. While the mythological imagery behind this assertion is obvious, the prophet chooses not

---

1. Von Rad, *Old Testament Theology,* 1:149.

2. Blank, *Prophetic Faith in Isaiah,* 9–12.

3. Ward believes that the Zion motif, more than any other, was subject to "secondary coloration" in the post-exilic era. See his *Amos and Isaiah,* 228.

4. See Seitz, *Zion's Final Destiny,* 146.

to develop it. Instead, Isaiah follows his assertion about the foundation of Zion with the specification that the city is to be a refuge for "the afflicted of [God's] people."[5] Ollenburger understands the prophet's reference to the city's underclass as his attempt to offer the poor as models for those who did not try to secure Jerusalem's safety through diplomatic or military means but left the matter in the hands of God alone. "The afflicted," then, are those who are "neither arrogant nor proud," that is, those who expect no help except that which God will provide.[6] Albert Gelin popularized this way of looking at the poor in *The Poor of Yahweh*.[7] Still, there is no evidence that the prophet uses the word *ʿny* in any way but in its literal sense: the poor who are made miserable by their economic and social position. The prophet is not trying to inculcate an attitude of dependence upon God, but he is trying to demythologize the Zion tradition by asserting that God "established Zion" as a place of refuge for the poor. Thus he humanizes the mythological motif of the establishment of Zion as the place of God's habitation on earth.[8] While the prophet uses Zion, a central theological symbol of the Jerusalem cult, he uses it to undermine the basic assumption of that pattern of thought. For the prophet the execution of justice for the poor was the reason for God's founding of Jerusalem.

Oracles of Judgment

Despite his belief that God has founded Zion, Isaiah holds that the city is about to experience terrible divine judgment:

> Woe to Ariel, Ariel
> the city where David encamped!
> Add year to year,
> let the feasts come round.
> But I will bring distress upon Ariel,
> with mourning and grief (Isa 29:1-2).

Ariel is Isaiah's unique name for Jerusalem. What the prophet implies by referring to Jerusalem as Ariel is not certain, although the word may mean

5. The Hebrew word the *NAB* renders as "afflicted" is one of several words biblical Hebrew uses to speak of the poor. The prophet's choice of this word, *ʿny,* serves to emphasize the miserable state of the poor.

6. See Ollenburger, *Zion,* 116.

7. Kathryn Sullivan, trans. (Collegeville: The Liturgical Press, 1964).

8. Ollenburger does admit that concern for the poor is a "required posture," though he holds that this text assumes the basis of Zion's security is "Yahweh's exaltation" in Jerusalem. See Ollenburger, *Zion,* 128. I suggest that for Isaiah the basis of Zion's security is a just social order in which the poor find protection from exploitation.

"lion of God." This is the only instance that the name appears in the book of Isaiah. "Ariel" appears a few other times in the Hebrew Bible: Ezra 8:16, where it is a personal name; 2 Sam 23:20 and 1 Chr 11:22, where it is a common noun for "champion" or "hero"; and Ezek 43:15-16, where it is a common noun for "an altar hearth."

The Ariel passage is part of a larger unit in the book of Isaiah: 28:1–29:8. Here the prophet blames the leaders of the two Israelite kingdoms for the fate of Samaria and Jerusalem. Isaiah is certain that judgment is coming to the capital cities of both Israel and Judah. At the same time, he believes that judgment is not God's last word to Jerusalem:

> The horde of your arrogant shall be like fine dust,
>> the horde of the tyrants like flying chaff.
> Then suddenly, in an instant,
>> you shall be visited by the LORD of hosts,
> With thunder, earthquake, and great noise,
>> whirlwind, storm, and the flame of consuming fire.
> Then like a dream,
>> a vision in the night,
> Shall be the horde of all the nations
>> who war against Ariel
>> with all the earthworks of her besiegers.
> As when a hungry man dreams he is eating
>> and awakens with an empty stomach,
> Or when a thirsty man dreams he is drinking
>> and awakens faint and dry,
> So shall the horde of all the nations be,
>> who make war against Zion (Isa 29:5-8).

Because these verses speak of the deliverance of Jerusalem, some interpreters deny them to the eighth-century prophet. Isaiah, however, makes a distinction between Jerusalem of the present and Jerusalem of the future. The former stands under divine judgment because of its injustice to the poor. The Jerusalem of the future will be a creation of divine grace where justice will reign. Denying 29:5-8 to the eighth-century prophet is based on an unjustified assumption that he did not have a vision of Jerusalem beyond divine judgment.

Chapter 28 begins with a woe oracle (vv. 1-4) directed at the people of means in Samaria who enjoy extravagant meals ("those bloated with rich food . . . those overcome with wine!" v. 1b), while those who produce the food and wine are living on the subsistence level. The prophet probably sees Assyria as "the one who is mighty and strong" (v. 2). Hayes and Irvine suggest that the prophet considered all the anti-Assyrian military and political planning going on in the northern kingdom as the activity of drunks.[9] The imagery of v. 4 is transparent. Isaiah concludes that Assyria will make short work of Samaria, absorbing the Israelite state and its capital into the Assyrian Empire.

The next section (Isa 28:5-13) is a prophetic instruction on leadership that begins with an announcement that a time is coming when God will assume the leadership of Israel. The rest of the subunit clarifies the reason for this: the current leadership of the community is hopelessly incompetent. Ollenburger argues that the introduction of the motif of rest in v. 12 is an allusion to the Zion tradition, implying that the basis of Judah's security is that Zion is the site of God's sovereign rule.[10] Still, as he admits, God's rule in Zion is not enough to ensure security for Jerusalem. The city's political establishment tried to ensure that security through alliances with foreign powers, while the prophet insists that Zion's future depends on the maintenance of a just social and economic system. Isaiah is certain that neither God's presence in Zion nor any political alliance can ensure Jerusalem's future. If, however, Jerusalem will become a place of rest for the weary (v. 12), then there can be hope.[11] The people's unwillingness to hear the prophet's words means that the word of God has become nonsense for the people. What appears to be nonsense is a very serious matter. It is nothing less than Judah's defeat by the Assyrians (v. 13).

The third subunit (Isa 28:14-22) further specifies the consequences of the failings of the leadership classes. Here the prophet explicitly includes the elite classes of Jerusalem in his indictment (v. 14). The prophet now takes his turn at mockery and puts words into the mouths of his opponents that equate their political actions as "a covenant with death" (v. 15).[12] A basic assumption of his message is that Jerusalem can secure its future by faith in the God who calls for the creation of a just society. His opponents, however, believe that they can secure the city's future with treaties and alliances. The prophet sees this as suicide.

9. Hayes and Irvine, *Isaiah, the Eighth Century Prophet,* 323.

10. Ollenburger, *Zion,* 115.

11. J. J. M. Roberts suggests emending v. 12d by inserting "let the needy repose" after "this is the resting place." See his "Note on Isaiah 28:12," 51. If one accepts this emendation, the argument that Isaiah demythologized the Zion tradition becomes stronger.

12. Jensen suggests that the prophet refers to an alliance with Egypt, which had "a preoccupation with death and the underworld," *NJBC* 15:41. Otto Kaiser sees v. 15 as reflecting a desire to be safe from a premature death by making a covenant with Mot; See his *Isaiah 13–39,* 251. It is easier to imagine the prophet criticizing Jerusalem's leadership for their political moves.

In a masterful analysis of Isa 28:16-18, J.J.M. Roberts shows that this portion of the oracle was occasioned by a violent rainstorm, which undermined the foundations of defensive fortifications made in Jerusalem to hold off potential invaders.[13] Evidently the fortifications were put up quickly without adequate foundations to resist the pressures that were brought to bear on any structure built on the Ophel's slopes. When a particularly heavy downpour fell on the city, the flimsy construction simply washed away. The site of the collapsed fortifications gave the prophet the opportunity to speak about the solid foundation that God was preparing for the city's future:

> Therefore, thus says the Lord GOD:
> See, I am laying a stone in Zion,
> a stone that has been tested,
> A precious cornerstone as a sure foundation;
> he who puts his faith in it shall not be shaken (Isa 28:16).

Justice and right will set this foundation in place (28:17). While it is true that Jerusalem's security was dependent on God's presence in the city, God's presence was, in turn, dependent on the righteous and just behavior of the city's people—especially of the city's political leaders. They, however, have not fostered justice. According to the prophet, this left God no choice but to begin an urban renewal project in Jerusalem. The project had to begin with demolition so that justice could become the foundation for Jerusalem's future.

While Jerusalem's leadership believe the city's fortifications will provide the city with security, Isaiah sees terror ahead (Isa 28:19). The metaphor in v. 20 asserts that the city will be without effective protection:

> For the bed shall be too short to stretch out in,
> and the cover too narrow to wrap in (Isa 28:20).

In v. 21 the prophet alludes to traditions about David's victory over the Philistines (2 Sam 5:17-25) and Joshua's over a coalition of Canaanite kings (Josh 10:7-14) but then implies that in the conflict with the Assyrians, God will intervene to defeat rather than save Judah. Isaiah characterizes this as "a strange deed" given the traditional view that God takes the side of Israel against its enemies. The prophet then calls for the city's powerful to change their attitude toward his message, suggesting that there is still time to avoid being caught up in the universal judgment that God is about to bring upon the world (v. 22).

13. Roberts, "Yahweh's Foundation in Zion," 27–45. Especially helpful is Roberts' handling of the complex textual problems that make analysis of this verse difficult.

The fourth subunit (28:23-29) is an allegory on the divine judgment that Jerusalem will experience. The allegory takes the form of a didactic poem on how God acts at the right time for the right purpose. While judgment is coming there will be a positive outcome, just as the farmer's purposeful activities lead to the harvesting of food. The plowing and planting take place during specific, limited periods and according to a plan (vv. 24-25). Similarly, the activities connected with harvesting and winnowing follow a pattern (vv. 27-28). All that will happen to Jerusalem will happen according to a plan that originates with God, whose counsel is "wonderful" and whose wisdom is "great."

Isaiah 29:1-4 begins with a woe oracle against Jerusalem addressed with the epithet "Ariel." What the prophet implied by referring to Jerusalem as Ariel is not certain. This name appears nowhere else in Isaiah. The two occurrences of the word in Ezekiel (43:15, 16) understand the term to refer to the altar as a place where sacrifices are burnt, that is, the altar as a hearth. By using Ariel as a name for Jerusalem, the prophet may be comparing the city to a burning altar hearth, implying that the city is going to be the place where the people and their leaders will be sacrificed.

Verse 1b ("Add year to year, let the feasts come round") suggests a setting for the oracle: the New Year's celebration. This celebration gives the prophet the ideal opportunity to speak about what lies ahead for Jerusalem. Isaiah asserts that after some years a hostile army will surround the city. This siege will lead the people to raise a lamentation, but Jerusalem's affliction will be God's doing, so the lamentation will be ineffective. The prophet announces that God is going to sacrifice the people of Jerusalem, but they will not be alone in their subjection to divine wrath. Ironically, the instrument chosen to effect the sacrifice will itself be subject to divine judgment (vv. 5-8). The prophet does not explicitly say that Jerusalem will be delivered but that the nations who make war against Zion will have their day of judgment. This does not mean that Jerusalem will escape unscathed but merely that the nations arrayed against it will also experience God's anger.

Chapter 28 introduces an oracle that first threatens Jerusalem and then ends with a promise of deliverance (29:1-8). Of all Isaianic oracles of judgment, 29:5-8 is the most subject to a reading that finds the book of Isaiah shaped by Zion theology. This subunit reflects the "Conflict with the Nations" motif that Rohland sees as the historical counterpart to God's victories over chaotic waters. While one solution is to view vv. 5-8 as a later expansion of an original Isaianic oracle,[14] it is possible to see this

---

14. See, for example, Clements, *Isaiah and the Deliverance of Jerusalem*, 47–8.

text reflecting Hezekiah's capitulation (2 Kgs 18:13-16) and the consequent lifting of the Assyrian siege. Still, the prophet does not advocate a simple reliance on divine guarantees. He does announce God's judgment on Jerusalem, though he also announces the passing of the agent of that judgment: the Assyrian Empire. God comes in judgment against Jerusalem, although this does not annul God's fidelity to the city. It is possible to read 29:1-8 as a judgment oracle upon Jerusalem without assuming that vv. 5-8 are a later expansion.

Isaiah contrasts the Jerusalem of the present with that of the future. "Jerusalem of the present" suffers from incompetent leadership. The city's rulers are concerned with ensuring their wealth and prosperity when they should be thinking about providing rest for the weary (28:12). Their failure to create a just society, their avarice, and their incompetence will bring about a terrible defeat for the city. Still, the difficult times that Jerusalem must face will be of limited duration and will serve the divine purpose. The Jerusalem of the future will be ruled by God, who will create a society in which justice will reign.

After Jerusalem experiences divine judgment, the nation executing that judgment will be punished for its excesses. God's instrument of judgment on Jerusalem was the mighty Assyrian Empire. In the second half of the eighth century B.C. the Assyrians led by Tiglath Pileser III (744–727), their vigorous and capable ruler, began to expand their empire to the west, subjecting some states to vassalage and absorbing others into their provincial system. In 10:5-23, Isaiah attempts to set Assyria's political and military actions within the context of the divine will for Jerusalem. The prophet portrays Assyria as a powerful tool that God will use in executing judgment on the city. Assyria's fall from power, however, is to come only after God has completed "all his work on Mount Zion and in Jerusalem" (10:12). Assyria then will experience divine judgment (10:24-27). There will be no miraculous intervention rescuing Jerusalem from the aggressively expansionist Assyrian Empire. On the contrary, Jerusalem will endure a fate similar to that experienced by Samaria, the capital of the kingdom of Israel (10:11), though the prophet does assure the people of Jerusalem that God will give them another opportunity to create a just social system in their city (Isa 10:20-23).

According to Isaiah, Jerusalem's social and economic system once reflected the divine will:

> How has she turned adulteress,
>   the faithful city, so upright!
> Justice used to lodge within her,
>   but now, murderers (Isa 1:21).

Isaiah 1:21-26, framed by Jerusalem's title as "the faithful city," describes the city's fall from its former state.[15] What once was, however, is no more, so Jerusalem stands under divine judgment. The most specific indictment the prophet makes reflects his evaluation of Jerusalem's political leadership (v. 23), whom the prophet derides as venal. Those who should be protecting Jerusalem's economically vulnerable do not. On the contrary, the city's powerful use their position and influence to exploit the poor and to increase their own economic well-being at the expense of those they should protect from such exploitation. This oracle of judgment identifies Jerusalem's elite as God's enemies against whom God must act. Verse 25 picks up the metaphor found in v. 22: God must refine away the dross of the city's corrupt and unjust leadership. The implication is that the goal of judgment is not merely vengeance but the elimination of the city's political and economic corruption. Verse 26 underscores this by asserting that God will restore the type of political leadership that once was characteristic of the city. With new leadership Jerusalem once again will be a just and faithful city. Unfortunately, the text does not identify the just leaders of the past.[16] Still, Isaiah is clear that the kings, politicians, and bureaucrats of his day are the cause of Jerusalem's imminent judgment. Obviously the prophet does not consider an ethically upright political system an impossibility, since he asserts that Jerusalem had such a system in the past. The prophet proclaims that God will have to set aside Jerusalem's current leadership so that God can provide the city with rulers who have a measure of integrity.

Joseph Jensen holds that 1:27-28 are an editorial comment on the oracle of judgment in 1:21-26:[17]

> Zion shall be redeemed by judgment,
> and her repentant ones by justice.
> Rebels and sinners alike shall be crushed,
> those who desert the LORD shall be consumed (Isa 1:27-28).

The shift from the second person address of vv. 21-26 to the third person announcement form in vv. 27-28 at least justifies treating the latter as a new structural unit. The prophet does not see Jerusalem's future as a consequence of its unique status as the dwelling place of God on earth. These words affirm that Jerusalem's salvation lies in its doing of justice. As such,

---

15. The Septuagint version of this passage specifically identifies Zion as the city in question.

16. The use of "judges" and "counselors" in v. 26 may imply non-monarchic, decentralized patterns of leadership and administration of justice.

17. *NJBC* 15:8 (F). Sweeney, *Isaiah 1–39*, 87, considers vv. 27-28 to be a mid- to late- fifth-century addition to chapter 1.

these verses are clearly Isaianic in spirit. Verses 27-28 are characteristic of the prophet's view of Jerusalem's future. The city's fate will be decided by the commitment of its people to justice. Here the prophet not only demythologizes the Zion tradition but also democratizes it as well. The city's future will not be shaped by the Davidic dynasty but by people who repent and who are just and righteous.

The prophet, however, threatens Jerusalem of his day with attack and destruction precisely because of the injustice of the city's economic system as manipulated by the city's elite (Isa 3:1–4:1). This oracle begins by asserting that Jerusalem has no leaders who can stave off the disaster (3:2-4, 6-7, 12). The prophet then specifies the defects of Judah's leadership class by accusing it of injustice toward the poor (vv. 13-15). Isaiah also pronounces judgment on "the daughters of Zion," whom he accuses of arrogance (v. 16). He lists the trappings of wealth that will be taken from them (vv. 18-24), concluding with the promise that their champions will suffer defeat in battle (v. 25). Jerusalem can look forward only to mourning (v. 26). This text makes no allusion to the Zion tradition. It simply indicts the people of means in Judah for failing to prevent the coming disaster. These people are totally occupied with divesting the poor of what little they have. The prophet describes the judgment to come in its effects on the wealthy women of the city, who will be deprived of their finery. Judah's army will suffer defeat, leaving Jerusalem to mourn its losses. The once-affluent women are left scrambling to find husbands to support them (4:1).

Oracles of Salvation

Though Isaiah is adamant in his announcement of the judgment that will come upon Zion for its failure to maintain a just social and economic system, the prophet is convinced that judgment will not be God's last word to Jerusalem. He believes that while Jerusalem is under the immediate threat of judgment, in the future the city will once again experience divine favor. Sweeney characterizes Isaiah as a prophet of salvation.[18] If that characterization is correct, it is necessary to look to the prophet's oracles of salvation to determine his views regarding Jerusalem. Here one expects the influence of the Zion tradition to be much stronger than in the prophet's oracles of judgment.

Of the prophet's oracles of salvation, Isa 2:2-4 makes the clearest allusion to the Zion tradition. For example, v. 2 refers to "the mountain of the LORD's house" as "the highest mountain." The prophet, however, makes a significant change in his adaptation of this tradition. Zion will become

18. Sweeney, *Isaiah 1–39*, 62.

the divine mountain at some point in the future. It is not now "the highest mountain." Zion's change in status will occur "in days to come" (v. 2a). Jerusalem of the prophet's own day is going to experience divine judgment. Primarily because of its current failed leadership, Jerusalem cannot expect to be spared from the consequences of its infidelity. Only after Jerusalem faces those consequences will it be in a position to fulfill its destiny as "the highest mountain." It is also significant that the motif of divine kingship is muted. In its place is Torah. Jerusalem's future status comes from its position as the place to which the nations come for instruction in the Law. Another important transformation of the Zion tradition is the defeat of the nations. Instead of speaking of God's victory over the enemies of Zion, Isaiah describes a future in which the nations will live in peace with one another. The enemy that is defeated is war. The prophet does make use of the Zion tradition, but the mythological elements of that tradition are humanized. Isaiah describes a future of peace based on universal observance of Torah.

Another eschatological formula, "on that day," introduces another oracle of salvation (4:2-6) and makes it obvious that the prophet is speaking of a future Jerusalem rather than the city of his day. What the people of Jerusalem can expect in the immediate future is a washing away of the city's filth and the purging of its blood by "searing judgment," (v. 4) which will leave only a remnant in Jerusalem (v. 3). Divine protection then will come upon the city and the inhabitants who survive the judgment (v. 5). Here there is no allusion to Jerusalem as the place of God's exaltation. It stands in need of purgation, which, when complete, will create a proper setting for the divine presence (v. 5b). The filth and blood of the present Jerusalem make the city unfit to be the dwelling place of God on earth.

Sometimes this oracle is seen as opposing the immediately preceding oracle of judgment in 3:16–4:1. The conclusion that 4:2-6 must be a later addition follows.[19] Such an approach assumes that the prophet did not see beyond the immediate political crisis of his day. This text shows that the prophet did have a vision of an ideal Zion that would emerge in the future. The prophet's view of Jerusalem's ultimate destiny transcended the realities of the Assyrian crisis. He was convinced that God was going to refound Jerusalem after it experienced the consequences of its unjust social system. It is true that Jerusalem's political leaders were corrupt and its wealthy women were vacuous (Isaiah 3:1–4:1). Still, their failures did not mean the end of Jerusalem. "On that day" (4:2) there will be a purifica-

---

19. For example, Sweeney, *Isaiah 1–39*, 111. He dates 4:2-6 to the late sixth century—some two hundred years after the ministry of Isaiah.

tion and God will be present in Zion as a "shelter." The use of *sukhah* ("shelter") in 4:6 is deliberate. The prophet wants to contrast his vision of the future of Zion with the inflated rhetoric of the Zion tradition. What God will provide Judah for its protection is a humble hut rather than a monumental structure like the temple. The word *sukhah* also is associated with the Sinai tradition, as is v. 5b (Exod 13:21-22; 40:34-38).

The announcement of salvation in 4:2-6 makes it clear that the divine judgment upon Jerusalem is not vindictiveness. Its purpose is to prepare a purified remnant in Jerusalem. The prophet has a vision of an ideal Jerusalem, which he considers to be a work of God to be revealed in the future. He condemns the Jerusalem of his day because of its social and economic sins. His vision of Jerusalem of the future does not even explicitly mention the Temple; rather, the prophet prefers to speak of the wilderness tradition when there could be no temple but only a *sukhah* to enclose the divine presence in Israel's midst.

Isaiah 30:18-26 is another of the prophet's eschatological visions of Zion's future. Predictably, some interpreters consider these words of salvation to be an interpolation of a devout redactor.[20] This text reflects the Isaianic notion that Jerusalem's future will not be finally determined by its infidelity. After Judah experiences divine judgment, there will come deliverance. Like Isa 2:2-4, which also describes an eschatological vision of Jerusalem's future, 30:18-26 uses motifs from the Zion tradition. But in v. 25 the prophet speaks about "streams of running water," which will grace every "high mountain and lofty hill." Thus God will guarantee the prosperity of all the land and not Zion alone. The oracle begins, however, with the assertion that Yahweh is a "God of justice" (v. 18). The key to the glorious future that awaits Zion is a just social and economic order. The people of Jerusalem should not depend on the city's supposed status as God's dwelling place.

In a passage (Isa 30:20-21) that reflects an idea that will be picked up later by both Jeremiah (30:33-34) and Ezekiel (36:26-27), Isaiah implies that the people of Jerusalem will be able to enjoy a secure future because they will be obedient. Their obedience results from the instruction that comes by way of Jerusalem's teachers, that is, the prophets.[21] While this passage is optimistic about Jerusalem's future, that future is not described

20. For example, Kaiser, *Isaiah 13–39*, 298.

21. Both the *NAB* and the *NRSV* translate *môrêkā* ("your teachers") as singular, although the form is plural. William H. Irwin suggests that this word should be translated as "giver of rain," since the root *yrh* also carries that meaning. This suggestion fits the context of vv. 23-6 very well, though it fits less well into the context of vv. 20-1. See his *Isaiah 28–33*, Biblica et Orientalia 30 (Rome: Pontifical Biblical Institute, 1977) 90–1.

in terms of the Zion tradition. Jerusalem will have a future only because of God's decision to provide it with peace and prosperity. God will ensure that the people of Jerusalem learn from the prophets and remain faithful, even when tempted to act otherwise (vv. 20-21).

A far more ambiguous promise of salvation is Isa 31:4-9. This oracle uses two metaphors. The first (v. 4) compares God to a lion who comes down upon its prey and will not surrender it when shepherds try to frighten it away by making noise. The second metaphor (v. 5) is less clear. The *NAB* and the *NRSV* both translate the verbs of this verse so as to leave the impression that the flight of birds above Jerusalem is somehow protective:

Like hovering birds,
     so the Lord of hosts
     shall *shield* Jerusalem
To protect and deliver
     to spare and rescue it. *(NAB)*
	Like birds hovering overhead,
	     so the Lord of hosts
	     will *protect* Jerusalem
	he will *protect and deliver* it,
	he will *spare and rescue* it. *(NRSV)*

Birds circling a city under siege does not conjure up an image of protection —quite the opposite. It presents an image of scavengers looking for carrion. Ward's translation, however, suggests the rescue of some Jerusalemites from the enemy:

Like a flight of birds
Will Yahweh of hosts *surround* Jerusalem,
Encircle and snatch away,
Dart over and help to escape.[22]

The value of Ward's rendering is that it is reminiscent of the remnant idea and does not require that this verse be ascribed to a late redactor, as does Clements.[23] The imagery, ambiguous as it is, does not derive from the Zion tradition. While the text does imply that God will not abandon Jerusalem, it also says that Jerusalem's salvation will be more like a timely escape than a glorious deliverance.

Isaiah 33 is another passage that is sometimes not ascribed to Isaiah but to later editors. Roberts has argued persuasively that this chapter is an authentic Isaianic text, although other interpreters have dated it as late as the Seleucid era.[24] Roberts believes that once readers recognize that the Zion tradition comes from the Davidic-Solomonic period and that Isaiah is dependent upon that tradition, it is relatively easy to recognize that this

22. Ward, *Amos and Isaiah,* 255.
23. Clements, *Isaiah and the Deliverance of Jerusalem,* 49.
24. Roberts, "Isaiah 33," 15–25.

text comes from the prophet. Chapter 33 begins with a woe oracle against an unnamed enemy who has threatened Jerusalem. The poem goes on to speak of the destruction of the enemy army, which will precede the glorification of the city. The poem is complex: it changes persons and is obscure at times. For example, the woe oracle with which the poem begins addresses the enemy (v. 1), but the verse following is a lament addressed to God (v. 2).

Verse 5 affirms God's rule in Jerusalem and asserts that God has filled Zion with "justice and righteousness." These, of course, are prophetic code words for a just social order in which the poor find protection against the venality, greed, and avarice of the rich. God's exaltation in Zion is connected with a just social order. While chapter 33 begins with an allusion to the defeat of the city's enemy, an element of the Zion tradition, the shift to the prophetic concern for justice—the move from the mythological to the humanistic—occurs. A similar shift is evident in vv. 14-16, where the prophet adapts the question-and-answer pattern of entrance liturgies (e.g., Psalms 15, 24) to underscore the need for a just social order in Zion.

Verses 17-24 conclude the poem with a picture of Zion after the removal of the threat and the establishment of justice. Here the prophet adapts mythological motifs to speak of God's rule in Zion. In particular, v. 21 has Yahweh's dwelling in Zion protected by "broad rivers and streams" as El's was (III AB C l. 4–5; *ANET,* p. 129). The prophet is comfortable using this metaphor to speak about Zion's security, although Jerusalem's geographical position did not leave the city open to attack from the sea. While the imagery has roots in the Zion tradition, it is important to note that this affirmation of Jerusalem's security occurs after the assertion that God will fill Zion with justice and righteousness (v. 5) and after the entrance liturgy, which affirms that "those who walk righteously and speak uprightly . . . will live on the heights" (v. 15). While the prophet uses the Zion tradition, he transforms it by including the establishment of justice as the goal of God's rule in Zion.

Zion's Fate

In his study of Isaiah 36–39 Christopher Seitz has shown that three main concerns of the final form of chapters 36–37 are the challenges put to Yahweh and Hezekiah by Sennacherib, the retreat of the Assyrian army, and the final punishment of Sennacherib.[25] These chapters center their

---

25. Seitz, *Zion's Final Destiny,* 96.

attention on Hezekiah, who stands in clear contrast with Ahaz as depicted in Isaiah 6–8. This contrast has the effect of demythologizing those elements of the Zion tradition that emphasize the hubris of those who attack the place of God's habitation on Zion. The taunt song in 37:22-29 needs to be seen in this context. Like a woman shaking her head at a scoundrel, Jerusalem can deride its enemies, since God protects Zion from defeat because of Hezekiah's response. Verse 32 is part of a sign (v. 30) given to Hezekiah.[26] The sign assures the king of the survival of the remnant from Jerusalem, a motif that sometimes is an expression of doom, as in 10:20-22 and 30:15-17, though here it appears to be an expression of divine blessing, as in 11:10-16 and 28:5-6. Another assurance given in chapter 37 has God promising to defend Jerusalem for God's own sake and for the sake of David (v. 35). This text has the effect of tempering the assertion that Jerusalem is saved solely because of Hezekiah's fidelity. Ultimately, the city's deliverance is an act of divine grace.[27] The thrust of chapter 37 is clearly theological, but the theological centerpiece is not the Jerusalem tradition but the sovereignty of God extending over all nations. God saves Jerusalem from Sennacherib not because of the city's status but because all the kingdoms of the earth must know that Yahweh is Lord (37:20). Here Isaiah ignores the mythological in favor of the theological.

Conclusion

The purpose of Isaiah's oracles of judgment against Jerusalem and its social system was not to announce the end of the city. On the contrary, the prophet believed in the city's future. Still, between Jerusalem of the present and Jerusalem of the future there lay divine judgment. The prophet took no pleasure in proclaiming the doom of the city: "I say, turn away from me, let me weep bitterly; do not try to comfort me for the ruin of the daughter of my people" (Isa 22:4). Isaiah recognized that he was asking people to believe the unbelievable (28:21). He did not want to believe it himself, but he was convinced that Jerusalem's supposed status as the dwelling place of Yahweh on earth would not save it from that judgment (28:22). Isaiah even uses a parable in his attempt to convince the people of Jerusalem that divine judgment lay ahead for them. He compares God to a farmer who employs a variety of planting and harvesting

26. This underscores the contrast with Ahaz, who refused to accept the sign the prophet offered during the Syro-Emphraimite crisis. See Isa 7:10-12.

27. Seitz, *Zion's Final Destiny*, 88, insists that Isa 37:35 is not evidence of a "doctrine of Zion's inviolability." God protected Zion because God's own honor was at stake and because of the promise made to David, whom Hezekiah ably represented.

techniques to ensure a successful farm. The particular technique used de-pends on the crop (28:23-29). The prophet tries to convince his audience that God will respond to them in a variety of ways, depending on their situation. Because they have created a society founded on injustice and op-pression, God will not take their city's side in the coming conflict with the Assyrians. On the contrary, the Assyrians will be instruments of judgment, allowing God to re-found Jerusalem as a city of justice for all—especially the poor.

The rationale behind God's actions against the city was not vindic-tiveness but the divine will to make Jerusalem what it always ought to have been: a city of justice (Isa 1:26-27; 2:2-5). The prophecy of Isaiah survived for at least two reasons. First, the prophet had an abiding faith in Jerusalem's future. He believed it was indeed "established" by God (14:32). Still, that did not exempt it from divine judgment. But judgment was not to be God's final word to Jerusalem. The oracles of salvation directed to the city and its people, which are too often ascribed to editors, are a prod-uct of the prophet's faith in Jerusalem's future. Second, Isaiah's "Zion theology" helped the people of Jerusalem and Judah cope with the cap-ture of the city, the destruction of its temple and the scattering of its priest-hood, and the fall of the national state and dynasty in 587 B.C. The key to this adaptability was the prophet's insistence that a just social order was a requisite for the city's security. Thus the events connected with Nabuchadnezzar's victory did not invalidate the prophet's affirmations about Jerusalem's future, although the city's fall to the Babylonians did stimulate a probing of Isaianic oracles about Zion. The prophet's insis-tence on justice for the poor made it possible for those who developed the Isaianic tradition to maintain that the city fell because of its sins (50:1-3) but that God forgave those sins (40:1-2), making possible the city's restoration. Similarly, the latest exponents of the Isaianic tradition were able to assert that the restoration did not proceed as expected because of a new failure to create a just society (58:1-12).

5

Zion Under Judgment: Jerusalem in Pre-Exilic and Exilic Prophecy

The prophets and Jerusalem's leaders had fundamental differences in identifying the crisis that lay ahead for the city. Everyone recognized the threat that the aggressively expansionist Assyrian Empire was to Jerusalem. Jerusalem's leaders responded to that threat in two ways. When necessary, they complied with the Assyrians' demands for tribute, all the while waiting for the opportunity to assert Jerusalem's independence. Several of the prophets who preached in the pre-exilic and the exilic periods tried to convince the city's political and religious leaders that Assyria and Babylon were not the cause of Jerusalem's problems—they were. By using their enormous power to increase their wealth at the expense of the poor, the people of means were calling divine judgment upon themselves. Assyria and Babylon were simply the instruments of executing that judgment. It was a mistake to expend energy and resources to deal with the expansionist empires of the day. What Jerusalem had to do was to reconstitute its social and economic system according to the ideals of traditional Yahwism, which portrayed Israel's God as the protector of the poor and which looked upon the oppression of the poor as an offense against the Deity.

The Book of Micah

Micah offers Jerusalem a message similar to that of Isaiah, but Micah casts it in more striking language. There is no misunderstanding what this prophet wants to say as he castigates Jerusalem's leadership and its people of means for creating a two-tiered society of the wealthy and the poor. Like Isaiah, Micah does not consider the words of judgment he proclaims in God's name to be the last word. He sees a future for Jerusalem, but on the way to that future, Jerusalem of the present will come to an end so that God can reestablish the city in justice and righteousness. The city's leaders are unwilling to shape Jerusalem according to the ideals of traditional Israelite morality. The society they have created will have to crumble before anything new is possible.

According to the title of the book (1:1), Micah's ministry began during the reign of Jotham (759–744 B.C.), the son and successor of Uzziah, who used an interlude of peace to prepare for war (2 Chr 26:9, 11-15). Micah also preached during the reign of the next two kings: Ahaz (743–728) and Hezekiah (727–699). Both these kings had to pay tribute to Assyria, since at Ahaz' initiative Judah became a vassal-state of the Assyrian Empire (2 Kgs 16:7-8). Hezekiah, planning to revolt against Assyria, began a program of rearmament and fortification (2 Chronicles 32). The policies of these kings placed a terrible burden on the poor, who had to pay for their implementation.

In 721 the Assyrian Empire ended the political existence of the kingdom of Israel, incorporating its territory into the Assyrian provincial system. One consequence of this event was that refugees from the north swelled the population of Jerusalem to three or four times what it had been.[1] This new population strained the resources of a city that was not blessed with the ability to support a larger population. This likely led to an increase of prices for basic necessities. At the same time, the larger labor market brought down wages. While this was a boon for the owners of large estates, it was another burden for the poor to bear. What Micah saw was the disintegration of Jerusalem's social fabric (7:1-6). He believed that what was happening to the poor was contrary to the divine will. But the prophet did more than condemn social injustice. He proclaimed the coming of a new, golden age for Jerusalem, when God would rule over the people from Zion. Before that day could come, however, judgment awaited the city. Micah was convinced that Jerusalem's injustice toward its poor made of its God a force that would bring about the city's destruction.

The book of Micah begins with an announcement of divine judgment against Samaria, the capital of the kingdom of Israel (1:2-7). The inclusion of Judah and Jerusalem in v. 5 appears as an afterthought, although it shows that Jerusalem should be ready to face the same judgment that is

---

1. Broshi, "Expansion of Jerusalem," 21.

coming on Samaria. Micah's lament over Jerusalem shows that he takes no joy in proclaiming its coming judgment. The prophet does not stand above the city and its people but with them. This leads him to react in horror and grief to the very message he is about to give: "I lament and wail, I go barefoot and naked. . . . There is no remedy for the blow she has been struck. . . . It reaches to the gate of my people, even to Jerusalem" (Mic 1:8-9). Still, the prophet is unrelenting in his criticism of those who steal the land of the poor (2:1-5).

In 2:1-2, Micah identifies those he is addressing:

> . . . those who plan iniquity,
>   and work out evil on their couches;
> In the morning light they accomplish it
>   when it lies within their power.
> They covet fields, and seize them;
>   houses, and they take them;
> They cheat an owner of his house,
>   a man of his inheritance.

The prophet is speaking to people who have economic and political power in Jerusalem and are eager to use it. He focuses on the use of power to amass property—something Isaiah decried as well (see Isa 5:8). Though Micah does not provide details of how the powerful were able to seize a person's ancestral holdings, it was probably by making loans with exorbitant interest rates and then foreclosing upon default. What the prophet condemns is not simple greed but the violation of a basic tenet of Israelite morality as found in the Decalogue. Micah even uses the word "covet," which recalls the commandment (Exod 20:17; Deut 5:21). The ideal Israel society was not to have a class of debt-slaves, laborers, or sharecroppers: "[S]ince the LORD, your God, will bless you abundantly in the land he will give you to occupy as your heritage, there should be no one of you in need" (Deut 15:4). Everyone was to have access to the means of production, which in an agricultural economy meant the ownership of land. Jerusalem's powerful were taking the ancestral holdings of subsistence farmers by "legal" means, and thus severely limiting the economic opportunities of a whole class of people. In other words, the actions of Jerusalem's wealthy were creating poverty. The prophet promises the wealthy that there will come a time when God will restore economic justice, but they and their descendants will find that they will have no share in that new allotment of land (2:3-5).

That there will be no mistaking his announcement of judgment, Micah uses a metaphor that is not merely blunt but horrific. He describes the actions of those responsible for maintaining a just society as cannibalism:

Hear, you leaders of Jacob,
  rulers of the house of Israel!
Is it not your duty to know what is right,
  you who hate what is good, and love evil?
You who tear their skin from them,
  and their flesh from their bones!
They eat the flesh of my people,
  and flay their skin from them,
  and break their bones.
They chop them in pieces like flesh in a kettle,
  and like meat in a caldron.
When they cry to the LORD,
  he shall not answer them;
Rather shall he hide his face from them at that time,
  because of the evil they have done (Mic 3:1-4).

Those whom Micah addresses here are the men responsible for the administration of justice. Most likely they were elders, respected members of families and clans who were usually consulted in matters under dispute. The story of Naboth's vineyard (1 Kings 21) illustrates how these elders could be co-opted by the powerful (see vv. 8-11). Though this story's setting is in the kingdom of Israel, matters were not different in Judah and Jerusalem. The judges that Micah castigates love bribes, and this makes them partners with those who are stealing the land of those who cannot pay the judges well enough (see Isa 1:23 for a similar critique). The greed of these judges for bribes is so great that the prophet does not hesitate to use shocking hyperbole: these judges are guilty of nothing less than eating the innocent.[2] The conclusion that the prophet arrives at is obvious: because the members of Jerusalem's wealthy class cheat the poor they are living under a curse—a curse pronounced on them by God (6:9-16).

  Micah's most bitter critique of Jerusalem's leadership and the unjust social system over which it presides occurs in 3:9-12:

Hear this, you leaders of the house of Jacob,
  you rulers of the house of Israel!
You who abhor what is just,
  and pervert all that is right;
Who build up Zion with bloodshed,
  and Jerusalem with wickedness!

  2. Micah was not the only biblical author to use such a metaphor. See Ezek 34:2-3; Pss 14:4; 53:5; Hab 3:14. This underscores the biblical tradition's aversion to the injustice of ancient Israel's social and economic system under the monarchy.

Her leaders render judgment for a bribe,
> her priests give decisions for a salary,
> her prophets divine for money,
While they rely on the LORD, saying,
"Is not the LORD in the midst of us?
No evil can come upon us!"
Therefore, because of you,
> Zion shall be plowed like a field,
> and Jerusalem reduced to rubble,
And the mount of the temple to a forest ridge.

Here the prophet's text assembles the themes of all that precedes. He begins with a general denunciation of Jerusalem's judicial system. Abuse of power by the judges makes it impossible for the people of the city to have sound relationships with one another—relationships based on the ideals of traditional Israelite morality. Micah becomes more specific when he accuses the city's leadership of building Jerusalem "with bloodshed" (v. 10). According to the mythological perspective, building "the city of God" was God's responsibility, which was transferred to the king, God's viceroy (Pss 51:20; 102:17). The prophet condemns the building of the city's fortifications, palaces, and Temple as anything but holy. Archaeology has underscored the biblical text witness to the amount of building activity that went on in Jerusalem during Micah's ministry. The work was necessary to accommodate the refugees from the north and to prepare for a probable siege by the Assyrians. Micah condemns this activity as nothing less than murder, since it makes the economic circumstances of ordinary folk even more precarious.

Micah includes Jerusalem's religious leadership in his criticism, since they offer theological support for an unjust social system, providing a divine warrant for the exploitation of the poor—the very opposite of the role they should be playing (v. 11b). Jerusalem's priests and prophets have sold out. Of particular interest is Micah's critique of the prophets. Ancient Israel had many more prophets than the few whose words are found in the Bible. Most, however, were creatures of the system that Micah hated (see 1 Kgs 22:9; Jeremiah 28). What angered Micah most was the venality of his colleagues (v. 11a). Still, the greatest folly perpetrated by Jerusalem's leaders was the assurance they gave regarding Jerusalem's status before God. They counseled a naive reliance upon God and the Temple when the city was doomed because of its injustice. The prophet ends his oracle by announcing the destruction of the city—a destruction so complete that land on which the city was standing could be returned to cultivation and the site of the Temple would revert to a habitat for wild animals (v. 12).

The prophet's message changes so abruptly in 4:1-5 that often commentators suggest this passage was inserted in the book of Micah in the post-exilic period, when the more common prophetic form was the oracle of salvation. Also, since vv. 1-4 appear in Isa 2:2-4, they are hardly ever ascribed to Micah. This passage does assert that in the future God's earthly dwelling will be changed and God will rule over all nations from Jerusalem. God's rule will bring justice and peace to the world and security to Israel:

> In days to come
>> the mount of the LORD's house
> Shall be established higher than the mountains;
>> it shall rise high above the hills,
> And peoples shall stream to it:
>> Many nations shall come, and say,
> "Come, let us climb the mount of the LORD,
>> to the house of the God of Jacob,
> That he may instruct us in his ways,
>> that we may walk in his paths."
> For from Zion shall go forth instruction,
>> and the word of the LORD from Jerusalem.
> He shall judge between many peoples
>> and impose terms on strong and distant nations;
> They shall beat their swords into plowshares,
>> and their spears into pruning hooks;
> One nation shall not raise the sword against another,
>> nor shall they train for war again.
> Every man shall sit under his own vine
>> or under his own fig tree, undisturbed;
>> for the mouth of the LORD of hosts has spoken.
> For all the peoples walk,
>> each in the name of its god,
> But we will walk in the name of the LORD,
>> our God, forever and ever (Mic 4:1-5).

The opening phrase of this text, "in days to come," is an important key to its interpretation. This prophetic formula cues the reader that what follows does not refer to the immediate future but to an ideal period that will come in God's good time. Here Micah and Isaiah agree: Jerusalem of the present will experience severe judgment because of its unjust social system. This judgment, however, is not God's last word upon the city, for God will re-found Jerusalem to make it what it always should have been: a city of justice. Like Isaiah, Micah appended a picture of an ideal future to his condemnation of the present. Notice that the text does not say "Jerusalem will not fall" but that at some time in the future the city will be the place from which God will rule the world with justice.

The prophet's rhetoric moves us beyond the present into an ideal future, as is clear from the assertion that "in days to come" the mountain of the Lord will be higher than all other mountains. The reality is that the hill on which the Temple is built is not even as high as the Mount of Olives, which is just across the Kidron Valley. Once the nations see this glorification of Jerusalem's Temple, they will engulf the city like pilgrims, wanting to learn the Torah so they can shape their lives according to its ideals. The problem the prophet cites in 3:9-12 was that the priests and prophets have not been teaching God's word. In his vision of Jerusalem's future, Micah affirms that it will be God who will teach and prophesy.

The familiar words of v. 4 need no comment except to note that the line that pictures Israelite farmers relaxing under the shade of their vines and fruit trees is missing from the Isaianic parallel but is particularly appropriate in Micah because of his complaints against the confiscation of land. Here the prophet draws a very attractive picture of the average Israelite farmers living in the security that comes from the land. The economic system of Micah's day has turned them into tenants and slaves, but in the ideal future they will rest on their own land. Verse 5 is an act of faith in the prophet's word. Since the nations still serve their gods, the fulfillment of this vision lies in the indeterminate future. The prophet's words give hope that the unjust economic system of the present is doomed.

The prophet assures his readers that God, who is responsible for the catastrophe that is coming upon Jerusalem, will restore the city and its people one day. He uses the imagery of a shepherd who gathers the strays from the flock—a familiar image in his culture (4:7-8). The ideal future the prophet describes will witness God ruling from Jerusalem (4:9). The people of Jerusalem worry about the difficulties they will have to face, but Micah assures them that God is in their midst to deliver them (4:9-10).[3] The plans of the political powers that threaten Jerusalem will ultimately be frustrated (4:11-13).

Micah's prophecy comes from someone who has given up on the possibilities of the present. The prophet sees injustice against the poor perpetrated by people of means and supported by Jerusalem's judges, priests,

---

3. The reference to Babylon in v. 10 is anachronistic, since the power that threatened Jerusalem in Micah's day was Assyria. Yehezkel Kaufmann suggests that the original text likely mentioned Assyria but was revised when Babylon became the dominant power a century and a half later. See his *Religion of Israel,* abr. ed. (Chicago: Univ. of Chicago Press, 1960) 352.

and prophets—the very people who are supposed to uphold justice. He sees the society to which he belongs disintegrating, and he concludes that this is God's judgment upon Jerusalem. Still, Micah does not despair, since he believes that a future is coming when the problems that dominate Jerusalem's present will not be part of its future. There will come a time of peace when God will re-found Jerusalem. In that city to which the nations will come and from which God will rule the whole earth, the ordinary Israelite farmer will find the security that comes from a just social order. It is important to note that while Micah sees a glorification of Jerusalem in the future, the city will have to experience its judgment. Jerusalem does stand under God's curse.

The Book of Zephaniah

The words of this prophet were the inspiration of the *Dies irae,* the sequence used in the Masses of the Dead before the revision of the Roman Missal following Vatican II (see Zeph 1:14-16). But the day of judgment that Zephaniah envisions is not that of the *Dies irae*—a judgment on the Last Day. Jerusalem's day of judgment is imminent. The prophet sees the city fast approaching judgment as the inevitable consequence of its people's failures (1:4). Their crimes are the consequence of serving the deities of Canaan and Assyria and shaping the moral norms of society in accord with the values of these foreign religious systems. The prophet uses the ancient belief in the "Day of the Lord" (see 1:7, 8, 14) to speak of the approaching judgment. This belief pictured God as a divine warrior who fought against Israel's enemies. It became the linchpin of the expectation that Judah's subservience to Assyria was about to end with God's glorious intervention on Israel's behalf. God was about to defeat the Assyrians and restore Judah and Jerusalem to their rightful place as God established divine rule on earth. More than any other prophet, Zephaniah explicitly turns this belief against Jerusalem. He speaks of the "Day of the Lord" as the "Day of the Lord's Anger"—anger directed at the people of Jerusalem (1:18; 2:2).[4]

According to the book's opening verse, Zephaniah's ministry took place during the reign of Josiah (1:1). Josiah came to the throne as a child of eight (2 Kgs 22:1) after the assassination of his father, Amon (2 Kgs 21:23-24). During Amon's two-year reign the pro-Assyrian policies that

---

4. The pervasiveness of the "Day of the Lord" concept is clear from how many prophets make use of it to instruct Israel and Judah that the Day of the Lord means that judgment will come upon them. See Amos 5:18-20; Isa 6:22; Ezek 7:5-27; Joel 1:15; 2:1-11; Mal 4:5.

made it possible for Manasseh to rule for fifty-five years remained in place. Assyria's deterioration enabled Josiah to change these policies, but it was difficult to undo the economic and religious consequences of policies that had been in place for half a century. Manasseh was able to rule this long, but he was a pliant Assyrian vassal. Of course, someone had to pay the price for Manasseh's collaboration. While all sectors of Jerusalem's economy were adversely affected, the people with the fewest economic resources had to pay the heaviest burden. Their taxes supported Jerusalem's royal establishment and paid Judah's tribute to Assyria. The peasants of Judah and Jerusalem were conscripted for service in the Assyrian army and for work on building projects in Nineveh. But commercial contacts with the peoples of the Assyrian Empire did benefit some people. That may be why the prophet singles out Jerusalem's merchants for judgment, promising that their profits will be wiped out:

> Wail, O inhabitants of the Mortar!
> > for all the merchants will be destroyed,
> > all who weigh out silver, done away with (1:11).

Contacts with other peoples were probably also the occasion for the religious innovations in Jerusalem. These went so far as to lead some Jerusalemites to believe that their ancestral deity was impotent:

> At that time I will explore Jerusalem with lamps;
> > I will punish the men . . .
> Who say in their hearts,
> > "Neither good nor evil can the LORD do" (1:12).

Zephaniah announces the harshest words of judgment any prophet ever addressed to Jerusalem:

> Woe to the city, rebellious and polluted,
> > to the tyrannical city!
> She hears no voice,
> > accepts no correction;
> In the LORD she has not trusted,
> > to her God she has not drawn near (3:1-2).

The prophet continues his diatribe by criticizing the city's political and religious leadership, which he regards as self-important and venal (3:3-4). Zephaniah cites God's promise to assemble all nations—including Judah—for judgment. Those guilty will be devoured by "the fire of [God's] jealousy" (3:8). But Zephaniah, like Isaiah and Micah, does not believe divine judgment is God's last word for Judah. He describes the salvation of a humble remnant (3:11-13). These people will be ashamed of their past. Their behavior in both the Temple and the marketplace will reflect their reconciliation with God. The prophet concludes his words to Jerusalem by calling for the city and its people to rejoice. And remarkably, Zephaniah has God joining in the singing and dancing:

> The LORD, your God, will be among you
> as a powerful savior;
> God will rejoice over you with a song,
> will renew you with love,
> will dance with shouts of joy over you (3:17).

While the prophet has no illusions about Jerusalem's failures and the divine judgment these will bring upon Israel, he believes in Jerusalem's future with God—a future in which God will join the city's citizens in festive singing and dancing.

The Book of Jeremiah

Jeremiah's mission to Jerusalem took place during the years immediately preceding its destruction by the Babylonians in 587 B.C. The city survived the Assyrian threat, but it could not survive the threat posed by the neo-Babylonian Empire. By the time Nabuchadnezzar absorbed Judah into the Babylonian provincial system, Judah was effectively reduced to Jerusalem and a few square miles surrounding the city. It appears as if Jeremiah was almost alone in his assessment of the great danger Jerusalem faced. Apparently, what kept the city from appreciating its precarious political situation was a belief that somehow, some way, God would find a way to save the city at the last moment—a belief expressed in Isa 37:33-35:

> Therefore, thus says the LORD concerning the king of Assyria: He shall not reach this city, nor shoot an arrow at it, nor come before it with a shield, nor cast up siegeworks against it. He shall return by the same way he came, without entering the city, says the LORD. I will shield and save this city for my own sake, and for the sake of my servant David.

The people of Jerusalem took these words, spoken at a specific time regarding a specific crisis, and turned them into a general promise by God to save the city when it was threatened. When Jeremiah announced that the city and its Temple were doomed to fall to the Babylonians (Jer 7:2-15; 26:2-6), his words sounded not only treasonous but blasphemous: "Put not your trust in the deceitful words: 'This is the temple of the LORD! The temple of the LORD! The temple of the LORD!'" (7:4). The prophet believed the true temple was the one in the heavens—not the one in Jerusalem, and so what the people of Jerusalem say about the temple in their city is appropriate only for God's temple in the heaven. Jeremiah would have been executed as a blasphemer were it not for the timely intervention of some elders from the city, who cited a precedent for Jeremiah's oracle that offended the people of Jerusalem. They cited the words of Micah spoken more than a century earlier (vv. 18-19; see Mic 3:9-12). The elders asserted that Micah also announced God's judgment on the city but was not punished for proclaiming his words of judgment.

Jerusalem has a central place in Jeremiah's prophecy. After all, the city was the setting for his prophetic mission. The book of Jeremiah mentions Jerusalem 105 times and Zion 17. At the beginning of his prophecy he speaks poignantly of the time of the city's fidelity:

> Go, cry out this message for Jerusalem to hear!
> I remember the devotion of your youth,
>   how you loved me as a bride (2:2).

Like Isaiah and Micah before him, Jeremiah announced that the city was under divine judgment for its crimes: idol worship (11:13; 19:7, 13), pride (13:9), and failure to keep the Sabbath (17:19-27)—for its infidelity as Yahweh's bride. But in the book of Jeremiah God's principal complaint against the city is its unjust social, political, and economic system. In a passage reminiscent of Abraham's bargaining with God over the fate of Sodom (Gen 18:16-33), God asks the prophet to find a single just person so that the city can be spared (5:1-9). Jeremiah looks among both the poor and the wealthy but finds not a single person who knows and does justice. God has little choice but to pronounce the sentence of death on the city and its people (v. 9).

The prophet depicts God as fighting against Jerusalem in a great battle that will bring judgment upon the city: 4:5-7, 14-17, 19-20, 29-31; 5:7-11; 6:2-8, 22-23; 8:18–9:3; 10:19-24; 12:7-13; 13:20-27. These oracles announce an imminent attack by the proverbial enemy from "the north" (Jer 4:6; 6:1, 22; 13:20).[5] God fights against Jerusalem because the city has rebelled against God (4:17) and has proved to be utterly faithless (5:11). The behavior of the city's wealthy women becomes a metaphor for Jerusalem's

---

5. Iron Age Jerusalem was built on the Ophel hill, which was surrounded on three sides by deep valleys that made approach from any direction other than the north foolhardy. Jerusalem was particularly vulnerable to attack from the north, since the northern approaches to the city were actually higher in elevation than the city itself.

folly: the city dresses in purple, wears jewelry, and uses cosmetics in a vain attempt to attract lovers, who spurn her (4:30). Jerusalem has acted like a shameless prostitute (13:27), and this brings about her destruction (4:18; 6:7). The city is the mother of its citizens, who are guilty of forsaking Yahweh for other gods, thus committing infidelity that is like adultery (5:7, 29). Jerusalem realizes her fate and laments her destruction and the loss of her children (4:19-20, 31; 10:19-20), but it is too late. While the dominant image of God in the poems of Jeremiah 4–13 is that of a military leader orchestrating the battle against Jerusalem, God is not without feeling toward Zion:

> I abandon my house,
>   cast off my heritage;
> The beloved of my soul I deliver
>   into the hand of her foes (Jer 12:7).

God weeps over the city's destruction (Jer 8:18–9:2), but the city's infidelity has turned God's love into hate (12:8). Then, in a most offensive image the prophet has God exposing Jerusalem's nakedness for all to see:

> I now will strip off your skirts from you,
>   so that your shame will appear (Jer 13:26).

What makes Jeremiah's prophecy so disturbing is his assertion that God intervened to ensure that Jerusalem would fall. God actually prompted Jerusalem's false confidence:

> "Alas! Lord GOD" they will say,
>   "You only deceived us
> When you said: Peace shall be yours;
>   for the sword touches our very soul" (4:10).

God does this to ensure the city's fall. Still, Jeremiah cannot but be moved at the prospect of Jerusalem's fate. He sees the city as a beloved young woman in dire anguish:

> Yes, I hear the moaning, as of a woman in travail,
> like the anguish of a mother with her first child—
> The cry of daughter Zion gasping,
>   as she stretches forth her hands:
> "Ah, woe is me! I sink exhausted
>   before the slayers!" (Jer 4:31).

The prophet seems mystified by the failure of Jerusalem's religious leadership to recognize the hand of God in the city's political problems (see 6:14). An illustration of this is the debate between Jeremiah and

Hananiah (Jeremiah 28). The prophet Hananiah announced God's intention to "break the yoke of the king of Babylon" (v. 2): the exiles of 597 B.C.[6] were coming back to Jerusalem and the Temple's vessels were going to be returned. It is important to note that Jeremiah never calls his antagonist a "false prophet." In fact, he prays that Hananiah's words find fulfillment (v. 6). Jeremiah has no reason to doubt that Hananiah is just who he claims to be: a spokesperson for God with a message for Jerusalem. Still, Jeremiah is convinced that Jerusalem has to face an even greater disaster in the immediate future. If Hananiah's words are misleading the people of Jerusalem, then it must be God's intention to have the people misled.[7] God is deceiving Jerusalem to ensure that the city will experience the full extent of divine judgment. What does this mean except that God is nullifying the covenant? God's relationship with Israel is over because the people have already abandoned the covenant themselves.

Oblivious to what is happening and discounting Jeremiah's warnings, some people ask with fatuous complacency, "Is the LORD no longer in Zion?" (8:19; see also 14:19). God responds with a question: "Why do they provoke me with their idols, with their foreign nonentities?" The problem with idolatry was not simply a matter of violating the exclusive claim that God had on Israel's worship. Foreign religious traditions were used as theological support for an exploitive and oppressive social system. Yahwistic religious traditions sustained an economic system that was designed to give all people access to the means of production, that is, land. It had mechanisms such as the sabbatical and jubilee years to ensure as far as possible that ancient Israelite society would preserve this economic system. Non-Yahwistic religious traditions provided support for a hierarchical social system, which led to the development of two distinct societies in Judah and Jerusalem: the society of the wealthy and that of the poor. What led Jeremiah to envision the fall of the city was its people's assumption that God was honor bound to uphold the city because it was God's own, so they ask: "Is the Lord no longer in Zion?" The prophet concludes that Jerusalem is beyond salvation:

6. Judah became a vassal state of the Babylonian Empire in 605 B.C. Seven years later King Jehoiakim withheld the tribute required of its vassals by Babylon. In 597 B.C. Nabuchadnezzar took Jerusalem, stripped the Temple, led the king and other important citizens of Judah into exile, and installed Zedekiah as king of Judah. See 2 Kgs 24:10-17.

7. There is another example of God's deception through the prophets. See 1 Kgs 22:1-40, especially v. 21. In this instance there was a single prophet, Micaiah ben Imlah, who predicted military disaster for Israel and Judah, while four hundred prophets promised victory. The text asserts that God placed "a lying spirit" in the four hundred, guaranteeing that they would give the wrong advice (1 Kgs 22:23).

> Who will pity you, Jerusalem,
>   who will console you?
> Who will stop to ask
>   about your welfare?
> You have disowned me, says the LORD,
>   turned your back upon me;
> And so I stretched out my hand to destroy you,
>   I was weary of sparing you (15:5-6).

Now, therefore, says the LORD God of hosts, the God of Israel: I will bring upon Judah and all the citizens of Jerusalem every evil that I threatened; because when I spoke they did not obey, when I called they did not answer (35:17).

The most striking aspect of Jeremiah's assessment of Jerusalem's status occurs in his letter to the citizens of Jerusalem whom the Babylonians took into exile in 597 B.C. (Jeremiah 29). The prophet tells the exiles that they have no hope for a quick solution to the problems caused by the Babylonians. Jeremiah advises them to settle down for a long stay, but he also assures them that God's ultimate plans for them are for restoration and peace (vv. 11, 14). He suggests that God granted the Babylonians hegemony over Judah and Jerusalem for seventy years (v. 10; see also 25:1-14).[8] Jeremiah assures the exiles that they can find God even in Babylon. Jerusalem, then, is not the only place where people can have an authentic encounter with God. If the exiles search for God sincerely, they will find God (29:12-13). On the other hand, what awaits Jerusalem is "the sword, famine and pestilence" (9:17-18). The city's people will experience divine judgment because of their refusal to obey God's words sent to them through the prophets (29:19). What is decisive for an authentic experience of the divine is not that a person be in Jerusalem but that a person be obedient. One can be obedient in Babylon and disobedient in Jerusalem.

The surrender of Jerusalem to the Babylonians and the exile of some of the royal family and other leading citizens in 597 B.C. gave the prophet another opportunity to reflect on the mode of God's presence to the people of Judah. Was an authentic experience of God dependent on people's being

---

8. The Chronicler considered Jeremiah's prophecy as fulfilled with the restoration under Cyrus after less than fifty years (see 2 Chr 36:21). Zechariah believed that the prophecy was fulfilled with the rebuilding of the Temple, which occurred about eighty-two years after the exile in 597 B.C. (Zech 1:12). Others believed that Jeremiah's prophecy was not fulfilled, and there was at least one attempt at salvaging it (see Dan 9:24). Christian fundamentalists have taken the reinterpretation in Daniel as an unfulfilled prophecy of the end of the world. See *The Scofield Study Bible* (New York: Oxford Univ. Press, 1917) 914, no.1.

in Jerusalem, the supposed "city of God"? After all, the power of God's word proclaimed by Jeremiah transcended space and time. He was able to announce that word to the exiles in Babylon. It was a word about present judgment and future salvation. That experience led the prophet to conclude that the power of God's presence is not limited to Judah and Jerusalem. The person who sincerely seeks God and lives in obedience can find God—even in Babylon.

While Jeremiah was convinced that Jerusalem was going to experience divine judgment because of its infidelity, he was confident that there was a divinely ordained future for the city. He demonstrated his faith in the city's future in a very tangible way: while the Babylonians were besieging the city, he bought some land. For thirteen years the prophet had been proclaiming that God's judgment on Jerusalem was irrevocable. Then, seemingly out of nowhere, came a hopeful word from God: "For thus says the LORD of hosts, the God of Israel: Houses and fields and vineyards shall again be bought in this land" (Jer 32:15). While the prophet's words of judgment against Jerusalem were in the process of being fulfilled, God revealed to Jeremiah a new word: a word of hope. He decided to act on that word himself. He bought a field for himself (32:6). This shift in the message he was to announce surprised the prophet, so he prayed that he was hearing correctly and was doing the right thing in buying the field (34:17-25). In answer to his prayer, God assured the prophet that his buying of land while the city was under siege will be a sign that "sword, famine, and pestilence" were not God's last words to Jerusalem:

> I will make with them an eternal covenant, never to cease doing good to them; into their hearts I will put the fear of me, that they may never depart from me. I will take delight in doing good to them: I will replant them firmly in this land, with all my heart and soul.
>
> For thus says the LORD: Just as I brought upon this people all this great evil, so I will bring upon them all the good I promise them. Fields shall again be bought in this land, which you call a desert, without man or beast, handed over to the Chaldeans. Fields shall be bought with money, deeds written and sealed, and witnesses shall be used in the land of Benjamin, in the suburbs of Jerusalem, in the cities of Judah and of the hill country, in the cities of the foothills and of the Negeb, when I change their lot, says the LORD (32:40-44).

This revelation was a turning point in Jeremiah's life and ministry.[9] It led him to see in the divine purpose more than retribution, rather, authentic restoration. Still, this was not a matter of cheap grace. Jerusalem was going

9. William L. Holladay, *Jeremiah 2*. Hermeneia (Minneapolis: Fortress Press, 1989) 220.

to experience the consequences of its failure to be faithful (9:10). Though Jeremiah witnessed the houses of the city being demolished during the siege, he was still convinced that God would restore the city one day (33:1-15). The prophet even gives the restored Jerusalem a new name, "the Lord is our justice,"[10] to emphasize that the foundation of the city's future is divine justice. It will require the creation and maintenance of an entirely new social, political, and economic order—one based on the will of God rather than on the power of the wealthy.

The Book of Lamentations

Settling on a date of composition for almost any book of the Bible is a notoriously perilous affair. That the catastrophe of Jerusalem's fall is reflected in the book of Lamentations seems fairly obvious.[11] Despite this, many interpreters of Lamentations have not taken seriously the idea that this book might actually have been spoken by the survivors of the victorious Babylonian siege of the city in 587 B.C.[12] While it may be true that the book in its final form may be later than the sixth century, it is safe to say that it owes its existence to the memory of the Jerusalemites who were trying to cope with the destruction of their city—indeed, the destruction of their world.

Though prophets like Isaiah and Jeremiah tried to prepare Jerusalem for its day of judgment, it was difficult for the city to accept God's verdict. There was the temptation to interpret the city's fall as the consequence of a heavenly duel between Yahweh, the patron deity of Jerusalem, and Marduk, the patron deity of Babylon. Since Babylon prevailed on earth, it must mean that Marduk prevailed in the heavens. One purpose of prophetic

---

10. The Hebrew form of this name is *yahweh-tsidqenu.* Some commentators see this as a play on the name of *tsidqiyyahu,* the last king of Judah (Zedekiah). The names have similar meanings. The king's name means "Yahweh is my righteousness." The name that the prophet gives to Jerusalem is "Yahweh is our righteousness." While a play on words is possible, more likely Jeremiah was concerned that the restored Jerusalem be built on the foundation of justice—the lack of which led to the city's fall.

11. The book of Lamentations can be classified as a lament over a fallen city. See W. C. Gewaltney, "The Biblical Book of Lamentation in the Context of Near Eastern Lament Literature," *Scripture in Context II,* ed. W. W. Hallo and others (Winona Lake, Ind.: Eisenbrauns, 1983) 191–211.

12. Claus Westermann, *Lamentations: Issues and Interpretation* (Edinburgh: T&T Clark, 1994) 62. For example, Iain Provan does not find firm evidence to fix the dating of Lamentations with any more precision than to assert that the book could be dated from the sixth to the second centuries. See his "Lamentations," *New Century Bible Commentary* (Grand Rapids: Wm. B. Eerdmans, 1991) 19.

preaching was to counter such an explanation. Yahweh has used the nations—first Assyria and then Babylon—as instruments of judgment over the city that had proven unfaithful. Shorn of any defense, the people of Jerusalem had but one alternative: to cry out in despair over the fall of their city, the destruction of its Temple, the scattering of the priests, the end of the Davidic dynasty, and the exile of so many of the city's important citizens. The book of Lamentations preserves these cries of despair, which become assertions of new hope as they express Jerusalem's acceptance of God's verdict on its past. Nabuchadnezzar and the Babylonian army were but the means God chose to express sovereignty over the city. What the book of Lamentations represents is both the confession of sin and the audacious hope that what God has destroyed God will build up again:

> For the Lord's rejection
>   does not last forever;
> Though he punishes, he takes pity,
>   in the abundance of his mercies (Lam 3:31-32).

Lamentations seeks to help Jerusalem deal with God's anger: "How the Lord in his wrath has detested daughter Zion!" (2:1). In the Bible the anger of God always has a purpose—usually to purify and renew. Indeed, a God who could not become angry over the injustice of Jerusalem's social and economic system and over the infidelity of the city's people could not really be God. Still, God's anger is not a permanent mode of God's relationship to Jerusalem. Anger flares up but then recedes. The question is "how long" will God's anger toward Jerusalem last (see 5:22). Above all, it is important to remember that despite its rhetoric, Lamentations does not consider anger to be the equivalent of rejection—otherwise the book would have never been written.

The book of Lamentations agrees with the prophetic announcement of divine judgment upon Israel.[13] The images the book uses to speak of Jerusalem make this clear. Zion is an adulterous woman (1:19), left without her children (2:21). She has no one to comfort her (1:2) in her shame and disgrace (1:8-9, 11, 17). Her suffering is without parallel:

> Come, all you who pass by the way,
>   look and see
> Whether there is any suffering like my suffering,
>   which has been dealt me
> When the LORD afflicted me
>   on the day of his blazing wrath (Lam 1:12).

13. Claus Westermann, "Boten des Zorns," *Forschung am Alten Testament: Gesalmmelte Studien III.* Theologische Bucheri 73 (Munich: C. Kaiser, 1984) 96–109.

Jerusalem was guilty before God. Divine judgment was unavoidable. Accepting the disaster that came upon the city as an act of divine judgment was an admission of Jerusalem's guilt. Lamentations, then, succeeded where the prophets failed. The leadership and the people of Jerusalem rejected the message that Isaiah, Micah, and Jeremiah announced to them. By joining in the laments over their devastated city, the remnant of the community finally accepted the judgment of the prophets. This made it possible for the people to plead for God's mercy upon their city. Those who experienced the full measure of God's judgment turned to that God for mercy. Though the city deserved the fate that came to it, the people of Jerusalem cried out to the very one who brought disaster on them. Moved by the death of many people, the destruction of the institutions that gave Jerusalem its identity, and witnessing the exile of its leadership, those left in the ruins of the city raised their laments.

The book of Lamentations comprises five poems. The poems present the people of Jerusalem grieving because of the disasters they have experienced: military defeat, the end of the national state, the destruction of the Temple, and exile. The first poem emphasizes Jerusalem's isolation: there is no one to grieve with the city (1:11, 21)—not even God, who has abandoned it to its fate. Several times the poem repeats that it is impossible to comfort the city: 1:2, 9, 16-17, 21. The text re-creates the feeling of despair that must have gripped the Jerusalemites following the destruction of their homes and their city in a way that makes it difficult for the reader not to empathize with the fallen city. While the poem agrees that the city has suffered for its sins, it asks how long Zion must suffer while its enemies, whose crimes are as great, do not (1:22).

The second poem focuses not so much on what has happened to Zion but why it has happened. The cause of Jerusalem's calamity is the destructive anger of God:

> How the Lord in his wrath
>   has detested daughter Zion!
> He has cast down from heaven to earth
>   the glory of Israel,
> Unmindful of his footstool
>   on the day of his wrath (Lam 2:1).

Speaking to the devastated Zion, the poet describes the victory of the city's enemies as God's doing (2:11-17). The poet advises Jerusalem to pray for the relief that can come only from God:

> Cry out to the Lord;
>   moan, O daughter Zion!

Let your tears flow like a torrent
   day and night;
Let there be no respite for you,
   no repose for your eyes (Lam 2:18).

Zion's response to the poet is similar to that in the first chapter. There is no confession of guilt but a subtle but clear questioning of God's justice: "Look, O LORD, and consider: whom have you ever treated thus?" (Lam 2:20). Zion again implies that its punishment is out of proportion to its guilt. Here is evidence that the fall of Jerusalem led some people to question divine justice.

In the first two poems Lamentations speaks of Jerusalem as "daughter Zion."[14] This expression occurs twenty-six times in the Hebrew Scriptures. All of the occurrence are in poetic texts. Of these, thirteen are found in a positive context (Isa 16:1; 52:2; 62:11; Mic 4:13; Jer 6:2; Lam 4:22; Zech 2:14; 3:14; Ps 9:15). The remaining instances use this expression to speak of Jerusalem as the object of divine anger (Isa 1:8; 10:32; Mic 1:13; 4:10; Jer 6:23; Lam 1:6; 2:1, 4, 8, 10, 13). The expression likely originated to depict Jerusalem and its people as victorious, secure, and prosperous.[15] This makes its use to speak of Jerusalem in its desolation as both ironic and poignant. What once was is no more. Jerusalem lies in ruins, and its people do not know how to make sense of what has happened to them. All they can do is lament their city's fate. The use of this metaphor makes it clear that while Jerusalem may be God's favorite, this does not exempt it from judgment when guilty of disobedience.

The third poem is a debate between those who find some hope of Jerusalem's situation (3:31-33) and those who find none (3:34-36). Despite appearances, the poet assures Zion that there is reason to have confidence about the future (3:37-39). Personal experience is the basis for that hope. The poet describes an experience of personal suffering (3:1-18) and the confidence in God's deliverance (3:22-23), but by the end of the chapter the poet's confidence appears to have dissipated (3:52-66). The book of Lamentations does not reflect the triumph of faith over doubt. It describes how people of faith try to overcome their doubts—without great success—about the future God has in store for them.

Like anyone dealing with serious problems, the book of Lamentations swings from one approach to another. The fourth poem describes Zion's

---

14. The singular form, "daughter Zion," is a poetic personification of Jerusalem, while the plural form, "daughters of Zion," which occurs only four times, refers to the female inhabitants of Jerusalem. See Elaine R. Follis, "Zion, Daughter of," *ABD* 6:1103.

15. Ibid.

suffering but ends with the most confident affirmation uttered by the poet to this point: "Your chastisement is completed, O daughter Zion, [God] will not prolong your exile" (Lam 4:22). The fifth and final lament brings the reader back to doubts and questions. Though the people of Jerusalem admit their failings (5:1), they imply that God has not kept the promises made to Israel (5:2-3, 5) and thus is guilty as well for Zion's fall. The book ends with questions and despair:

> Why, then, should you forget us,
>   abandon us so long a time? . . .
> For now you have indeed rejected us,
>   and in full measure turned your wrath against us (5:20, 22).

The book of Lamentations is the product of a people in that terrible place between faith and doubt. Faith urges them to look for some meaning in the fall of their city and in the suffering of the innocent along with the guilty. Doubt tells them there is no meaning. While Zion was guilty of infidelity, the suffering of the innocent—the poor, children, women with infants—renders any attempt to explain Zion's problems as the result of sin to be folly. Theoretically speaking, suffering is a consequence of sin, but Jerusalem's experience shows that God must be arbitrary in the administration of divine justice. One must wonder how "in control" God really is (3:34-36) and, therefore, whether hope makes any sense at all (5:22). Reading these words of faith and hope, doubt and despair, reveals the isolation and abandonment, the anger and frustration, the questions and desperation, that must have gripped the people of Jerusalem after the fall of their city.

The book of Lamentations did not arise to deal with the problem of suffering or to resolve tensions between the Zion tradition and the experience of 587. These laments are the immediate reaction of people who have experienced the collapse of their world. The theological issues that emerge in the laments are not the result of profound and systematic reflection. The real significance of Lamentations is that they are the means by which the people of Jerusalem can express their grief. What is important to note is the ending of the work. Nothing is really resolved with the final verses of chapter five. There are still questions and doubts. But the book has allowed people their disillusionment and grief. The fall of Jerusalem did give rise to a more systematic analysis, but that did not appear in the book of Lamentations. What does appear invites contemporary readers to relate their own experiences of isolation, abandonment, and anger, which come from intense suffering, to their faith in God. The book of Lamentations shows that it is no simple task, for how can one speak when

God's voice is drowned out by the disruption that suffering introduces into our lives?

The Book of Ezekiel

Ezekiel was among the Judahites who were taken to Babylon following Jerusalem's surrender to Nabuchadnezzar in 597 B.C. From that vantage point the prophet looks at Jerusalem and offers an assessment of its immediate future, which is as bleak as that given by Jeremiah. Ezekiel tries to convince the Judahites that the worst is yet to come for Jerusalem. He sketches the outline of Jerusalem on the soft clay of a brick that is being air dried. Then the prophet adds trenches and earthworks around the brick to portray the city's siege. He does this at the behest of God to show the severity of the divine judgment that is still to come on the city (4:1-3, see also 24:2). The reason for the new attack on the city is its rebellion against God (5:1-9). It may appear that the city is going to fall because of another ill-advised rebellion against Babylonian domination of Judah, but that is only what human eyes see. The prophet asserts that Jerusalem's fall is God's doing—a necessary response to Jerusalem's infidelity.

The prophet then goes on to describe what we would call a "mystical experience" in which he is transported to Jerusalem's north gate. There he sees what the people have done in the vain hope of preventing the total collapse of their city. They have set up images of foreign deities in the Temple (8:3-6). The walls of the Temple's forecourt have been decorated with relief work depicting unclean animals (8:7-12). The elders excuse this departure from tradition by asserting: "The LORD cannot see us; the LORD has forsaken the land" (v. 12). When the prophet enters the Temple itself, he sees women engaged in ritual lamentation for the god Tammuz (8:14-15). Finally, in the very sanctuary of Yahweh, the priests are worshiping the sun (8:16). Instead of dealing with the social evils that have turned God against Jerusalem, the people turn to foreign rituals. Apparently, they have concluded that the traditional Yahwistic rituals were ineffective, so they hope their worship of other gods will prevent the disaster they see approaching their city. After having those innocent of these crimes marked, God orders Jerusalem's total destruction (9:4-10). But before this death sentence can be executed upon the city, the divine presence must leave the Temple, for this presence is all that is standing between Jerusalem and the full measure of divine judgment. "The glory of God" leaves the Temple. At first, it goes only as far as the eastern gate of the Temple, but then it vanishes (10:18-21). Ezekiel uses the Zion tradition that honors Jerusalem as "the city of God" only to turn that tradition against itself.

He describes God abandoning Jerusalem to leave the city and its Temple to its total destruction. Ezekiel agrees with his prophetic predecessors, who proclaimed divine judgment against the city.

What sets off Ezekiel's treatment of Jerusalem from that of other prophets is his thorough exploitation of the metaphor that portrays Jerusalem as Yahweh's wife.[16] Chapters 16 and 23 personify Jerusalem as a woman married to Yahweh. Both stories show that Jerusalem came to represent all Israel in microcosm. These stories are both poignant and repulsive at the same time. In neither story does Ezekiel depend upon the elements of the Zion tradition to speak about Jerusalem. In fact, the word "Zion" never appears in the book of Ezekiel. He prefers images that come from the sphere of personal relationships to those that derive from monarchic institutions.

Chapter 16 tells the story of a Canaanite foundling. The prophet's story recalls that Jerusalem was a Canaanite enclave in the central highlands that were home to the Israelite tribes. It became integrated into Judah during the monarchic period, eventually becoming the political and religious center of the Judahite state. Underscoring God's graciousness, the prophet tells how God saved the foundling from certain death and endowed it with wonderful gifts. Eventually God married the foundling—now grown. She bore God children only to sacrifice them to idols. Jerusalem, God's wife, proved to be unfaithful by worshiping other gods and becoming entangled in political alliances with the nations. Her infidelity was greater even than that of Sodom to the south and Samaria to the north. Like her sister cities, Jerusalem will suffer the consequences of its infidelity—that is unavoidable. In fact, Jerusalem will become a more infamous example of disgrace than even Sodom. Still, God's mercy will overwhelm God's justice. Jerusalem will be forgiven and restored (16:59-63).

The prophet tells a similar story in chapter 23 with a similar goal: to strike at the heart of Jerusalem's self-assurance as "the city of God." This story is about two sisters with similar names: Oholah, the elder sister, and Oholibah, the younger one.[17] The prophet identifies the former with Samaria and the latter with Jerusalem (v. 4). Here it is not the prophet who speaks but God, and God's figurative address on the two sisters is far more harsh

16. See Galambush, *Jerusalem in the Book of Ezekiel,* 78–88, for a discussion of the distinctiveness of Ezekiel's use of the marriage metaphor.

17. The names are likely allusions to the supposed pastoral origins of the ancient Israelites. The patriarchs were thought of as shepherds who lived in tents (Hebrew: *ʾohel*). Scholars have not reached a consensus about the significance of these names. See Walther Zimmerli, *Ezekiel 1.* Hermeneia (Philadelphia: Fortress Press, 1979) 483–4. This story may be inspired by Jeremiah 3:6-13, which speaks of the kingdoms of Israel and Judah as sisters.

than the Ezekiel story about Jerusalem's infidelity in chapter 16. God excoriates the two sisters for their promiscuity. What the story alludes to is the attempt by both Samaria and Jerusalem to seek their political security through alliances with the nations. Of course, both come to grief for their misguided policies. What they should have done is relied upon God by living in obedience to the covenant. Both Samaria and Jerusalem sought safety though political entanglements—never realizing that the nations were seeking to achieve their own goals and not the security of the Israelite and Judahite kingdoms.

Verses 5-10 describe the liaison of Oholah (Samaria) and the Assyrians. From the very beginning of its existence as a political entity, the kingdom of Israel struggled with Aram for supremacy in the Levant. To settle this conflict in Israel's favor, Jehu, who reigned in Israel from 839 to 822 B.C., made an alliance with the Assyrians.[18] What began as an attempt to secure Israel's future ended one hundred years later with the absorption of the territory of the kingdom of Israel into the Assyrian provincial system. Verses 11-17 describe in lurid detail the activities of Oholibah (Jerusalem) with her lovers. Though Jerusalem witnessed what had happened to Samaria, it chose to follow the same path, so the prophet concludes that her guilt is even greater than that of her sister. Jerusalem made a string of alliances, first with Assyria under Ahaz (2 Kgs 16:7), then with Babylon under Josiah (2 Kgs 23:29),[19] and finally with the Egyptians under Jehoiakim (2 Kgs 23:24). Ezekiel probably was aware of Zedekiah's alliance with Egypt against Babylon (see Jer 44:3) and considered it rank stupidity. That is why he portrays Oholibah's dalliance with Egypt with such demeaning images (vv. 19-21). The rest of the chapter details the judgment that God brings upon Oholibah. She will suffer the same fate as her older sister.

In chapters 16 and 23 Ezekiel demolishes any hope that the people of Jerusalem had for their city based on the election traditions. They will not be able to depend upon God's choice of Jerusalem as they ponder their political fate. Jerusalem is the unfaithful wife. She has shamed her husband by her cultic and political infidelity. The city will have to face the consequences of that infidelity. The problem the prophets had with foreign

18. Jehu has the distinction of being the only Israelite or Judahite king of whom we have a contemporary portrait. The Black Obelisk (*ANE*, 192, pl. 100) depicts Jehu kneeling in obeisance to the Assyrian king Shalmaneser III.

19. Egypt under Pharaoh Neco was going to engage the Babylonians, who were about to take the Assyrian capital. Josiah tried to intercept the Egyptians—probably to ingratiate himself with the Babylonians. His attempt to halt the Egyptians failed. Josiah died in battle at Megiddo.

alliances is that they introduced a non-Yahwistic political and economic ideology into Israel. A hierarchical social system was characteristic of the nations with whom Israel and Judah made their alliances. It was not long before the nations brought their influence to bear upon the Israelite and Judahite social systems. Second, since Israel and Judah were invariably the weaker partners in the alliances they made with the nations, they were required to offer tribute to their senior partners. This put an unbearable burden on the ordinary Israelites, who had to contribute their labor and their tithes to pay this tribute. Israel and Judah had to mortgage their traditions of morality and faith to pay for their political security. For Ezekiel this sealed Israel's fate. Jerusalem came to stand for the whole of Israel for the prophet, so he pronounces this verdict:

> Thus says the Lord GOD of the inhabitants of Jerusalem [to the land of Israel]: They shall eat their bread in anxiety and drink their water in horror, that their land may be emptied of the violence of all its inhabitants that now fills it. Inhabited cities shall be in ruins, and the land shall be a waste; thus you shall know that I am the LORD (Ezek 12:19-20).

The imagery of Ezekiel 16 and 23 is particularly troublesome, since the prophet uses feminine imagery to depict Jerusalem's infidelity. The use of such imagery to speak of capital cities was not invented by the prophet; he simply adopts conventional patterns of speech.[20] The problem with this imagery is that it helps perpetuate a negative image of women. Of course, those most responsible for Judah's failures were its leaders. The king, the royal establishment, the priesthood, the wealthy landowners, were men. They created and maintained an unjust social system that flaunted the norms of traditional Israelite morality. While the women in Judahite society were not blameless, the social standing and political power of men determined the fate of Judah. Ezekiel's use of feminine imagery in speaking of Judah's infidelity is explicit and even crude, making it a difficult text for people to read today. Unfortunately, Ezekiel speaks of Jerusalem as Yahweh's spouse only in oracles of judgment. He does not use this imagery when describing Jerusalem's restoration.

On January 19, 586 B.C., Ezekiel's prophecy underwent a profound transformation. It was on this day, according to Ezekiel 33:21, that a fugitive who escaped from the second Babylonian siege of Jerusalem informed the prophet that the city had fallen. Ezekiel was right about the judgment Jerusalem experienced. Still, the prophet's words were remembered, treasured, and transmitted over the centuries not because his political

20. See Fitzgerald, "*BTWLT* and *BT* as Titles," 167–83.

analysis was correct—not because he recognized that Judah and Jerusalem could not survive the incursions of the Babylonian Empire. People came to value Ezekiel's words not simply because he was able to see that the Babylonians were merely instruments of divine judgment upon an unfaithful people. We have Ezekiel's words today because he gave Jerusalem a vision of the future, but he would never speak of Jerusalem as the bride of Yahweh again. Still, he was able to offer the city hope once he heard that the full measure of divine judgment had come upon it.

Chapters 33–39 are oracles of salvation for all Israel. They promise restoration: a return to their land and a renewal of their relationship with God:

> Therefore, thus says the Lord GOD: Now I will restore the fortunes of Jacob and have pity on the whole house of Israel, and I will be jealous for my holy name. They shall forget their disgrace and all the times they broke faith with me, when they live in security on their land with no one to frighten them. When I bring them back from among the peoples, I will gather them from the lands of their enemies, and will prove my holiness through them in the sight of many nations. Thus they shall know that I, the LORD, am their God, since I who exiled them among the nations, will gather them back on their land, not leaving any of them behind. No longer will I hide my face from them, for I have poured out my spirit upon the house of Israel, says the Lord GOD (39:25-29).

The prophet promises that Judah's devastated cities will be repopulated (36:38). In 38:12 the prophet speaks about "the navel of the earth." Though the prophet does not explicitly mention Jerusalem, it is likely that he does envision Jerusalem as the center of the world (see 5:5). Chapters 40–48 contain the prophet's vision of the restoration. It is clear that Jerusalem is to be rebuilt, but it is no longer personified, for Ezekiel has abandoned the metaphor of Jerusalem as Yahweh's bride, which he exploited so skillfully in the first part of his prophecy. What becomes the center of the restoration is the Temple. A building becomes the substitute for Yahweh's bride in Ezekiel's mind. It is as if the stone of the Temple seems a less dangerous and more reassuring substitute for the flesh-and-blood city.[21] Ezekiel sees God's glory returning to the Temple (43:5) to take possession of a new temple. The prophet sees the fulfillment of a word he heard from God during the last days of the old Jerusalem—a word that promised that one day there would be worship pleasing to God offered on "my holy mountain" (20:40).

The prophecy of Ezekiel has a significant place in the development of Jerusalem as a theological idea because the prophet has linked the hopes

21. Galambush, *Jerusalem in the Book of Ezekiel*, 157.

of his people to the fate of this city. For Ezekiel Jerusalem was the representative of all Israel. It was becoming the symbol of its future. That city experienced the full measure of divine justice, but the prophet saw the great future for Jerusalem, so he proclaimed to a people in exile—a forlorn and downcast people—that God was beginning to build a new temple in faithfulness to God's promises. Judgment is never God's last word to Jerusalem, for God is full of gentleness and compassion. The last verse of the book suggests that in the future the name of the temple-city will be "the LORD is here" (48:35).[22] The prophet ends by picturing God dwelling among Israel once again.

Conclusion

The prophetic task was complicated by a view prevalent in Judahite society that it was a matter of divine honor for God to protect Jerusalem. When the prophets spoke of the city's coming judgment, it sound like blasphemy to many. Still, the prophets consistently spoke of the judgment that Jerusalem was going to face. The prophets believed in this message, since they were convinced that God would not allow the unjust social system of Judah to continue unchecked. They believed that the wealthy and powerful of Jerusalem sealed their city's fate by their exploitation of the poor. The prophets spoke this message of judgment only because they believed that Jerusalem had a future beyond judgment. The prophets believed in the ultimate triumph of justice.

---

22. The name "Jerusalem" never appears in Ezekiel 40–48. Still, it is clear that the prophet is speaking of Jerusalem. Also, the book of Deuteronomy never mentions Jerusalem, although its formula "the place where the Lord will make his name dwell" does, of course, refer to the city. See p. 44, above. Similarly, the name of Jerusalem does not appear in Qumran's Temple scroll *(11QTemple)* or the fragments of an Aramaic composition that clearly describes the "new Jerusalem" (e.g., *1Q32*).

6

A Vision of Restoration:
Jerusalem in Second Isaiah

Among the questions the worshipers of Yahweh asked themselves after the fall of Jerusalem and the destruction of its Temple was one about the future of the city they believed to be the place God chose to dwell on earth. Is there any future for the city in view of the Temple's destruction? One reason for the city's survival through the ages is the answer to that question, as found in Isaiah 40–55. Jerusalem's future as the symbol of hope for the worshipers of Yahweh dominates this part of the book of Isaiah.

It would have been so easy for the exiles to forget Jerusalem, believing that God's actions on behalf of the city were a matter of its past—not of its future. Still, one of Judah's poets wrote: "If I forget you, Jerusalem, may my right hand wither" (Ps 137:5). Who was responsible for keeping hope alive during the exile? Toward the end of the exile one person who kept the Judahites from slipping into despair about their future was the poet and prophet whose words have been preserved in Isaiah 40–55. He spoke in such lyrical terms of Jerusalem that he helped a defeated, dispirited, and exiled people maintain their identity, their unique religious belief and practices, and their hope of return. The prophet did not have a simple task. The Babylonians settled exiles of Judah in underpopulated and agriculturally marginal regions of Mesopotamia. The exiles were not kept as chattel—they had a modicum of freedom. They even prospered. Many took Jeremiah's advice (Jeremiah 29) and established roots in the place of their exile. Some even rose to important positions in Babylon's civil service. Then a prophet spoke, reminding the exiles that they belonged somewhere else, and promised them that God was going to lead them back soon.

The prophet's fellow exiles were likely skeptical about his message. The loss of Jerusalem, its Temple, and the Davidic dynasty left the exiles with the feeling that Yahweh's action in the world was something that belonged to the past—or at best that Yahweh had forgotten them:

> But Zion said, "The LORD has forsaken me;
> my Lord has forgotten me." (Isa 49:14)

To the exiles it appeared that Marduk, the god of Babylon, was the one who was controlling events. Could the prophet convince his fellow exiles otherwise? His strategy was to boldly assert that God could never forget the exiles of Jerusalem:

> Can a mother forget her infant,
> be without tenderness for the child of her womb?
> Even should she forget,
> I will never forget you.
> See, upon the palms of my hands I have written your name;
> Your walls are ever before me (Isa 49:15-16).

Second Isaiah was certain that a new exodus was on the horizon—one so spectacular it would eclipse the escape of the Hebrew slaves from Egypt:

> Thus says the LORD,
> who opens a way in the sea
> and a path in the mighty waters,
> Who leads out chariots and horsemen,
> a powerful army,
> Till they lie prostrate together, never to rise,
> snuffed out and quenched like a wick.
> Remember not the events of the past,
> the things of long ago consider not;
> See, I am doing something new!
> Now it springs forth, do you not perceive it? (Isa 43:16-19a).

These words were proclaimed to the exiles as Babylon's star began to fall. The empire was suffering from internal divisions. Nabonidus (559–539), the last Babylonian monarch, angered the religious establishment by favoring the god Sin and neglecting Marduk, Babylon's patron deity. In a ploy to garner popular support for his policies, Nabonidus brought the images of gods worshiped at local shrines in his kingdom to the city of Babylon.[1] This move backfired, and the people deserted Nabonidus because he took away their gods. Also, the king detached himself from his

---

1. Weinfeld, "Cult Centralization," 202–12.

administrative responsibilities, taking up residence in Teima, a town in the Arabian peninsula, and leaving his son Belshezzar to rule in his stead. While the Babylonian Empire was beginning to unravel, a new imperial power was beginning to assert itself: Persia. Its armies were led by a vigorous and successful general named Cyrus. The prophet took these events as his cue and began to speak about Yahweh's return to center stage. Judah's God was not hidden or powerless before Babylon. In fact, the new political events that were stirring things up were directed by Yahweh for one purpose: the restoration of Judah and Jerusalem:

> I [Yahweh] say of Cyrus: My shepherd,
>   who fulfills my every wish;
> He shall say of Jerusalem, "Let her be rebuilt,"
>   and of the temple, "Let its foundations be laid" (Isa 44:28).

In his enthusiasm at the rise of Cyrus and the inevitable fall of Babylon, the prophet called Cyrus Yahweh's "messiah" (45:1), a title once reserved for kings of Judah's own Davidic dynasty. Certainly the use of this word had to astonish the prophet's fellow exiles. Choosing this word for its shock value, the prophet spoke in the name of a God who was about to use every resource and set aside hallowed traditions in order to answer the exiles' laments. Since there was no descendant of David to lead them, God chose a Persian general—not to be an instrument of judgment as God used Sennacherib and Nabuchadnezzar. Cyrus the Persian, "the anointed one," was to be an instrument of salvation, fulfilling a role once reserved for Judah's own kings.

Isaiah 40:1-11

Second Isaiah, the greatest of all ancient Israel's prophets, did not speak as his predecessors did. He did not threaten or cajole. He did not simply proclaim God's message and leave the people to decide how they were to respond to it. The prophet tried to persuade his fellow exiles, appealing to them with logical arguments and beautifully evocative rhetorical technique. Perhaps none of his words are more familiar to an English-speaking audience than the beginning of his prophecy, which served as the inspiration for one movement of Handel's oratorio *The Messiah:*

> Comfort, give comfort to my people,
>   says your God.
> Speak tenderly to Jerusalem, and proclaim to her
>   that her service is at an end,
>   her guilt is expiated;

Indeed, she has received from the hand of the LORD
> double for all her sins (Isa 40:1-2).

Chapter 40 is indeed a new message for Jerusalem. Unlike his prophetic predecessors, Second Isaiah did not ask the people to recognize and confess their infidelity. The exile brought the Judahites beyond confession of sins. Unlike Hananiah and the other prophets of false hope, Isaiah of Babylon offered his fellow exiles no cheap promises or vain expectations. Unlike those who composed the book of Lamentations, he did not give voice to the grief of his fellow exiles. Unlike the Deuteronomists, he explicitly asserted his hopes for the future. Isaiah of Babylon believed that the fall of Jerusalem was an act of divine judgment (42:24-25), but he was equally convinced that he was living at the beginning of a new day for the city and its people. The prophet saw divine providence controlling the destinies of powerful nations for one purpose: to restore Jerusalem. He believed that this insight was given him by God to offer comfort to the exiles of Jerusalem.

The prophet's message begins with a series of commands. The imperative forms ("comfort," "speak," "proclaim") in Isaiah 40:1-2 are plural, and it appears that the prophet wants his readers to understand the commands as given by one member of the "divine council"[2] to others. They make clear God's orders to console the exiles of Jerusalem with the news that their suffering is about to end. Next, the prophet hears a member of the council commanding that another prepare the way for God's imminent manifestation on earth. The prophet wants his audience to imagine God's coming as if it were an even grander triumphal procession than the ones they probably witnessed in Babylon honoring Marduk:

A voice cries out:
In the desert prepare the way of the LORD!
> Make straight in the wasteland a highway for our God!
Every valley shall be filled in,
> every mountain and hill shall be made low;
The rugged land shall be made a plain,
> the rough country, a broad valley.
Then the glory of the LORD shall be revealed,
> and all mankind shall see it together;
> for the mouth of the LORD has spoken (Isa 40:3-5).

2. The image the prophet is painting is a heavenly council over which Yahweh presides. The other members of the council carry out his orders. This common ancient Near Eastern metaphor is found also in Jer 23:18, 22; Amos 3:7; 1 Kgs 22:19; Isaiah 6. In the text from Isaiah 6 and 1 Kings 22 the prophet, in question form, hears the voice of God speaking to the council. In Isaiah 40, the prophet hears members of the council relating God's decree, but God's authority lies behind the words the prophet hears.

It is clear that the return of the exiles and the restoration of Jerusalem will be a miraculous movement of God and not the result of any human efforts. Next comes what some see as God's call to the prophet to announce salvation for the exiles:[3]

> A voice says, "Cry out!"
>   I answer, "What shall I cry out?"
> "All mankind is grass,
>   and all their glory like the flower of the field.
> The grass withers, the flower wilts,
>   when the breath of the LORD blows upon it.
> [So then, the people is the grass.]
> Though the grass withers and the flower wilts,
>   the word of our God stands forever" (Isa 40:6-8).

The translation "What shall *I* cry . . ." (v. 6) follows the Septuagint and Vulgate, while the Masoretic text reads "What shall *he* say. . . ." It is important to note that in Qumran's Isaiah scroll v. 6 can be translated "A voice said, 'Cry aloud!' and *she* said . . ." implying that it is not the prophet but Jerusalem itself that is commissioned to proclaim God's coming.[4] The transformation of Jerusalem will be so complete it will take on the prophetic role after being the object of prophetic judgment oracles for so long.

Jerusalem fulfills its prophetic role by announcing the good news to the other cities of Judah:

> Go up onto a high mountain,
>   Zion, herald of glad tidings;
> Cry out at the top of your voice,
>   Jerusalem, herald of good news!
> Fear not to cry out
>   and say to the cities of Judah:
>   Here is your God (Isa 40:9).

Like Jerusalem, the other cities of Judah were sacked during the Babylonian invasion. They too lost many of their citizens to exile. In anguish they called out to God for deliverance. Zion is to tell them of the great victory God has won.[5] Indeed, God is coming back to Judah, and with God are coming the exiles. No longer would the whims of an oppressor

3. For example, Claus Westermann, *Isaiah 40–66,* OTL (Philadelphia: Westminster Press, 1969) 40.

4. Cf. Clements, "Zion as Symbol and Political Reality," 7.

5. The Hebrew word translated as "herald" refers to a military runner, who in this case brings news of a great victory.

determine their fate, for they are coming home to the land where they will be able to live in freedom as God promised their ancestors.

Jerusalem uses two metaphors to eliminate the doubts of those who no longer believe in God's love for Judah. In v. 10 the city-turned-prophet presents Yahweh as a victorious general coming with the exiles—the prize he won by defeating Babylon:

> Here comes with power
>   the Lord GOD,
>   who rules by his strong arm;
> Here is his reward with him,
>   his recompense before him (Isa 40:10).

The second image (v. 11) is just the right counterpoint, for it portrays God as the gentle shepherd who takes care of the newborn lambs, leading them to their mothers:

> Like a shepherd he feeds his flock;
>   in his arms he gathers the lambs,
> Carrying them in his bosom,
>   and leading the ewes with care (Isa 40:11).

Jerusalem affirms that its God still has the power to change the course of history yet is concerned about each individual personally. The juxtaposition of these two metaphors may appear jarring to the reader today, but the Judahites in exile needed to hear what both implied. Their primary experience of Yahweh had been the experience of absence. This led them to a pessimism that drew all the wrong conclusions about their God and their future. Jerusalem announces to its people in captivity that God has both the power to end their exile and the love to begin their restoration. Chapter 40 incorporates the prophet's entire message in just eleven verses. This text makes the astonishing announcement that God has forgiven Jerusalem and its people and that their agony is about to end, and that God has commissioned Jerusalem to proclaim that good news. The rest of chapters 40 to 55 is simply an elaboration of this basic message.

Isaiah 49:8–50:3

The oracle begins by characterizing the restoration of Jerusalem as a theophany, a manifestation of the divine presence and activity in the world (49:13). Zion's response is a lament:

> But Zion said, "The LORD has forsaken me;
>   my Lord has forgotten me" (Isa 49:14).

Evidently, the Jerusalemites in exile thought of their situation as hopeless. God responds to this lament by evoking the memory of Zion's lost children (Lam 1:16; 2:11-12):

> Can a mother forget her infant,
>   be without tenderness for the child of her womb? (Isa 49:15).

God assures Jerusalem of God's love for her. God then commands the city to look around and see all the people coming to her. Her isolation is over. Her shame will turn into joy because those gathering around Zion are her children (49:19-21). She will have so many children she will be overwhelmed. Jerusalem is surprised at the reversal of her fortunes. In contrast with the tragic trek into exile, the restoration of Zion will be a royal parade in which kings and princesses will see to Zion's needs. All Jerusalem has to do is wait (49:23). God anticipates Zion's questions and assures her that God will fight on her side and defeat her enemies. To make this clear God evokes the terrible memory of the siege of Jerusalem, when mothers ate their own children to ensure their survival (Lam 2:20; 4:10). God will make Zion's oppressors eat their own flesh so that all "flesh" will recognize God's special care for Jerusalem (49:26). The poem ends with another striking reversal, as God turns to speak with Jerusalem's children. God asks to see their mother's bill of divorce (50:1), implying that the divorce never took place. They were responsible for their mother's suffering. Second Isaiah reunites mother and children in this poem. The prophet asserts that Zion's suffering was caused by her children and that God has determined to end that suffering.

Isaiah 51:1–52:12

In developing his message, the prophet provides a prominent place for Jerusalem in 51:1–52:12. The passage begins with an address to the exiles who have remained faithful to God (51:1a). The experience of exile has tested their faith and affected their self-image. Apparently they looked to the restoration the prophet announced with some misgivings: how could their small community be equal to the task God has given them? To reassure the exiles, the prophet reminds them that they are the offspring of Abraham and Sarah. God promised these two several times that their descendants would become a great nation (Gen 12:2-3; 15:5; 18:18; 22:17). What God did for Abraham and Sarah whose hopes for a child were gone, God will do for Zion. Despite its political and economic insignificance and its military impotence, the exilic community will have its profoundest hopes realized (51:1b-3). The exiles will return to a fertile land with flourishing cities. Even the arid regions of the country will flourish like Eden, the wonderful garden God gave to Adam and Eve (Gen 2:8-9).[6] The prophet was not simply describing an agrarian utopia. The restoration they will experience is the triumph of God's saving justice (Isa 51:1, 4, 8). While this text emphasizes the certainty of the restoration, it also underscores the character of the Eden spoken of in v. 3. It is a place where the victory of justice is manifest–something that was absent from Jerusalem in the years immediately preceding its fall to Babylon. In fact, it was this lack of justice that was responsible, in part, for the fall of the city. The restored Jerusalem will have to display wholehearted devotion to traditional Israelite morality, whose foundation is justice.

In a departure from his usual style, the prophet uses mythological imagery to assure the exiles of the certainty of the restoration of Zion:

> Awake, awake, put on strength,
>   O arm of the LORD!
> Awake as in the days of old,
>   in ages long ago!
> Was it not you who crushed Rahab,
>   you who pierced the dragon?
> Was it not you who dried up the sea,
>   the waters of the great deep,
> Who made the depths of the sea into a way
>   for the redeemed to pass over?
> Those whom the LORD has ransomed will return
>   and enter Zion singing,
>   crowned with everlasting joy;
> They will meet with joy and gladness,
>   sorrow and mourning will flee (Isa 51:9-11).

The theology of Second Isaiah is so clearly monotheistic that the reference here to a great battle during which God killed a sea monster known as Rahab seems out of character. Myths of this type were common enough in the ancient Near East. Similar stories are told about both Baal and Marduk. The prophet is referring to the Israelite form of the myth, which has not survived except for allusions here and in Ps 74:13-14 and Isa 27:1. Perhaps the prophet uses this imagery to make certain there can be no doubt about Yahweh's power to topple Babylon and bring the exiles back to Jerusalem. When they do return to the city, they will be shouting for joy (51:11).

To those who still have doubts about the future (51:12), the prophet quotes God saying to Zion: "You are my people" (51:16). This assurance

6. Other prophets use Eden as a symbol of the ideal agricultural existence. See Ezek 31:8-9; 36:35; Joel 2:3.

comes at the end of a series of clauses, all of which assert that Yahweh is the world's creator (51:13-15). There can be no question of God's power, and so the entire thrust of the prophet's message is that God's unique relationship to the people of Jerusalem and Judah is particularly important. All questions and doubts should dissipate before the assurances given by the creator, who not only consoles but redeems Zion. The prophet calls Jerusalem to awake from the stupor of despair (51:17-20) caused by its suffering in exile. God assures Jerusalem that these sufferings are at an end. In fact, Zion's oppressors will experience what they inflicted on the city and its people. In the name of God, the prophet insists that the people's punishment has been sufficient and will end (51:21).

After the prophet has answered all the exiles' questions and relieved their doubts about the future, he makes a rousing call to Jerusalem—the exiles and the city—to prepare for the restoration. For the exiles, it will mean going home. For the city, it will be a return to its former glory—the glory of the "holy city" (52:1).[7] Verse 2 implies that Jerusalem will change places with Babylon:

Come down, sit in the dust,	Shake off the dust,
O virgin daughter Babylon;	ascend to the throne, Jerusalem;
Sit on the ground, dethroned,	Loose the bonds from your neck,
O daughter of the Chaldeans	O captive daughter Zion!
(Isa 47:1).	(Isa 52:2).

God is about to topple Queen Babylon from her throne and enthrone the slave-girl Jerusalem in her place—a striking and unexpected reversal of fortunes. But the unexpected is what the prophet announces to Jerusalem in exile.

The exiles are not the only ones to hear the good news about Zion's redemption. A runner from Babylon takes the message to the city of Jerusalem, still lying in ruins. He is sent to tell the city and its inhabitants that after years of humiliation and exile he can say to Jerusalem, "all is well":[8]

How beautiful upon the mountains
    are the feet of him who brings glad tidings,
Announcing peace, bearing good news,
    announcing salvation, and saying to Zion,
      "Your God is King!" (Isa 52:7).

7. None of the prophets whose ministry took place in Jerusalem ever referred to it as "the holy city," but this is the second time Isaiah of Babylon has (see also Isa 48:1).
8. This is the connotation of the Hebrew word *shalom,* which the *NAB* translates as "peace."

It has been a very long time since anyone has been able to say that to Zion. The exclamation "Your God is king!" is reminiscent of the opening lines of the psalms of God's kingship that were so often sung in the Temple, for example, Ps 97:1: "The LORD is king; let the earth rejoice." Here the acclamation does not celebrate God's presence in the Temple but in Jerusalem's life. The acclamation assures the exiles that this statement of faith will be acted out as God is victorious over Babylon and leads the exiles back to Jerusalem. The response is predictable. The watchmen on the city walls see the runner approaching. They are first to hear his message, and they respond with joyous shouts because God is restoring Zion (51:8).[9] Actually, at this time Jerusalem was in ruins. It had no walls on which lookouts could position themselves. This bit of poetic license is corrected in 52:9 as the city responds to the good news brought to it:

> Break out together in song,
>   O ruins of Jerusalem!
> For the LORD comforts his people,
>   he redeems Jerusalem.

Isaiah 54:1-17

The theme of Jerusalem's impending restoration continues in chapter 54. Though this poem does not mention Zion by name, it is clear that God addresses God's cast-off spouse, the destroyed Zion, the woman to whom God has returned. Again, the prophet has to deal with people's doubts and questions. For them Zion is both a barren woman abandoned by her husband (vv. 1a, 6) and a widow (v. 4). She believes God has forgotten her (vv. 6-7). Each of these complaints is answered. Zion will find herself with innumerable children (v. 1b). Her husband will take her back with "great tenderness" (v. 7). God announces the end of Zion's humiliation. Yahweh, Zion's husband, assures her:

> Though the mountains leave their place
>   and the hills be shaken,
> My love shall never leave you (54:10).

God even admits to Zion that God was responsible for their long separation (54:5-8). In a remarkable admission, God admits abandoning Zion. It

---

9. The text of this verse in Qumran's Isaiah scroll adds a word that is easily understood but difficult to translate. One attempt is "with tender affection." The word is related to the Hebrew word for "womb." It refers to the natural love that a mother has toward her children. While commentators see this as an addition to the original text, it does reflect the basic thrust of the runner's message to Jerusalem.

was not the other way around. God assures Zion that this will never happen again. These reassurances given, God now speaks of the Jerusalem to be rebuilt (54:11-17). Its beauty will eclipse that of Babylon, whose magnificence was a byword in the ancient world. It is interesting that the prophet does not mention the rebuilding of the Temple. What is important for him in the restoration of the community of those who are heirs to the promises made by God to Israel. For the prophet Jerusalem's foundation in justice is more important than the liturgy that takes place in the city (v. 14). The city's social, economic, and political structures must conform to the divine will. The prophet associates Zion's restoration with the triumph of justice (see also 46:12-13).

Conclusion

In the Christian interpretation of Second Isaiah, the figure of the Servant of the Lord (42:1-9; 49:1-7; 50:4-11; 52:13–53:12) almost completely obscures the image of Zion because of the use the New Testament makes of the Servant to explain the person and work of Jesus.[10] But in Second Isaiah, Zion is the more significant figure. The opening poem and hence the entire book is addressed to her. Chapters 40 and 54 create a striking envelope around the book, underscoring the importance of the prophet's message to Zion. The city is no longer the object of divine judgment, the unfaithful bride, the woman bereft of her children. In Second Isaiah, Jerusalem is the "holy city" (48:2; 52:1). She appears in unprecedented transcendence (54:4-5), giving birth to new children (49:21; 54:1). It is to this holy city that the exiles are to return. Zion is their joyous mother, anxious to receive them. Even more striking that this, Second Isaiah diminishes Zion's sin and blames God for Zion's exile. In contrast, the story of the Servant of the Lord is grim and tragic. The Servant poems speak to Jerusalem's experience of suffering and its meaning for Judah and the nations. The prophet suggests that the Servant's suffering is redemptive and that God will vindicate the Servant at some future time. While Zion too is a figure who endures suffering, the whole point of the prophet's message is that her suffering has ended and what she can look forward to is joy. Zion is a figure that suggests healing and comfort. She is no longer the shamed and abandoned woman but a loving mother reunited with her children and living under the love and protection of her husband.

The message Isaiah of Babylon brought to the exiles is deceptively simple: they will return to Jerusalem and enjoy political independence

10. For the similarities between the Servant of the Lord and Zion, see Sawyer, "Daughter of Zion and the Servant of the Lord," 89–107.

and economic prosperity in their own land. Indeed, restored Jerusalem will move to a position of dominance over other peoples. The exiles have paid the price of their infidelity. Now they will enjoy God's favor again and nothing will ever disturb them. Still, the prophet's message is not like that of earlier prophets such as Hananiah (see Jeremiah 28), who denied the depth of divine anger at Jerusalem's infidelity. They could not entertain the possibility that God would allow Jerusalem to fall. Second Isaiah was speaking to a people who did not enjoy the possibility of such denial. The fall of Jerusalem, the destruction of the Temple, and the end of the Davidic dynasty brought the exiles to their senses. They experienced the consequences of their infidelity and could no longer ignore its gravity. These people were prepared for the repentance that leads to deliverance.

The irony that surrounds the prophetic vision recorded in Isaiah 40–55 is that very little of it was ever realized. Yes, Cyrus did take Babylon. He not only allowed the exiles to return to Jerusalem, he actually encouraged them to rebuild the city's Temple (see 2 Chr 36:22-23). Still, the return did not proceed as the prophet had promised. The years immediately following the exiles' return to Jerusalem were difficult ones economically. Despite the funds supplied by the Persians for the rebuilding of the Temple, it took almost twenty-five years to complete the project, and then those who remembered the first Temple wept when they saw its replacement (Ezra 3:12). Needless to say, the nations did not come in streams to worship Yahweh there. Jerusalem did not become the capital of a new imperial power. It was a small city in a minor Persian subprovince. It would be an understatement to say that the restoration was a time of frustration and disappointment due, in part, to the grandiose expectations that Isaiah of Babylon encouraged. It would be almost four hundred years before the Jews would enjoy political independence under the rule of a native dynasty, the Hasmoneans. Still, it is not an exaggeration to call the unnamed prophet whose words are found in Isaiah 40–55 the greatest of ancient Israel's prophets. Were it not for his ministry to the exiles, the story of ancient Israel would rate a brief mention in the history of the ancient Near East. He gave the exiles of Jerusalem hope—hope that made it possible for the city and its people to survive a great loss.

7

Zion Rebuilt:
Jerusalem in the Post-Exilic Period

The glorious portrait of Zion's future painted by Second Isaiah failed
to materialize. While the Persians allowed the Jews to return to Jerusalem
and encouraged them to rebuild the city's Temple, the restoration did not
have the miraculous edge the prophet promised. The Temple was still in
ruins, the city's walls were not rebuilt, the economy was shattered, and
Judah was politically impotent. Still, there were voices calling Judah to
lift itself out of the doldrums caused by unfulfilled dreams. For Haggai
and Zechariah, the first step was the rebuilding of the Temple. The structure would not only reestablish sacrificial worship, it would invigorate the
economy and prepare Judah for the future God had in store for it. The
Chronicler, too, saw Israel's future through the lens of Israel's past. Claiming Judah's past—especially its liturgical traditions—was the way to guarantee its future. Malachi, however, reminded Jerusalem that simply
restoring the Temple's liturgy was not enough. Moral integrity must be
the soul of worship.

Haggai

When Haggai began his prophetic ministry in December of 520 B.C. (see
Hag 1:1), Jerusalem was in the midst of a serious economic depression (1:6).
The prophet suggested that the reason for the city's economic difficulties
was the people's failure to rebuild the Temple. Before the modern reader dis-
misses Haggai's analysis as a flight of pious fancy, it is important to recognize the function a temple played in ancient Near Eastern societies. Temples

were more than simply places of sacrificial worship. They were administrative institutions dealing with political, economic, and judicial matters along with religious and liturgical concerns. The Persians, unlike the Assyrians and Babylonians, sought to pacify territories under their control not with harsh measures such as exile but by offering subject peoples the opportunity for semi-autonomous rule. Judah became a minor subprovince in the Persian Empire. Its principal city was to have its Temple rebuilt at the Persian emperor's expense, which was nothing less than his claim to legitimacy as a ruler of Judah and Jerusalem. The opening verse of Haggai implies support for this claim: "In the second year of King Darius . . ." (1:1a). Note that the reign of a non-Judahite king provides the framework for Haggai's prophecies—something without parallel in the biblical tradition.

Besides their role in providing theological support for their political sponsors, ancient Near Eastern temples and their priesthoods had very significant economic functions. It is estimated that Egyptian temples controlled 80 percent of the country's arable land. They were Egypt's principal employers and the main producers of its food. This gave Egypt's priests immense political and economic power—power that even the pharaohs had to recognize. Also, from an ancient Near Eastern perspective, the building of a temple brought economic prosperity. One purpose of its rituals was to ensure the fertility of the land. People brought the first fruits of their harvest to the temple with the expectation that, in exchange for their gifts, the gods would make their land produce during the next growing season. Ancient Near Eastern temples, then, were pivotal centers for the management of a country's economic resources. In the agricultural economies of the region this meant the temples controlled the agricultural surpluses. Temples served as communal storehouses for its produce and clearinghouses in its distribution.

Haggai notes that the people of Judah did bring sacrificial offerings to the site of the ruined first Temple but asserts that God blew them away (1:9). The benefit of these gifts for the community was lost because, as v. 10 notes, the Temple had not been rebuilt; that is, there was no central administration of the community's economic output. In addition to the lack of a temple building, the administrative structure was gone as well. Before the exile the monarchic system had supplied the necessary administrative apparatus, but now there was no Judahite monarchy. While there were, of course, the Persian bureaucrats, their main concern was the collection of taxes, not the economic welfare of Jerusalem and its people.

While Haggai knew that the Persians supported the rebuilding of the Temple and that the project was an economic necessity in the first years of the restoration, the prophet's words expressed the religious belief that the Temple's reconstruction was God's will. According to Jeremiah, God's anger against Jerusalem would take seventy years to abate (Jer 25:11-12; 29:10). Haggai began his ministry about three years before the end of the seventy-year period. He was convinced that the Temple's reconstruction and its dedication to the service of Yahweh would mark God's return to Jerusalem. Haggai believed that God had called him to urge the people of Jerusalem to rebuild the Temple. The people's response to Haggai's message (1:12-15) was immediate and gratifying. Without dissent the community united in fulfilling the divine will—a striking contrast to the response given to the preaching of the prophets who ministered before the exile.

While work proceeded on the Temple's reconstruction, some people were disheartened by the prospects for Jerusalem's future. They believed the reconstruction of the building would not mean the restoration of Jerusalem's former status. What the Temple symbolized was the Judahite national state ruled by a member of the Davidic royal family. Few people believed that the national state and the Davidic dynasty had any chance of restoration. Jerusalem's Temple had a significant political role: it represented Judah's national identity and independence. The first Temple stood in the capital of the Judahite state, but the second one would find itself in an insignificant city in an obscure corner of the Persian Empire. Certainly the people of Jerusalem wondered about the significance of a temple without a state. What kind of status would the reconstructed building have, given the realities of Jerusalem's undistinguished place in the empire of a foreign power?

Haggai assures the people of Jerusalem that God has a future for the Temple they are building:

> For thus says the LORD of hosts:
> One moment yet, a little while,
> > and I will shake the heavens and the earth,
> > the sea and the dry land.
> I will shake all the nations,
> > and the treasures of all the nations will come in,
> And I will fill this house with glory,
> > says the LORD of hosts.
> Mine is the silver and mine the gold,
> > says the LORD of hosts.
> Greater will be the future glory of this house
> > than the former, says the LORD of hosts;
> And in this place I will give peace,
> > says the LORD of hosts (Hag 2:6-9).

What lay behind these words was the image of a great national state like that which the tradition associates with David and Solomon. The story of the first Temple's construction described the exotic materials used in its building. These were supplied by the nations that recognized the important role Israel was playing in the eastern Mediterranean region (1 Kings 5; 10). The sight of all these materials coming into Jerusalem from distant places served to legitimate the monarchy in the people's eyes.[1] Haggai describes the Temple's future in terms of traditions about its past. It will have a place not only in Judah's national life, but it will be a magnet attracting the attention of the nations to Judah—nations that will bring gifts for Jerusalem's Temple. But Haggai insists that this will not happen because of human efforts. No military campaigns, political machinations, or powerful monarchs will bring this about. God will reign from Jerusalem. All peoples will acknowledge this divine sovereignty and express that recognition by bringing gifts to the Temple. For Haggai, it is no exaggeration to say, "Greater will be the future glory of this house than the former" (2:9). Jerusalem's Temple, then, will not be a symbol of the royal status of the Davidic dynasty. It will stand for the rule of God over the whole world—a rule that will mean well-being *(shalom)* for both Judah and the nations.

Neither the word "Jerusalem" nor "Zion" appears in the thirty-eight verses that make up the prophecy of Haggai. Still, the prophet's words concern the rebuilding of the Temple, and so they deal with Jerusalem at least indirectly. The Temple, of course, is to be rebuilt in Jerusalem. The prophet notes that the people of the city have rebuilt their homes but have neglected that of God (1:4). The reason for this was the economic depression and political situation in Judah during the early part of the restoration. For Haggai, the key to changing these for the better was the reconstruction of Jerusalem's Temple. He was right. He was also able to persuade the people of the city that rebuilding the Temple was necessary for their well-being *(shalom)*. The success of Haggai's ministry prepared for later reflections on the role of Jerusalem and its Temple in Jewish life.

Zechariah 1–8

Jerusalem has an explicit and important role in Zechariah's prophecy. Like Haggai, Zechariah began his ministry almost twenty years after the

1. It is important to remember that the Israelite tribes existed in their land for many years without a monarchy, which some people regarded as an illegitimate usurpation of God's place as king and an undue limitation on the people's freedom (see 1 Samuel 8).

return of the Jewish exiles to Jerusalem, and he too believed that the rebuilding of the Temple had been delayed for too long. Unlike Haggai, who linked the Temple with Jerusalem's economic prosperity, Zechariah viewed the project in more comprehensive terms. First, he presented it as the fulfillment of Jeremiah's prophecy of the seventy years:

Thus says the LORD: Only after seventy years have elapsed for Babylon will I visit you and fulfill for you my promise to bring you back to this place (Jer 29:10).

Then the angel of the Lord spoke out and said, "O LORD of hosts, how long will you be without mercy for Jerusalem and the cities of Judah that have felt your anger these seventy years?" (Zech 1:12).

Second, the prophet considered the Temple as an essential component of God's universal rule, as is clear from three short oracles that appear at the beginning of his prophecy:

And the angel who spoke with me said to me, Proclaim: Thus says the LORD of hosts: I am deeply moved for the sake of Jerusalem and Zion, and I am exceedingly angry with the complacent nations; whereas I was but a little angry, they added to the harm. Therefore, says the LORD: I will turn to Jerusalem in mercy; my house shall be built in it, says the LORD of hosts, and a measuring line shall be stretched over Jerusalem. Proclaim further: Thus says the LORD of hosts: My cities shall again overflow with prosperity; the LORD will again comfort Zion, and again choose Jerusalem (Zech 1:14-17).

These oracles are a response to a question raised in the prophet's first vision: "O LORD of hosts, how long will you be without mercy for Jerusalem and the cities of Judah that have felt your anger these seventy years?" (Zech 1:12). The answer is unequivocal: God is devoted to Jerusalem. The first oracle (vv. 14-15) has God losing patience with the nations that have kept the city prostrate.[2] God's anger toward the nations contrasts with God's compassion toward Jerusalem (vv. 15-16). The second oracle (v. 16) asserts that God's love toward the city had led to God's return to it. The sign of that return is the Temple's reconstruction. Zechariah announces the beginning of a new era in God's relations with Jerusalem. This leads to the third oracle in v. 17, which speaks about the consequence of this new era for the prosperity of the land. Here Zechariah, like Haggai, links the reconstruction of the Temple to economic prosperity. Note the central

2. Though the Persian emperors allowed the Jews to return from exile and encouraged them to rebuild the Temple, they did not permit the reestablishment of an independent Jewish state with a Davidic king at its head. Perhaps this is the reason behind the prophet's assertion of divine anger directed against the nations.

role Jerusalem plays in each oracle. It is Jerusalem to which God is devoted. It is to Jerusalem that God returns. It is God's return to Jerusalem
that ensures the land's prosperity.

Despite these encouraging words, the people of Jerusalem had to face
harsh economic and political realities. Jerusalem in Zechariah's day was
surrounded by unwalled settlements in the nearby hills. The hill country
was barely fertile and could sustain a population of only about two thousand in the city. During the monarchic period Jerusalem was the head of a
network of Judahite cities, each of which contributed to the capital's support. In the post-exilic period, the revenues of these towns went to the imperial Persian government. Jerusalem could scarcely survive—let alone
prosper—given these economic realities. Second, Jerusalem's walls had
not yet been rebuilt. A city's battlements were signs of its political power.
Its walls still lying in ruins were a sign of Jerusalem's political impotence.
What good was a new temple if the economic and political realities it
symbolized reflected Jerusalem's low status in a foreign empire?

Zechariah responds with words that begin the process of Jerusalem's
transformation from an ancient Near Eastern political and religious center
to a suprahistorical symbol of the divine presence:

> Again I raised my eyes and looked: there was a man with a measuring line
> in his hand. "Where are you going?" I asked. "To measure Jerusalem," he
> answered; "to see how great is its width and how great its length."
>
> Then the angel who spoke with me advanced, and another angel came
> out to meet him and said to him, "Run, tell this to that young man: People
> will live in Jerusalem as though in open country, because of the multitude
> of men and beasts in her midst. But I will be for her an encircling wall of
> fire, says the LORD, and I will be the glory in her midst" (2:5-9).

God's presence in the Temple will guarantee that Jerusalem will be not
only inhabitable but prosperous. As for city walls, God will be a "wall of
fire" for the city. Here the prophet may be playing with two different images. Of course, there is the Israelite tradition that remembered Yahweh as
a pillar of fire guiding and protecting the tribes in the wilderness (Exod
13:21-22). Another referent for the "wall of fire" image comes from Pasar-
gadae, the royal city of the Persian emperors. It was built without walls,
but around it were a number of fire altars that symbolized the protective
presence of the Persian deity, Ahura Mazda.[3] Like the Persian royal city,
Jerusalem will be impregnable because of the presence of Yahweh in its
Temple (Zech 2:9). But the detail about the measuring of the city (2:6) im-

---

3. David L. Petersen, *Haggai and Zechariah 1–8,* OTL (Philadelphia: Westminster Press, 1984) 171.

plies that the whole city is holy. The whole city—not just the Temple—is God's dwelling place. This, of course, guarantees the city's material prosperity: it will be filled with people and animals (2:8b), but more than this, it speaks of Jerusalem in a way that goes beyond any historical, concrete reality. Jerusalem is on the way to becoming a transcendent reality.

Zechariah is convinced that Jerusalem has a bright future ahead of it—despite its economic and political impotence—because God has chosen it as God's dwelling-place: "Sing and rejoice, O daughter Zion! See, I am coming to dwell among you, says the LORD" (Zech 2:14). In his enthusiasm, Zechariah has the holiness attached to the Temple touch not only Jerusalem and Judah. God's presence has made all the territory of the former Israelite kingdoms holy: "The LORD will possess Judah as his portion in the *holy land,* and he will again choose Jerusalem" (Zech 2:16). Though similar expressions occur elsewhere in the Bible (Exod. 3:5; 15:13; Ps 78:54; Jer 31:23), this is the only time the phrase "holy land" appears in the Hebrew Bible.[4] In Zechariah this term serves to highlight the role of Jerusalem. Of course, God is the source of the land's sacred character, but its holiness extends from Jerusalem because God dwells in that city's Temple.

Another important motif connected with Zechariah's idealization of Jerusalem is universal significance of God's choice of Zion. It will benefit not only the Jews but the other people who will come to the city as believers. Jerusalem will become the place where God will manifest God's universal love. Any visitor to Jerusalem today sees that the prophet's vision has become reality. Every day people from around the world—Jews, Christians, and Muslims—come to Jerusalem to pray—to experience God in the place that God chose to dwell on earth. This is both Jerusalem's glory and its burden. While the universalism the prophet foresaw has come about, the city's peace is still the hope and dream of all believers.

---

4. Here this term is concrete and specific. This is clear from Zechariah's choice of words. The Hebrew word translated as land here is *ʾădāmâ.* The word refers to the actual ground or soil, whereas *ʾeretz,* a Hebrew synonym, has a social or political connotation. See Carol L. Meyers and Eric M. Meyers, *Haggai, Zechariah 1–8,* AB, 25B (Garden City, N.Y.: Doubleday, 1987) 170–1. The phrase "holy land" here refers to the territory that was home to the Jews who recognized it as promised to their ancestors by God. In the rabbinic period Jews from the Diaspora sought to be buried in this land because of its holiness. The belief in the sacredness of the land is what has caused some religious Jews in Israel to resist the establishment of a Palestinian State on land that was once the territory of the Israelite kingdoms. Christians too acknowledge the land's holiness through their practices of pilgrimage and the building of shrines to commemorate events of Jesus' life.

The prophecy of Zechariah concludes with seven oracles about Jerusalem (8:1-17).[5] The first oracle (v. 2) insists on God's eternal love for Jerusalem. In the second (v. 3) Zechariah coins another expression. He says that Jerusalem will be called "the city of truth" (8:3). The prophet uses this epithet to underscore the importance of a just social order in the city. Toward the end of this passage (8:16) Zechariah lists a few specific moral principles that are to guide the lives of the people in Jerusalem. The prophet insists that the reason God has come back to Zion is so that the ideals of justice that characterize traditional Israelite morality might be realized in the city. The third oracle (vv. 4-5) paints a charming picture of Jerusalem's elderly sitting in the city's squares, while the city's children are at play, to convey the peace and prosperity that will be part of Jerusalem's future. The fourth oracle (v. 6) affirms God's power to restore the city. The passage concludes with three oracles that envision a return of exiles from the Diaspora (vv. 7-8), promise the blessings of prosperity (vv. 9-13), and call for the restoration of Jerusalem (vv. 14-15). The passage concludes with moral exhortations (vv. 16-17). Although God's initiative is paramount in Jerusalem's restoration, the people are not to be simply passive recipients of God's blessings. They are to respond to God's goodness with patterns of behavior that reflect the ideals of traditional Israelite morality. Jerusalem's future depends upon God, to be sure. But if Judah has learned anything from its past, it is that the city's future depends as well on the moral choices its people make.

The Books of Chronicles

Certainly the greatest disappointment for the Jewish people during the restoration was that Judah and Jerusalem remained totally subject to the Persian emperor. The restoration did not bring with it the reestablishment of the Judahite state ruled by a member of the Davidic family. There were several attempts to deal with this disappointment. The most successful was the Deuteronomic tradition's defining the people's relationship with God solely in terms of obedience to a written authoritative law. Though this law made a place for a king (Deut 17:14-20), the king's sole duty was to study the law so that he would not think of himself as superior to his people (see Deut 17:20). The failure to reestablish the native dynasty led to the development of messianism: the belief that God's final intervention

5. Zechariah 9–14 contain two collections of prophetic material from the fifth and fourth centuries B.C., which have been appended to the words of Zechariah, whose ministry took place in the sixth century.

in Judah's life would be the establishment of God's kingdom on earth. A scion of the royal Davidic dynasty was to rule over this kingdom. The New Testament reflects the belief of a small number of Jews who saw Jesus of Nazareth as this messiah (see Matt 16:13-20; Acts 1:6). The Qumran community has highly developed messianic expectations. Similar expectations fueled the Jewish revolts against Rome in A.D. 67–70 and 132–5. Other Jews despaired of ever experiencing the triumph of justice in this world. They were looking for a new world that would come through a dramatic exercise of divine power that would bring this world to a climactic end, establish God's reign, and reverse the fortunes of the pious. This perspective inspired Daniel 7–12. A less dramatic but still effective way of dealing with the problems of a failed restoration was the product of priestly circles. They believed that the Jews were to fulfill their destiny through their support of and participation in temple worship.

With some help from Persian authorities and encouragement of the prophets Haggai and Zechariah, Jerusalem's Temple was rebuilt. This made it possible to worship Yahweh in accord with traditional practice. The priests encouraged the people of Judah and Jerusalem to join them in worshiping their God as their ancestors did. The problem faced by the priests was to show that temple service was still relevant. After all, throughout its existence the first Temple had served as the "royal chapel" of the Davidic kings.[6] Its hymns celebrated the election and achievements of the kings (e.g., Psalms 2, 20, 21, 89). Its rituals sought God's blessings of peace and prosperity for the kingdom of Judah. Without the monarchy, what was the point of temple worship? What the priests did to convince their people was to show that the monarchy existed to serve the Temple. The Temple did not necessarily exist to support the monarchy. The clearest expression of this ideology appears in the books of Chronicles.

The Chronicler tells the story of Israel from David to Cyrus' edict regarding the return from exile.[7] Much of this story had already been told in 2 Samuel—2 Kings. But it is important to pay attention to what the Chronicler omits from and adds to the earlier narratives. For example, First Chronicles makes it absolutely clear that God chose Jerusalem as the site for the Temple, while First Kings implies this but is not as explicit as

6. For the ancient Near Eastern background for the ideology of a temple city and its relationship to the monarchy, see Moshe Weinfeld, "Zion and Jerusalem as Religious and Political Capital," 75–115.

7. Actually, First Chronicles begins with Adam (1:1) and continues with genealogies to the time of David (1 Chronicles 1–9). Narratives in Chronicles begin with David's story.

Chronicles. A comparison of parallel passages that report Solomon's prayer at the Temple's dedication makes this clear:

Since the day I brought my people Israel out of Egypt, I have not chosen a city out of any tribe of Israel for the building of a temple to my honor; but I choose David to rule my people Israel (1 Kgs 8:16).	Since the day I brought my people out of the land of Egypt, I have not chosen any city from among all the tribes of Israel for the building of a temple to my honor, nor have I chosen any man to be commander of my people Israel; but now I choose Jerusalem, where I shall be honored, and I choose David to rule my people Israel (2 Chr 6:5-6).

For the Chronicler there is no question about Jerusalem's status—it was the place chosen by God as the place for the Temple. The Chronicler made this choice explicit: sacrificial worship in his day took place only in Jerusalem, and he wanted to show that this is by divine choice and not because of the vagaries of Persian imperial policy.

If one compares the narratives of David and Solomon as found in Samuel and Kings with those found in Chronicles, it is clear that the latter are not interested in the political, military, or administrative achievements of the two kings. Chronicles focuses on David and Solomon as the founders of temple worship (1 Chronicles 22–29; 2 Chronicles 2–8). The Chronicler suppresses the most unflattering stories about the two found in Samuel and Kings, presumably because these clashed with the image of David and Solomon the Chronicler is trying to create. For example, David's adultery with Bathsheba (2 Samuel 11) does not appear in Chronicles, nor does the story of Solomon's succession (2 Samuel 9–20; 1 Kings 1–2) with its unflattering portrait of Judah's royal family. For the Chronicler, David and Solomon are the two kings principally responsible for enabling Israel to worship God according to the divine will.

The Chronistic narratives dealing with other kings of Judah also focus on their actions related to the Temple of Jerusalem. A most telling story is that of a war fought between Jeroboam of Israel against Abijah (Abijam) of Judah (2 Chronicles 13). First Kings notes in passing that Abijah and Jeroboam "made war on each other" (1 Kgs 15:6). Second Chronicles expands this note and has Abijah addressing the Israelite army on the eve of battle, advising them that their cause is doomed because they have rejected the rule of the Davidic dynasty and the worship of God in Jerusalem (2 Chr 13:4-12). Of course, the Chronicler has Abijah inflicting a serious defeat on the Israelite army after it refuses to accept his message (2 Chr 13:13-19). If there is any historical basis for this story, Abijah enjoyed only temporary success. The kingdom of Israel usually dominated its southern neighbor.

Still, Jerusalem's status as the city that God had chosen did not prevent it from being the object of divine anger because of its infidelity (2 Chr 12:7). That is one reason for the attention the Chronicler gives to the attention of several kings to the purification of temple worship and obedience to the Torah: Asa (2 Chr 14:1-2; 15:8-18); Jehoshaphat (2 Chr 17:2-9); Jehoiada (2 Chr 23:16-19); Joash (2 Chr 24:4-14); Hezekiah (2 Chr 29:3–31:21); Manasseh (33:11-17); and Josiah (34:3–35:18). The Chronicler's portrait of Manasseh clashes with that in Second Kings, which portrays him as the most evil of Judah's kings. It was his infidelity that sealed Jerusalem's fate (2 Kgs 21:13). According to the Chronicler, Manasseh's captivity in Assyria leads him to recognize that Yahweh is God (2 Chr 33:13). Clearly, the Chronicler intends his portrait of Manasseh to serve as an object lesson for the Judahites. In focusing on the efforts of David and Solomon to establish the sacrificial worship of Yahweh in Jerusalem and by lifting up the example of many Judahite kings as religious reformers, the Chronicler wants to imply that the efforts of the people of his day to rebuild the Temple and reestablish its ritual puts them in continuity with the great leaders of the past. What David, Solomon, Hezekiah, Manasseh, and Josiah did centuries before, the Jews of the fourth century must do for their day. Because they stand in continuity with these great kings of the past, the Jews of Jerusalem can be sure their efforts are not in vain. Their temple rituals are legitimate expressions of the worship that pleases God. The priests and the Levites of the temple are God's genuine servants.

Unlike the Deuteronomists, who ended their story of Israel's life in the land in such an ambiguous way (2 Kgs 25:27-30), the Chronicler ends his story on a most positive tone. The conclusion of the Chronicler's history is the decree of Cyrus, the Persian king whose victories ended Babylonian hegemony in the ancient Near East. Cyrus not only allows the Jews in exile to return to Babylon, but he urges them to rebuild the Temple. In fact, the express purpose for the return from exile is the rebuilding of the Temple:

> In the first year of Cyrus, king of Persia, in order to fulfill the word of the LORD spoken by Jeremiah, the LORD inspired King Cyrus of Persia to issue this proclamation throughout his kingdom, both by word of mouth and in writing: "Thus says Cyrus, king of Persia: 'All the kingdoms of the earth the LORD, the God of heaven, has given to me, and he has also charged me to build him a house in Jerusalem, which is in Judah. Whoever, therefore, among you belongs to any part of his people, let him go up, and may his God be with him!'" (2 Chr 36:22-23).

It is important to note that the arrangement of books in the Hebrew Bible differs from that in Christian Bibles. The latter adopted the arrangement of books found in the Septuagint, a second-century B.C. Greek translation of the Hebrew Bible, with several additional books included. It made sense for the Greek-speaking Christians to use the Septuagint as their "Bible." In Christian Bibles, the last section of the Old Testament is the Prophets, and the last book is Malachi, whose final words about the return of Elijah (Mal 3:23) have been understood by Christians to refer to John the Baptist (see Matt 11:14; 17:10-12). The Hebrew Bible concludes with the books of Chronicles, so the last word in that Bible is a call to return to Jerusalem: "Whoever, therefore, among you belongs to any part of [God's] people, *let him go up,*[8] and may his God be with him." This is one reason for the longing for Jerusalem among Jewish people during their nearly two thousand years of exile from that city. This last verse of the last book of the Hebrew Bible has been calling Jews back to Jerusalem for two millennia.

Ezra and Nehemiah

Questions about these two books abound. What is their relationship to each other and to the books of Chronicles? Who came to Jerusalem first, Ezra or Nehemiah? What are the dates of their respective ministries? No firm consensus has developed around answers offered to these questions. Fortunately, it is not necessary to resolve these issues in order to appreciate what these books thought of Jerusalem. Each book tells the story of a man who, with the authorization of the Persian authorities, leads a group of Jewish exiles back to Jerusalem. Among Ezra's achievements is the restoration of the Temple and its altar on their original sites (Ezra 3:2-13). The book credits Haggai and Zechariah with encouraging the elders in taking up the rebuilding project (5:1) and describes the dedication of the completed building (6:16-18). Nehemiah's task is to rebuild the city's walls (Neh 2:11-18; 12:27-43) and to repopulate the city (11:1-3). The text notes that the leadership of the Jewish community moved to Jerusalem and the rest of the community drew lots for the privilege of living in what Nehemiah calls "the holy city" (11:1, 18).

Both books simply assume Jerusalem's privileged status. For Ezra, there is no question that the Temple has to be rebuilt on the precise site occupied by Solomon's structure. This and the returned temple vessels will ensure continuity between the Jews of the post-exilic period and their

---

8. The modern Hebrew word for immigration to Israel is *aliyah,* which is derived from the Hebrew verb ʿ*alah* found in this verse: "to go up."

ancestors who worshiped in the first Temple. Though Nehemiah calls Jerusalem "the holy city," he is concerned as much with practical necessities as with religious matters. The city's walls have to be rebuilt. He is careful to apprise the Persian authorities so they will not misinterpret his action as preparation for a revolt against imperial authority. In fact, when he asks permission of Artaxerxes, the Persian emperor, to return to Jerusalem, Nehemiah refers to it as "the city where my ancestors are buried" (Neh 2:3-4). Still, Jerusalem's walls were potent symbols of the city's viability and an affirmation of its future. The new walls were dedicated with a solemn religious ceremony led by priests and Levites. There were two choirs who "sang loudly" during the ceremonies (12:27-43). Nehemiah notes—probably with some pride—that the joy of Jerusalem on that day "could be heard from far away." The reason for this activity derived from Jerusalem's status as the site of Yahweh's Temple. It was, therefore, "the holy city." It could not remain in ruins. Nehemiah believed that God had inspired him to rebuild the walls and repopulate the city (Neh 2:11; 7:4-5).

Ezra and Nehemiah ignore the relationship of Jerusalem to David and the monarchy. In Nehemiah "the city of David" refers not to the whole of Jerusalem but to its southernmost neighborhood, located on the Ophel hill near the Pool of Siloah (Neh 3:15; 12:46). Most of the references to David in these two books reflect the Chronicler's portrait of David as one who founded the cult of Yahweh at Jerusalem (Ezra 3:10; 8:20; Neh 12:24, 36, 45-46). David is not mentioned in the prayer of repentance that rehearses Israel's history from Abraham to the Persians (Neh 9:5-37). The prayer simply notes that Israel's kings, princes, and priests were among those who did not keep the law (v. 34).

For Ezra and Nehemiah, Jerusalem was the site of Yahweh's Temple. They found the Temple and the city in ruins. Their mission was to rebuild the Temple, reconstruct its wall, and repopulate the city. But they also had to fill the city with people devoted to the service of the ancestral deity of the Jews. They led the Jewish community in a confession of sins (Neh 9:5-37) and a recommitment to the Law (Neh 8). With worship in the Temple restored, the city surrounded by its wall, and the community's pledging its allegiance to Yahweh and the Law, Ezra and Nehemiah fulfilled their mission.

Malachi

Jerusalem's Temple served as the religious center for the Jews of the Persian province of Yehud (Judah). Malachi reflects on the words of Isaiah of Babylon, Ezekiel, and Haggai that promise that this Temple will be bathed in God's splendor, and on his own experience of the Temple's rituals. The prophet concludes that there is something terribly wrong. He charges the priests with malfeasance because he observes their contempt for the very altar upon which they offer sacrifice (1:13). The prophet also accuses them of false teaching (2:8). Of course, Malachi is not the only one who felt the great disparity between prophetic visions of the restored Temple and the reality of what takes place in the Temple's services. Malachi writes to encourage people in the midst of this conflict.

The prophet engages the priests of the Jerusalem Temple in a lengthy dispute (1:6–2:9). They are responsible for the integrity of worship there but have disregarded their responsibilities. Of course, the prophet sees Jerusalem's relationship with God as involving more than ritual activity. The prophet bases his notion of morality on the image of God as "Father":

> Have we not all the one Father?
>   Has not the one God created us? (2:10a).

Though this means that the people of Jerusalem should have been brothers and sisters to one another, this is not the case. They are guilty of violating the most fundamental precepts of traditional Israelite morality (2:10b).

The prophet observes that the people have profaned the Temple, which God loves (Mal 2:11a). The rituals that take place there offer only the appearance of piety. What makes temple service an "abomination" is the casual way the people of Jerusalem are treating their marriage commitments (2:11b-16). The prophet views the frequency of divorce as a paradigm of the people's infidelity to God. Temple service ought to be a celebration of Jerusalem's commitment to its God. But if the men of the city cannot remain committed to their wives, it is little wonder they are not faithful to God. The prophet also sees himself as God's messenger to Jerusalem, sent to reform its liturgical life (3:1).[9] The prophet's coming will involve divine judgment. The people do need to be purified. The two metaphors that make this clear describe the prophet's activity as a refining fire that eliminates the dross from ore containing precious metal and as the cleansing soap of the person preparing cloth for use. The result of the purification will be that offerings made by the people of Jerusalem will be acceptable (3:4). It is clear, then, that the revitalization of the community's worship will be a consequence of the revitalization of its moral life (3:5).

While Jerusalem is not among Malachi's specific concerns, he does assume that it is the place of sacrificial worship. He complains that this

---

9. The name Malachi means "my messenger" and may not be the prophet's actual name. The book's title may be derived from 3:1.

worship is going on without the requisite care by the priests and without the moral uprightness of the worshipers. The prophet criticizes both the priests and laity for allowing the worship of Yahweh to be less than it should be. He depicts God as the father of Israel and tries to move people toward lives of integrity based on this image, for it is only through Israel's moral integrity that its worship can have any value.

Conclusion

For Haggai and Zechariah, the first step in completing the restoration had to be taken by the people of Jerusalem themselves. They had to complete the rebuilding of the Temple. This meant more than simply reestablishing temple worship. It is the fulfillment of the divine will that will have repercussions in the economic and political sphere. More than this, the Temple is a symbol of the divine presence that transcends the vagaries of human events. God has chosen Zion, and the Jewish community has to make that choice visible through the reconstruction of the Temple.

The community addressed by the books of Chronicles, Ezra, Nehemiah, and Malachi was a different one from the one to which Jeremiah, Isaiah of Babylon, and Ezekiel were sent. It was a different community than the one that produced the book of Lamentations and the Deuteronomistic History. It was a community that was different even from that addressed by Haggai and Zechariah. The communities of the exilic and early post-exilic period experienced the loss of their political, economic, and religious institutions. This led to a fundamental reassessment of their relationship with God and the religious traditions of which they were heirs. How were they to understand the fall of Jerusalem, the destruction of the Temple, and the end of the Davidic dynasty? Was Yahweh powerless before Marduk, the god of Babylon? Did God not care what happened to Jerusalem and its people? What had gone wrong? Are the promises made to Abraham and David still valid? Is there a future for Jerusalem?

The people who first read the works of the Chronicler, Ezra, and Nehemiah began to see that the exile, while necessary and justified, was not God's last word to Jerusalem. Isaiah of Babylon preached this message with great conviction and evoked the first stirrings of hope in the exiles. The Chronicler, Ezra, and Nehemiah gave that hope concrete shape. Though there was no chance that the Persians would permit the restoration of the native dynasty, they actually encouraged the rebuilding of the Temple. The second Temple was put on the very site of the first, and the worship of Yahweh resumed. The city's walls were rebuilt, leading to its repopulation. Here was the initial fulfillment of the hopes of an earlier generation of Jerusalemites. The old institutions were coming back to life, mediating the same promise and handing on the same tradition that nurtured the people of Israel from the time of the Exodus. What the Chronicler, Ezra, and Nehemiah did for the people of Jerusalem was to assure them of the validity of their religious institutions. Continuity and legitimacy—these were the issues of the day. Assured that it was, in fact, a new day, the people of Jerusalem rejoiced in a way that was not possible for many years, and Nehemiah observes that "the rejoicing at Jerusalem could be heard from afar off" (Neh 12:43). Malachi reminded the people of Jerusalem that the restoration of temple worship was not enough. Authentic worship comes from people of moral integrity.

8

The New Jerusalem

When will life get better? When will the words of the prophet be fulfilled? When will Jerusalem be free and be ruled by a descendant of David?
These are the questions that the people of Jerusalem asked themselves as
it became clear that Jerusalem's future was not going to be as glorious as
they were led to believe by prophets such as Second Isaiah. Jerusalem
continued to be nothing more than the religious, commercial, and administrative center of a backwater Persian subprovince. Though the Persians
allowed the Jews some measure of autonomy, it was clear that the imperial authorities expected nothing less than complete loyalty expressed in a
concrete way by regular payment of taxes. The prophets promised that the
nations would bring their wealth to Jerusalem. Instead Jerusalem's people
had to funnel their meager surpluses to an already wealthy imperial
power. The prophets promised that the nations would join Judah in the
worship of Yahweh in Jerusalem's Temple. Instead the Persians imposed
a special tax on sacrifices offered in the Temple.[1] Apart from these economic burdens, the Jewish community in Jerusalem was not troubled by
the international political situation, since the Persian empire was running
smoothly. The priests of the Temple provided leadership for the community, which tried to shape its life according to the Torah. For some Jews
this was enough. They adjusted to the modicum of self-determination the
Persians allowed, but others expected more, wanted more. They remembered and treasured the words of the prophets with their magnificent visions of Jerusalem's glorious future. These people wondered when those
visions would become reality.

1. Josephus, *Antiquities* 11. 297, 301.

Isaiah 56–66

For some Jews, like the prophets Haggai and Zechariah, Jerusalem's future was tied to the Temple. They believed its reconstruction to be an essential component of Jerusalem's restoration. But there was another prophetic voice that dissented:

> Thus says the LORD:
> The heavens are my throne,
>   the earth is my footstool.
> What kind of house can you build for me;
>   what is to be my resting place?
> My hand made all these things
>   when all of them came to be, says the LORD.
> This is the one whom I approve:
>   the lowly and afflicted man who trembles at my word (Isa 66:1-2).

The prophet who uttered these words saw Jerusalem's restoration from a perspective quite different from that of his predecessors, Haggai and Zechariah. There have been attempts to identify this anti-temple perspective as reflecting the experience of those who believed that the vision of Jerusalem's restoration as articulated in Isaiah 40–55 was being ignored in favor of one that gave the priests of the Temple sole control over Judah's religious life.[2] While this hypothesis may not enjoy universal acceptance, it is clear the reconstruction of the Temple was not a priority for the prophet whose words are found in the last eleven chapters of the book of Isaiah. More important was obedience to God's word.

Despite this prophet's devaluation of the Temple's importance, Jerusalem still held a significant place in his prophecy. His anti-temple rhetoric serves to underscore the belief that the status of Jerusalem as God's chosen city was actually independent of the Temple's fate.[3] In 59:20 the prophet insists that God is coming to Zion as a redeemer for those "who stop rebelling."[4] Following that assertion is a glowing picture of the redeemed Zion, which rivals Jerusalem's portrait in Isaiah 40–55. The Hebrew grammatical forms in 60:1-3 have God addressing Jerusalem personified as a woman:

2. See Hanson, *The Dawn of Apocalyptic.*
3. Clements, "Zion as Symbol and Political Reality," 10.
4. It is important to note that Isaiah 56–66 sees a division in the Jewish community—a division based on obedience to the divine will. According to the prophet, God's salvation is for the obedient.

Rise up in splendor! Your light has come,
> the glory of the LORD shines upon you.
See, darkness covers the earth,
> and thick clouds cover the peoples;
But upon you the LORD shines,
> and over you appears his glory.
Nations shall walk by your light,
> and kings by your shining radiance.

Jerusalem basks in the glow of God's light. The nations see reflected glory and come to Jerusalem to offer her their tribute.[5] The following section (vv. 4-9) develops this theme as it speaks of Yahweh's dominion over the world from Jerusalem. This is a dramatic reversal for the city that has been a vassal state of Mesopotamian empires for more than three hundred years. Now these foreign kings, who have held Zion in subjection, will serve as workmen to rebuild the walls of the city (60:10-11). The nations will also contribute to the outfitting of the new Temple (v. 13). The future prosperity and security of Jerusalem are direct consequences of God's presence in the city, for the nations that once subjected Zion will now address it as "the City of Yahweh" and "Zion of the Holy One of Israel" (v. 14). Of course, the prophet is painting a utopian picture that has no correspondence with the experience of Jerusalem at the end of the sixth century B.C., so he concludes his description of the city's future by having God say, "I, the LORD, will swiftly accomplish these things when their time comes" (Isa 60:22).

The prophet exploits the figure of Jerusalem as a woman by using the bridal metaphor very effectively in 62:4-5 to speak of the city's restoration and glorification:

No more shall men call you "Forsaken,"
> or your land "Desolate,"
But you shall be called "My Delight,"
> and your land "Espoused."
For the LORD delights in you,
> and makes your land his spouse.
As a young man marries a virgin,
> your Builder shall marry you;
And as a bridegroom rejoices in his bride
> so shall your God rejoice in you.

5. In Isa 2:2-3 the nations come to Zion to learn God's ways. Here, the emphasis is not on this universalist theme but on the glorification of Jerusalem. Here, the nations come to serve Jerusalem. What we have in Isaiah 60 is not universalism but religious nationalism.

The prophet has God taking back Jerusalem as a husband takes back an estranged wife. The land will be "wedded." Here the prophet uses an ancient pre-Israelite image of the patron deity making the land fertile. This restoration has not taken place, so the prophet provides further assurance that God has not forgotten their cause (62:6-7). He concluded this chapter by addressing "daughter Zion": ". . . your savior comes" (62:11). The prophet speaks to people whose hopes for Jerusalem's restoration have been shaped by Isaiah of Babylon. That his vision of the restoration has not found immediate fulfillment does not mean his disciples have abandoned it. They reaffirm their faith in God's intention to restore Jerusalem by developing the images and metaphors that Isaiah of Babylon had used (see Isa 54:1-10). In the face of an economically depressed and politically impotent city, the prophet whose words are found in Isaiah 60–62 speaks only of the city's splendor. While that splendor is yet to be revealed, it is coming. The "spirit of the Lord" has anointed the prophet to make these assurances to the afflicted and brokenhearted in the city (Isa 61:1). They will rebuild the city (Isa 61:4).

It is becoming clearer to the prophet that the Jerusalem of his visions may not be the same as the Jerusalem he lives in. The Jerusalem the prophet envisions is part of a new world that God will bring into existence:

> Lo, I am about to create new heavens
>   and a new earth;
> The things of the past shall not be remembered
>   or come to mind.
> Instead, there shall always be rejoicing and happiness
>   in what I create;
> For I create Jerusalem to be a joy
>   and its people to be a delight;
> I will rejoice in Jerusalem
>   and exult in my people (Isa 65:17-19).

The prophet has come to realize that this world will not be the place of the ultimate triumph of God's justice. God will create a new world and, of course, a new Jerusalem. This new Jerusalem will be a joy and a delight— not like the Jerusalem of this world. Here Jerusalem becomes a symbol of that new world. It is a world in which there will be no infant mortality. People will live into old age. They will enjoy their homes and vineyards. Their children will grow to honorable adulthood. God will answer their prayers before they finish them (Isa 65:19-24). In short, it will be a perfect world—a world in which "the wolf and the lamb feed together" (Isa 65:25). This utopian image of the Jerusalem that God will create was born of the disappointment and despair of the restoration period. It is the first step in the direction of Revelation's "new Jerusalem coming down out of heaven" (Rev 21:3).

The prophet ends his meditation on Jerusalem's future by adopting another image from Isaiah of Babylon: Jerusalem as mother (66:7-14; see 49:18-23; 54:1-3). The prophet uses this image to counter the depressing experience of a severely depopulated Judah. The massive return from Babylon to Jerusalem never took place.[6] Here the prophet speaks of the return of the Jews of the Diaspora as a kind of miraculous birth. Mother Zion's children will repopulate Judah and ensure its peace and prosperity. Those who will witness the repopulation of Jerusalem will be encouraged (66:14).

Zechariah 9–14

Chapters 9–14 of Zechariah did not come from the same hand as the first eight chapters of the book. The most obvious clue is that while Zechariah 1–8 anticipates the rebuilding of the Temple and the new day which that will bring for Jerusalem, Zechariah 9–14 presupposes that the new Temple has been built and is functioning (9:8; 11:13; 14:16-21). Though there is a wide consensus about the composition of the book, the date for Zechariah 9–14 is another matter. Portions of these chapters have been dated to as early as the eighth century B.C. and as late as the fourth century B.C.[7] The following comments will assume that the latter half of Zechariah comes from a time in the first half of the Persian period—sometime after the completion of the Temple and the resumption of its rituals, that is, some time in the late sixth or early fifth century B.C.

The Jerusalem community reflected in the book of Haggai and in Zechariah 1–8 was a relatively small community confined to the city of Jerusalem and the surrounding countryside. Some of the people in this region were not taken into exile and remained on the land. Another component of the community was the first group of returnees. Against long odds, both groups tried to reestablish their community life based on their ancestral religious traditions. Their great achievement was the rebuilding of the

---

6. Jews continued to live in Mesopotamia through the Arab period (12th c. A.D.). The Jewish community there was a vibrant one. Almost a thousand years after Cyrus allowed Jews to return to Palestine, the Jews of Mesopotamia produced the Talmud, a collection of Jewish Law that is still the basic source for Jewish life and study. Jewish scholars of Palestine never completed their version of the Talmud.

7. See Paul L. Redditt, *Haggai, Zechariah, Malachi*, NCB (Grand Rapids: Wm. B. Eerdmans, 1995) 94–100, for a summary of scholarly views regarding the date of Zechariah 9–14.

Temple. Some years later other groups of Jews returned from exile. The Bible speaks of two such groups, one led by Ezra and another by Nehemiah. The latter helped rebuild the walls of the city by enlisting the help of 10 percent of the population of the countryside around Jerusalem (Neh 11:1-2). But Neh 5:1-5 sounds a discordant note:

> Then there rose a great outcry of the common people and their wives against certain of their fellow Jews. Some said: "We are forced to pawn our sons and daughters in order to get grain to eat that we may live." Others said: "We are forced to pawn our fields, our vineyards, and our houses, that we may have grain during the famine." Still others said: "To pay the king's tax we have borrowed money on our fields and our vineyards. And though these are our own kinsmen and our children are as good as theirs, we have had to reduce our sons and daughters to slavery, and violence has been done to some of our daughters! Yet we can do nothing about it, for our fields and our vineyards belong to others."

The old economic disparity between the elite class of Jerusalem and the subsistence farmers in the area—condemned by the earlier prophets—was beginning to emerge once again. Factions were emerging in the Jewish community. Like his prophetic predecessors, the prophet whose words are preserved in Zechariah 9–14 rises to condemn this economic disparity.

Factionalism was a fact of Jewish life during the restoration. Those returned from exile thought of themselves as a purified remnant. As a self-styled religious elite, they were determined to control the Jewish community's land resources and its religious life. There was some tension between the people of Jerusalem and those who lived in the rural areas surrounding it. Though it was a small city, Jerusalem was the commercial and administrative center for Judah. Peasant farmers saw the urban elite as living off their work. The Jewish community in the Persian period was anything but monolithic, and it had to deal with tensions that arose from the divisions within it. In addition to these tensions there were problems with the worshipers of Yahweh who lived in the territory of the former northern kingdom. The Samaritans, as they came to be called, wanted to contribute to the rebuilding of the Temple but were rebuffed by the people of Judah. The rift between the two groups began to grow wider. There were competing groups with different agendas, each claiming to be the authentic Israel. Zechariah spoke to these divisions among the worshipers of Yahweh.

The author of Zechariah 9–14 does not show much interest in the Temple, mentioning it only twice (11:13; 14:21). Instead, he thinks of himself as the authentic interpreter of earlier prophetic tradition. Zechariah 13:3-6 shows that he does not think much of the prophets of his day. Also, he seems to consider the restoration of the Davidic dynasty as a forlorn hope, due to the sins of Judah's rulers (11:1-7). He believes that God will rule Judah directly from Jerusalem. Like Isaiah of Babylon, the author of Zechariah 9–14 believes that Jerusalem is to be the center of worship for all nations (14:6-9). Still, Zechariah insists that before the city can assume that role, it has to be purged of all its sinful inhabitants (13:8-9; 14:2, 5).

Zechariah begins his prophecy by describing Yahweh's victory march that will end in Jerusalem (9:9-13). God promised Jerusalem a new king, the return of its inhabitants from exile, and victory over the Greeks.[8] The treachery of Judah's "shepherds," that is, its rulers, have made it impossible to reestablish the Davidic dynasty (11:4-17). Also, Jerusalem will have to undergo a purge to cleanse it of its sins. Zechariah 12–14 contains two accounts of Jerusalem's future. Both use the motif of "the nations against Jerusalem." The first account occurs in chapter 12. It appears to be a composite whose first scenario depicts God protecting the city and elevating its citizens to royal status and its royal house to divine status:

> On that day, the LORD will shield the inhabitants of Jerusalem, and the weakling among them shall be like David on that day, and the house of David godlike, like an angel of the Lord before them (Zech 12:8).

At the same time, the prophet insists that Jerusalem's deliverance does not give it status above the rural areas of Judah:

> The LORD shall save the tents of Judah first, that the glory of the house of David and the glory of the inhabitants of Jerusalem may not be exalted over Judah (Zech 12:7).

Though the prophet assures Jerusalem of its victory over the nations, that victory will come at a price:

> On that day the mourning in Jerusalem shall be as great as the mourning of Hadadrimmon in the plain of Megiddo (Zech 12:11).[9]

The results of God's intervention on Jerusalem's behalf will not result in rejoicing but in mourning. It will purge the city of its sinful element (Zech 13:1).

8. Some interpreters consider the reference to the Greeks in 9:13 as a reference to the campaign of Alexander the Great in the region. Contact with Greeks occurred long before Alexander the Great, as Ezek 27:13 testifies. Greeks from Mycenae had a trading colony in the region centuries before Israel emerged in Canaan.

9. "Hadad-rimmon" may be a place name, although it is also the name of a god whose worship included ritual mourning. See Ezek 8:14, which speaks about the women of Jerusalem weeping for the god Tammuz.

Chapter 14 contains another description of Jerusalem's future. Here the scenario clearly depicts God's final intervention for Judah.[10] The prophecies in this chapter are typically introduced with the formula "on that day," which often marks prophetic sayings about God's final and decisive actions on Israel's behalf. The chapter begins with God gathering the nations in order to punish half of Jerusalem's people. When that is complete, God will use the forces of nature to defeat those nations and so bring peace to the city. The survivors will join in the worship of God in Jerusalem, bringing their wealth into the city. The holiness of Jerusalem will extend beyond its city limits to the whole of Judah.

Verses 4-5 depict God as standing on the Mount of Olives:

> That day his feet shall rest upon the Mount of Olives, which is opposite Jerusalem to the east. The Mount of Olives shall be cleft in two from east to west by a very deep valley, and half of the mountain shall move to the north and half of it to the south. And the valley of the LORD's mountain shall be filled up when the valley of those two mountains reaches its edge; it shall be filled up as it was filled up by the earthquake in the days of King Uzziah of Judah. Then the LORD, my God, shall come, and all his holy ones with him.

God will cause an earthquake to split the mount, allowing the people of Jerusalem to escape the city. Later rabbinic Judaism, Islam, and evangelical Christianity associated these verses with the end of the world and the final judgment.[11] Verse 8 depicts Jerusalem as a source of continually flowing water. A significant weakness of the city, which complicated its defense, was its inadequate water supply. After God's final intervention, Jerusalem will have more than enough water. Another of the city's weaknesses is the quality of its leadership. Verse 9 has the perfect solution: God will be Jerusalem's king and rule the world from that city:

> The LORD shall become king over the whole earth; on that day the LORD shall be the only one, and his name the only one.

10. Some see chapter 14 as an early example of apocalyptic. For example, see Hanson, *Dawn of Apocalyptic,* 369. Others, such as Robert North, "Prophecy to Apocalyptic via Zechariah," *VTSupp* 22 (Leiden: Brill, 1971) 70–1, see this chapter as simply having a few characteristics of genuine apocalyptic. The characterization of this chapter depends upon one's definition of apocalyptic and its essential components. It is important to note that the prophet is speaking about the final days of this age, when God will save Jerusalem.

11. According to rabbinic teaching, the messiah will appear on the Mount of Olives, cross the Kidron Valley, and enter the Temple, which will be rebuilt directly across from the Mount of Olives. That is the reason religious Jews wish to be buried on the Mount of Olives. This will allow them to join the messiah on the day of the resurrection when "he will bring his holy ones with him" (Zech 14:5).

Jerusalem will then be exalted, secure (vv. 10-11). The nations will come to Jerusalem to worship Yahweh, in particular for the feast of Booths (vv. 16-19; see Isa 56:3-8).[12] The final two verses in the book assert that the holiness traditionally associated with Jerusalem will be shared with all of Judah. Even the people's cooking pots will be as holy as the vessels used in the Temple itself (vv. 20-21). God's presence will be so pervasive that the distinction between the sacred and the profane will be meaningless. What the prophet seems to imply is that the basis for all the factions within the Jewish community of his day will end. The great effect of God's final movement in Israel's life will be the complete transformation of Jerusalem and Judah. Both the city and the rural areas surrounding it, all their people, even their cooking pots, will be holy. There will be no religious elite. Claims of superior status will be irrelevant.

Zechariah clearly is not satisfied with the Jerusalem of his day. Religious reform is a sham. The community's leadership is venal and its internal divisions potentially destructive. Zechariah's study of earlier prophets leads him to a solution to these problems. He comes to see that there is one more great battle in Jerusalem's future. God will incite the nations to attack the city in order to cleanse it of its sins. Once this is complete, God will strike those nations. The survivors will join in the worship of Yahweh. What Zechariah describes is the world after the final battle. Most characteristic of that world will be its holiness, the pervasive presence of God that will transform even cooking pots into sacred vessels. Above all, this new day the prophet sees will bring an end to every division within the Jewish community.

Joel[13]

Joel takes up an old prophetic theme and pursues it relentlessly. It is the "Day of the Lord." When Amos made use of this motif almost four hundred years earlier, it must have already been well known. The Day of the Lord marked the decisive intervention of God to place Israel at the

12. Evangelical Christians from around the world gather in Jerusalem each year during the Jewish feast of Booths *(Sukkot)*. They consider this gathering a fulfillment of Zechariah's prophecy.

13. Stephen Langton, who first introduced chapter divisions into the Bible during the thirteenth century A.D., divided the Vulgate version of Joel into three chapters. Since the sixteenth century, however, it has been customary to divide the Hebrew text into four chapters. The *New American Bible* follows this four-chapter division, while the *Revised Standard Version* preserves the three-chapter division. In the four-chapter division 3:1-5 is the same as 2:28-32 of the three-chapter division. Also, 4:1-21 is the same as 3:1-21. The citations here will follow the *New American Bible* usage.

head of the nations. Amos, however, insisted that it would be a day of judgment for Israel (Amos 5:18-20). Other prophets, following Amos' lead, spoke of the Day of the Lord as a time of judgment for which Israel must prepare: Isa 2:12-17; Ezek 13:5 and Zeph 1:14-18. Still other texts did affirm that God's judgment was coming on the nations: Isa 13:6, 9; Jer 46:10; Obadiah 15. Joel believes that God has commissioned him to bring a new word about the Day of the Lord.

His prophetic predecessors gave Joel alternative patterns in speaking about the Day of the Lord. He could speak about that day as decisive either for Jerusalem's final deliverance and glorification or for its final judgment and destruction. Joel chooses to lay both alternatives before Jerusalem. In the first part of his book (1:4–2:17) the prophet speaks about two agricultural disasters that destroyed Judah's crops like invading armies intent on conquest. In the second part (2:18–4:21) the prophet describes Jerusalem's deliverance and the defeat of the nations that sought to conquer it. Joel and many of his contemporaries did not consider the restoration of Jerusalem, which began with the return from exile and was consolidated by Ezra and Nehemiah, as the fulfillment of prophetic expectations about either the Day of the Lord or the restoration of Jerusalem. While the Temple was rebuilt and sacrificial worship was resumed according to the requirements of the Torah, Joel believes there must be something wrong. The prophets did not envision Judah being a minor subdivision of the Persian empire. That is why Joel begins speaking about new acts of God for Jerusalem. To speak of these new acts, the prophet resurrects an old prophetic motif: the Day of the Lord.

As his starting point, Joel used two successive crop failures. The first was caused by an attack of locusts that devastated the crops of one season. The following year's harvest was ruined by a searing east wind that pulled the moisture out of every plant in its path (1:4-20).[14] The prophet sees these agricultural disasters as harbingers of momentous disasters in Jerusalem's future:

> Hear this, you elders!
>   Pay attention, all you who dwell in the land!
> Has the like of this happened in your days,
>   or in the days of your fathers? (1:2).

---

14. The prevailing winds in the region are westerly, bringing moisture off the Mediterranean Sea. Sometimes during the change of seasons, the winds will come from the east, off the Arabian desert. If they last long enough, these east winds can dehydrate and kill the crops ready for harvest.

Joel believes it is his responsibility to open Jerusalem's eyes so the people can see that God is still acting in their lives and that the fulfillment of the prophetic word about the Day of the Lord is as yet incomplete. Raising lamentations in the Temple over the economic crisis brought on by the two calamitous agricultural years (1:16-20) is not an adequate response to what God is doing in Jerusalem's life. A far more dramatic and comprehensive response is necessary because something unprecedented is about to happen:

> Blow the trumpet in Zion,
>> sound the alarm on my holy mountain!
> Let all who dwell in the land tremble,
>> for the day of the LORD is coming (2:1).

The Day of the Lord can bring either judgment or salvation to Jerusalem. The people of Jerusalem will decide which by the quality of their repentance. Joel's mission, as he sees it, is to lead the people of Jerusalem to repentance. Clearly, he believes the reestablished temple worship is not helping people become aware of the new acts of God toward Jerusalem. Joel begins his message of salvation by assuring Jerusalem that God will end the food shortage caused by the natural disasters over the previous two years (2:19-27). Beyond simply preventing a famine, God's providence is the basis for the prophet's affirmation that the Day of the Lord will bring fulfillment of the ancient promises of salvation for Jerusalem:

> And you shall know that I am in the midst of Israel;
>> I am the LORD, your God, and there is no other;
>> my people shall nevermore be put to shame (2:27).

What the prophet promises transcends the hope of political restoration, economic prosperity, and a renewed cult. The prophet promises that God will pour out the divine spirit on the people of Jerusalem, giving new shape and purpose to the community. What the prophet foresees is nothing less than the complete renewal and deliverance of Jerusalem:

> Then everyone shall be rescued
>> who calls on the name of the LORD;
> For on Mount Zion there shall be a remnant,
>> as the LORD has said,
> And in Jerusalem survivors
>> whom the LORD shall call (3:5).

Following this promise of Jerusalem's salvation, the prophet paints a picture of a disintegrating Gentile world. There is little hope for the nations because of the injustice they have done to Israel:

> Yes, in those days, and at that time,
>> when I would restore the fortunes
>> of Judah and Jerusalem,
> I will assemble all the nations
>> and bring them down to the Valley of Jehoshaphat,
> And I will enter into judgment with them there
>> on behalf of my people and my inheritance, Israel;
> Because they have scattered them among the nations,
>> and divided my land (4:1-2).

After completely defeating the nations (4:9-14), God will settle in Jerusalem, keeping it safe from every Gentile power:

> Then shall you know that I, the Lord, am your God,
> Dwelling on Zion, my holy mountain;
> Jerusalem shall be holy,
> and strangers shall pass through her no more (Joel 4:17).

While Joel does not establish a time sequence for the fulfillment of his prophecy, it is clearly not something for the immediate future. He speaks about the ultimate time of salvation—not simply a restoration of the old Judahite state. He is concerned about the final fate of Jerusalem and the nations—not simply the renewal of the temple cult. Clearly the vision of the prophet contrasts sharply with the circumstances of Jerusalem during the first half of the fourth century B.C. He believes that the priests have gotten too complacent simply because they are able to carry out their duties in the new Temple. The prophet is certain that God has something far greater in mind for Judah and Jerusalem. The catastrophes that threaten Judah's present are nothing more than the harbingers of the Day of the Lord. If Jerusalem repents, that day will be a day of total renewal. The prophet is to broaden the vision of Jerusalem's people so they can see beyond the circumstances of their life as citizens of the Persian empire. He wants them to imagine a future in which the earlier prophets' proclamation about the Day of the Lord will find fulfillment. Joel speaks about an ideal future—a future that will not be the fruit of the restoration as Jerusalem experienced it but a future born of the last and greatest of God's deeds for the city.

Isaiah 24–27

Chapters 24–27 of the book of Isaiah are of a different character than the rest of First Isaiah. These four chapters have provoked much scholarly discussion, though most of the topics are not immediately relevant to the study of Jerusalem's role in Israel's future. Isaiah 24–27 has been called "the Isaiah apocalypse," though it is unlikely that Isaiah composed these chapters and they are certainly not an apocalypse. Their subject matter is the final fate of the nations—including Israel. It is because they deal with the final intervention of God in history that they have received the designation of "apocalypse." They are among the last texts to be introduced into the Isaianic corpus and have been placed following the oracles against the nations (Isaiah 13–23) because of the similarity in content. While Jerusalem is not among these chapters' primary concerns, some attention to the city and its fate is unavoidable.

Isaiah 24 begins with a description of a catastrophe that will envelop the whole world (vv. 1-6). Although the form this disaster will take is not clear, it will happen because of people's sins. Whatever form it takes, the catastrophe will be an act of God alone. The text does not mention human instruments of the coming judgment. Verses 14-20 describe the terror of the coming judgment, while vv. 21-23 affirm the cosmic nature of the kingdom that God will establish as the final act of judgment over the nations of the world. The divine judgment, then, will close one period of history and begin another. The final verse of chapter 24 asserts that God will rule from Jerusalem:

> For the LORD of hosts will reign
> 　on Mount Zion and in Jerusalem,
> glorious in the sight of his elders (Isa 24:23b).

The elders will witness the inauguration of God's rule from Zion just as they did when God founded the nation (see Exod 24:9-11).

The song of triumph in 26:1-6 does not mention Jerusalem by name, but "the strong city" of 26:1 could be none other than Jerusalem. After God's final victory it becomes a fortress city for all loyal Jews, especially the poor (v. 6). This song is an expression of trust in God's final victory over the powers of evil and serves to bridge the gap between the experience of the present and hope for the future. During the restoration period following the exile, Jerusalem became a central symbol of hope for the future. The city and its Temple were the tangible signs of the people's survival.

The Isaiah apocalypse ends with a description of the great return of God's people:

> On that day,
> The LORD shall beat out the grain
> 　between the Euphrates and the Wadi of Egypt,
> 　and you shall be gleaned one by one, O sons of Israel.

> On that day,
> A great trumpet shall blow,
>> and the lost in the land of Assyria
>> and the outcasts in the land of Egypt
> Shall come and worship the LORD
>> on the holy mountain, in Jerusalem (Isa 27:12-13).

The Jews will leave their places of exile in Egypt, Assyria, and Babylon and return to their own land. The great return begins with God's "threshing." God will separate those who are loyal from the apostate Jews and the Gentiles who are within the territory once ruled by David. They will form the nucleus of a nation that is obedient. Then the ram's horn will sound to announce the great return. The returning Jews will join in the worship of God on the holy mountain, which is in Jerusalem. This emphasizes that the final destiny of Jerusalem is not to be merely a political center. God's final intervention in Israel's life is not to reestablish the Davidic empire but to make it possible for the Jews to worship on the holy mountain.

Daniel

Centuries have passed since the people of Jerusalem first heard about the glorious future in store for their city, which God had chosen, but still nothing has happened. In fact, Jerusalem's situation had deteriorated. The Greeks replaced the Persians as masters of the world. At first their rule was benign. Like the Persians, the Greeks allowed the Jews to worship their ancestral deity in Jerusalem's Temple according to their unique traditions. Then Jerusalem and Judah were caught up in the conflict between competing Greek kingdoms: the Ptolemaic with its center in Egypt and the Seleucid with its center in Syria. Each claimed the territory of the old Israelite kingdoms as its own. The Jews could only watch as the economic and political status quo was becoming unraveled, for they had no power to influence events. Some Jews abandoned their ancestral religion to improve their social standing and economic situation under Greek rule (see 1 Macc 1:11-15). Most Jews continued to hope for "that day" promised by the prophets to come. Matters took an ominous turn when the Seleucid king, Antiochus IV, frustrated in his attempt to take Egypt, took his anger out on Jerusalem. He stripped the Temple of its precious appointments and massacred the people of the city (1 Macc 1:16-28).

Antiochus made careful preparations for another campaign against the Ptolemies. He decided that he needed a united people to support his military adventurism (1 Macc 1:41-42). This decision had a disastrous effect on the Jews. They were required to renounce their ancestral religion and end their distinctive religious practices such as circumcision and observance of the Sabbath and the dietary laws. Torah scrolls were confiscated and Yahweh's Temple was converted to a temple in honor of Zeus (1 Macc 1:44-61). While some Jews obeyed Antiochus' decrees banning their religion (1 Macc 1:43), many did not (1 Macc 1:62-63). The result of their disobedience was severe persecution, which sparked the Maccabean revolt (1 Macc 2:15-28). The faithful endured the persecution and wars, but certainly they wondered what happened to the promises about Jerusalem. What will its future be like? When is the "day of the Lord" coming? The book of Daniel attempts to answer some of those questions.

The significance of Jerusalem and its Temple is assumed in the book of Daniel, whose central character prays three times a day, facing Jerusalem (6:11). Several chapters deal explicitly with Antiochus' conversion of the Temple into a sanctuary for Zeus, which Daniel describes as "the horrible abomination" (9:27; 11:31; 12:11). When Antiochus disrupted the worship of Yahweh in Jerusalem's Temple, his actions made it painfully clear that the prophecies about Jerusalem's glorious future have yet to be fulfilled. In particular, people remembered the prophecy of Jeremiah, who predicted that the Babylonian domination of Judah would last seventy years (Dan 9:2; see Jer 25:11-12; 29:10). Daniel 9 takes two different tacks in dealing with "the horrible abomination" that occurred so long after Jerusalem's desolation was supposed to have ended. The first is a prayer of confession (vv. 3-19). The second is an account of a revelation given to Daniel that provides an interpretation of Jeremiah's prophecy.[15]

The prayer in vv. 3-19 is a communal confession of sin and a petition for God's mercy by the people of Judah and Jerusalem (v. 7). The people admit that they have violated the terms of the covenant (vv. 5-11a); acknowledge acquaintance with God's justice (vv. 7-8; 14); recall God's past mercies (v. 15); and ask for God's mercy for God's own sake (vv. 16-19).[16] There is tension between the prayer and the revelation that follows it. In the prayer the people of Jerusalem acknowledge that God has justly punished them for their sins, and they appeal for mercy. In the visions of Daniel, including the one in chapter 9, the primary sin is that of Antiochus. Still, God has arranged the course of history so that Antiochus' evil will be punished. One purpose of the visions in Daniel is to make the

---

15. It is important to remember that the book of Daniel is set in the time of the Babylonian exile, though it was actually written in the second century B.C., more than four hundred years later. See John J. Collins, *Daniel,* Hermeneia (Minneapolis Fortress Press, 1993) 29–33.

16. Other prayers of confession follow the same pattern. See Psalm 106; Ezra 9:6-15; Neh 1:5-11; 9:5-37; Tob 3:1-6; Dan 3:24-45.

pious aware of the divine decrees that will mean the eventual vindication of the just. Apart from this prayer, Daniel never explicitly asserts that the sins of the Jews have led to divine judgment expressed through Antiochus' persecution, since the book of Daniel sees the primary cause of the desolation of Jerusalem as the arrogance of Antiochus—not the sins of its people.[17] Also, when Gabriel describes the deliverance that is coming, he does not indicate that it is God's response to the people's confession of sins. In fact, the deliverance predicted in the vision will not come for more than five hundred years. The end of the "horrible abomination" will come because it has been decreed by God in advance, not because of the repentance or prayer of the people. The prayer is simply an act of piety on the part of the people of Jerusalem; it does not move God to deliver them from Antiochus.[18] The king's destruction had already been determined by God long before the prayer was uttered, as is clear from Daniel's reinterpretation of Jeremiah's seventy years:

> Seventy weeks are decreed
>   for your people and for your holy city:
> Then transgression will stop and sin will end,
>   guilt will be expiated,
> Everlasting justice will be introduced,
>   vision and prophecy ratified,
>   and a most holy will be anointed.
>   Know and understand this:
> From the utterance of the word
>   that Jerusalem was to be rebuilt
> Until one who is anointed and a leader,
>   there shall be seven weeks.
> During sixty-two weeks,
>   it shall be rebuilt,
> With streets and trenches,
>   in time of affliction.
>
> After the sixty-two weeks
>   an anointed shall be cut down
>   when he does not possess the city;
> And the people of a leader who will come
>   shall destroy the sanctuary.
> Then the end shall come like a torrent;

---

17. Even Zech 1:12-17, which does see the seventy years spoken of by Jeremiah as punishment for Jerusalem's sins, blames the Gentiles more for Jerusalem's troubles.

18. W. Sibley Towner, "Retributional Theology in the Apocalyptic Setting," *USQR* 26 (1971) 213.

until the end there shall be war,
   the desolation that is decreed.
For one week he shall make
   a firm compact with the many;
Half the week
   he shall abolish sacrifice and oblation;
On the temple wing shall be the horrible abomination
   until the ruin that is decreed
   is poured out upon the horror (Dan 9:24-27).

Although Daniel does not cite Jeremiah by name, it is most likely that the "seventy weeks" decreed for Jerusalem refer to the well-known prophecy in Jeremiah. By offering his reinterpretation of that prophecy, Daniel rejects the interpretations of both the Chronicler (see 2 Chr 36:20-21) and Zechariah (see Zech 1:12), both of whom hold that the prophecy was fulfilled during the Persian period when the decision was made to rebuild the Temple. Daniel attempts to put the crisis caused by Antiochus' actions into perspective for his fellow Jews. He wants to show them that all that has happened to them was decreed by God, as is the resolution of the crisis. Gabriel, who interprets Daniel's vision, tells the seer that the whole post-exilic period will last 490 years, that is, "seventy weeks of years." That is why Jeremiah's prophecy has not been fulfilled: the time of fulfillment has not come. Antiochus' desecration of the Temple will last for a half a week (v. 27), that is, three and one-half years.[19] This is a relatively short time when seen against the sweep of history that makes up the restoration. Gabriel does not refer to Antiochus as an instrument of God's judgment on Jerusalem, though earlier prophets implied that God used Assyria and Babylon to punish Israel for its sins. Jerusalem will be delivered from the power of this evil king. That is certain, for God has decreed it.

First Enoch[20]

Like the book of Daniel, *1 Enoch* is an apocalyptic work that wants to assure its readers that the triumph of the just and the destruction of the wicked is imminent.[21] It envisions the coming of a messiah-like figure

19. For the chronology of the seventy weeks of years, see Devorah Dimant, "The Seventy Weeks Chronology (Dan 9, 24-27) in the Light of New Qumranic Texts," *The Book of Daniel in the Light of New Findings*, ed. A. S. van der Woude (Leuven: Univ. Press, 1993) 61–70.

20. For the text see Charlesworth, *Old Testament Pseudepigrapha*, 1:5-89.

21. *First Enoch* is a composite work. The passage that is relevant to Jerusalem comes from about the same time as the book of Daniel, that is, the beginning of the

called "the Righteous One" or "the Son of Man," who will establish his kingdom following the resurrection of the just. This will bring about a new Jerusalem. In the purposely cryptic language of apocalyptic, *Enoch* speaks of the new temple that the Righteous One will bring into existence:

> Then I stood still, looking at that ancient house being transformed: All the pillars and all the columns were pulled out; and the ornaments of that house were packed and taken out together with them and abandoned in a certain place in the South of the land. I went on seeing until the Lord of the sheep brought about a new house, greater and loftier than the first one, and set it up in the first location which had been covered up—all its pillars were new, the columns new; and the ornaments new as well as greater than those of the first, (that is) the old (house) which was gone. All the sheep were within it (*1 Enoch* 90:28-29).

Jerusalem and its Temple will be part of the kingdom to be established at the end of this age. How could it be otherwise? But that new city will not simply be a continuation of the earthly Jerusalem. It will be something entirely new—the result of a miraculous transformation.

The Testaments of the Twelve Patriarchs[22]

Though roughly contemporaneous with the book of Daniel and *1 Enoch, The Testaments of the Twelve Patriarchs* are not apocalyptic works. They purport to be the final words of the twelve sons of Jacob, exhorting their children to avoid sin and lead exemplary moral lives. Still, the *Testaments* exhibit clear eschatological overtones. The blending of moral instruction with eschatological expectations reminds one of the Gospels, although the *Testaments* predate the Gospels by at least two hundred years. In describing the end of this age, the *Testament of Levi* foresees the destruction of Jerusalem and its Temple as God's judgment on Israel's sins (10:3; 15:1; 16:4-5), a common enough explanation for the disaster that befell Jerusalem.[23] The *Testament of Benjamin* assumes that the Temple will be rebuilt in the final days of this age and asserts that its glory will be unsurpassed (9:2). The *Testament of Dan* describes the "new Jerusalem" as a paradise for the righteous:

Maccabean Revolt, around 165–161 B.C. See E. Isaac, "1 (Ethiopic Apocalypse of) Enoch," Charlesworth, *Old Testament Pseudepigrapha,* 1:7.

22. The text is available in Charlesworth, *Old Testament Pseudepigrapha,* 1:775-81.

23. Other intertestamental works offering a similar explanation for ill fortunes of Jerusalem are 2 *Bar* 6:1–8:5 and the *Psalms of Solomon* 2:1-25; 8:1-34.

And the saints shall refresh themselves in Eden;
the righteous shall rejoice in the New Jerusalem,
which shall be eternally for the glorification of God.
And Jerusalem shall no longer undergo desolation,
nor shall Israel be led into captivity,
because the Lord will be in her midst (5:12-13).

Though the future of Jerusalem is not a central motif in the *Testaments,* it is clear that their eschatological expectations assume that Jerusalem will have a central role in the kingdom of God. After all, it is the place of God's dwelling within Israel's midst.

The Dead Sea Scrolls

The Dead Sea scrolls are the product of a community made up primarily of priests who believed that the priests who controlled the Temple in Jerusalem were corrupt and their rituals illegitimate. Two antagonists in the scrolls are the "Teacher of Righteousness," the leader of the Qumran community, and the "Wicked Priest," the leader of the Jerusalem priesthood. The Qumran community believed that after a great conflict between themselves ("the sons of light") and the priests of Jerusalem ("the sons of darkness"), God would restore legitimate worship to the Temple with the priests of Qumran as the ministers of that worship. It is true that Jerusalem is not a primary motif in the Dead Sea scrolls. The city appears only incidentally in most texts. However, the Temple and its worship are major concerns of the scrolls. There are several texts in Qumran documents that are particularly relevant to the community's vision of Jerusalem.

The most important, however, exists only in fragmentary form and is known as the New Jerusalem scroll from the first century B.C.[24] Like Ezekiel 48, this document gives a detailed plan for a walled temple city that will exist in the future. Though Ezekiel's new city is square (48:16), that of the Qumran texts is an immense rectangle. Still, it is likely that Qumran texts are dependent upon the book of Ezekiel.[25] The city plan in the Qumran texts envisions a city that is 15 miles long and 11 miles wide. While this is certainly larger than Jerusalem of the first century B.C., these dimensions are not the fantastic ones that Rev 21:15-17 gives for the heavenly Jerusalem, which will be 331 miles on each side. The Qumran text also provides realistic descriptions of the city's wall, streets, and housing

24. The text of the New Jerusalem scroll is available in Michael Chyutin, *The New Jerusalem Scroll from Qumran: A Comprehensive Reconstruction,* JSP Supplement Series 25 (Sheffield: Sheffield Academic Press, 1997) 15–32.

25. F. García Martínez, *Qumran and Apocalyptic* (Leiden: Brill, 1992) 186.

blocks.[26] It reflects the tradition of planning the ideal city found not only in the Bible but in Greek and Roman texts. The city plan that the New Jerusalem document uses is one developed by Hippodamos of Miletus and exemplified in the layout of the Ionian city of Pirene from the late fifth century B.C. and spread throughout the eastern Mediterranean by the Seleucids. Though this plan is based on the geometric principles of the Pythagoreans, similar temple-city plans are found in Egypt as far back as the second millennium B.C.[27] Unlike the heavenly Jerusalem of Revelation, in which there is no temple (21:22), the Qumran text includes a temple and outlines the rituals performed in it. This document, then, does not envision a heavenly Jerusalem—a city beyond time. It describes how the Qumran community envisioned Jerusalem and its Temple at the end of this age just prior to the final battle between the children of light and the children of darkness. However, this new city and temple will not be the work of human hands but of God.[28]

The New Jerusalem scroll has been reconstructed from many fragments; no complete copy of this document has emerged among the finds at Qumran. Nowhere does the word "Jerusalem" appear in any of the fragments. Of course, neither Ezekiel nor Deuteronomy mention Jerusalem, but it is clear that all three texts have Jerusalem in mind.[29] Another fragment from the Dead Sea scrolls makes clear the status accorded to Jerusalem by the Qumran community:

> And we think that the Temple [is the place of the Tent of Meeting and Je]rusalem is the place which [He chose from among all the tribes of Israel . . .] (4QMMT 2:34-36).[30]

This passage, from a letter dealing with matters of Jewish law, identifies Jerusalem with the tent of meeting from the wilderness tradition and sets

26. See Jean Starcky, "Jerusalem et les manuscrits de la Mer Morte," *Le Monde de la Bible* 1 (Nov./Dec. 1977) 38–40, who asserts that the New Jerusalem document is more utopian than Ezekiel 48 and that it would be difficult to reproduce its image of the city in reality. Of course, the document assumes that God will build the city, although it will be in this world.

27. Chyutin, *New Jerusalem Scroll,* 113–21.

28. Ibid., 202.

29. Chyutin, *New Jerusalem Scroll,* 111, explains this by a reference to the controversy over Jerusalem's status during the time of the first Temple. But certainly by the middle of the first century B.C. this issue had been settled in Jerusalem's favor.

30. See John Strugnell and E. Qimron, "An Unpublished Halakhic Letter from Qumran," *Biblical Archaeology Today* (Jerusalem, Israel Exploration Society, 1985) 400–7.

it apart from all the other cities of Israel. According to the New Jerusalem document (col. 22), the city will have a significance not only for the Jews but for all nations. At the end of the age, when God will save Israel from its enemies, those who survive God's intervention will join Israel in worshiping the Lord in the temple (see Zech 14:16).

The Temple scroll (11QTemple) contains what the Qumran community understood as the basic requirements of legitimate worship. Because Jerusalem and its Temple, contemporary with the Qumran community, did not meet the listed norms, they were considered as defiled, that is, unfit for divine worship. The people at Qumran were not the only ones to criticize the Temple and its priests, but the Qumran community was the most radical in its critique.[31] Because the Jerusalem Temple did not reflect the requirements of the Temple scroll, the Qumran community did not participate in it but believed that its own rituals provided the only legitimate form of expiation and adoration that was possible. The community then became the temple. This situation, however, was not to be permanent, for the Qumran community fully expected that the Jerusalem Temple would one day be brought into conformity with the requirements of the Temple scroll. Even this situation is temporary. It will last only until the "day of the creation when I (God) shall create my temple and establish it forever" (11QTemple 29:9-10). This temple is not the heavenly temple that transcends time. It is a temple that will exist in this world after God's final intervention in Israel's life, which will sweep away the evil priests. When the temple will be cleansed of its impurities, its holiness will extend beyond its precincts to the whole of Jerusalem, which the scroll refers to as "the city of the temple." This had practical effects in the realm of ritual purity. Men living in the temple city had to abstain from sexual intercourse, and women, because of their menstrual periods, could not be permanent residents there, although they could live in other cities.[32] The legislation on purity in the temple city derives from Num 5:2-3, which held that the laws of purity applied to the entire wilderness camp: the tabernacle, the camp of the Levites that surrounded it, and the camp of the rest of the tribes around the Levites. Since Qumran identified Jerusalem with the wilderness camp, more stringent rules of purity had to be observed there than in any other city. The Qumran community applied all the laws for the purity and cleanliness of the temple also to Jerusalem.

31. R. G. Hamerton-Kelly, "The Temple and the Origins of Jewish Apocalyptic," *VT* 20 (1970) 1–15.

32. For other examples of the concern for the purity of the temple city, see Yigal Yadin, *The Temple Scroll* (London: Weidenfeld & Nicolson, 1985) 170–91.

The Psalms of Solomon[33]

These eighteen hymns, which date from the mid-first century B.C., reflect the problems facing the Jewish community in Palestine at that time. There were internal conflicts within the community that were quite serious. The Pharisees, Sadducees, the Qumran community, various Zealot groups, and messianic movements each claimed to be the true Israel. This made it impossible for the community make a common response to the Romans who invaded the Jewish homeland in 63 B.C., incorporating it into their empire and transforming the Hasmoneans into a puppet dynasty. These prayers provide an insight into the response of a group of Jews living in Jerusalem to the events they see as destroying their community. The key to the future that they propose is messianism. The faithful are looking for an ideal son of David who will come to establish an everlasting kingdom of God on earth. Of course, Jerusalem will have a central role in that kingdom.

The immediate crisis that the *Psalms of Solomon* responded to was Pompey's conquest of Jerusalem and violation of the Temple. The psalms do not know what to make of this outrage, so they repeatedly raise the issue of divine justice (2:1, 15-18; 3:3-5; 4:8; 8:3, 23-26; 9:2). Of course, the first answer to the problem of justifying God's actions is to assert that the people's sins have brought this disaster on Jerusalem and the Temple. But this disaster has the potential of doing more than chastising the Jewish community. It could end that community's very life, so the psalms remind God that Israel is the people God has chosen and loved (7:8-9; 9:8-11; 11:7; 14:5; 17:4). However, the answer that solves the theological problem that is the subject of these hymns is the messiah, whose coming is not to be in the distant future but the immediate present. When the messiah comes, all the Gentile nations will be subject to him. Jerusalem will then enjoy its glory. Because the psalms are convinced of the messiah's imminent coming, they call for a revolt against the Romans that will usher in the messianic kingdom.

Though Psalm 1 does not mention Jerusalem by name, it is clear that the "I" of the psalm is Jerusalem personified: "I cried out to the Lord when I was severely troubled" (v. 1). Jerusalem claims to be righteous but acknowledges that her children have been "arrogant" (vv. 4-7). Their sins have brought an invasion worse than any other Jerusalem has experienced (v. 8). Psalm 2 expands on these themes and provides historical allusions to Pompey's three-month siege of the Temple. Its capture and desecration

---

33. The text of the psalms is available in Charlesworth, *Old Testament Pseudepigrapha,* 2:639-70.

are described as an insult to Jerusalem (v. 19). When the psalmist considered what the Romans did to Jerusalem, "the holy city," it made him physically ill (8:4-5). After describing the siege in some detail (8:1-22), the psalmist begs for God's mercy (8:23-34). Psalm 11 is an address to Jerusalem that is full of confidence about the city's future:

> Stand on a high place, Jerusalem, and look at your children
>> from the east and the west assembled by the Lord . . .
> Jerusalem, put on the clothes of your glory,
>> prepare the robe of your holiness,
> for God has spoken well of Israel forevermore (11:2, 7).

Psalm 17 asserts that the messiah "will purge Jerusalem and make it holy" (v. 30). Once this is accomplished, the Gentiles will recognize the glory of God in the city (v. 31) and pay homage to Jerusalem and its king.

The theology in the *Psalms of Solomon* is traditional. Most of its principal themes were already present in the biblical and post-biblical literature. The contribution these prayers make is to assure Jerusalem that Pompey's invasion is actually the harbinger of the messiah's coming. The hopelessness of Jerusalem's political situation and the theological crisis occasioned by still another disaster for "the holy city" are what convince the psalmist that God cannot allow matters to continue as they are. With profound faith in God's compassion and hope for Israel's future, the psalmist assures the oppressed city that the ancient promises will be fulfilled through the messiah, who is coming soon to establish his kingdom in Jerusalem.

The Sibylline Oracles, **Book Five**[34]

While the *Psalms of Solomon* reflects the views of one portion of the Jerusalem community to the desecration of the Temple by Pompey in 63 B.C., *The Sibylline Oracles,* book 5, reflects the reaction of the Jewish community in Egypt to the destruction of the Temple at the end of the first revolt in A.D. 70. The book was written in the period between the first revolt and the second, which began in A.D. 132. The hatred of Rome expressed in this work is undisguised by cryptic language. Its bitterness toward the great imperial power is without parallel. While it denounces Rome for its immorality, it underscores Rome's sin in destroying Jerusalem (vv. 160-1). The *Sibylline Oracles* envision a restored Jerusalem, which it calls "the city of God in the middle of the earth." The new city

---

34. The text is available in Charlesworth, *Old Testament Pseudepigrapha,* 1:390–405.

will be the envy of the nations. In vv. 249-55 the Sibyl foresees the extension of the city's wall to Joppa, a city on the Mediterranean Sea almost forty miles from Jerusalem. The new Jerusalem will be safe from any military threat because of this great wall. A savior figure will come from God and restore the Temple, ending all immorality (vv. 420-33). Its dimensions will be such that all the righteous will be able to see it and recognize God's victory. While the Sibyl's description of the restored Jerusalem is extravagant, it is likely that Jerusalem's restoration is to be in this world.[35]

Conclusion

The Deuteronomic tradition dealt with the fall of Jerusalem, the destruction of the Temple, and the exile by making these the consequence of Judah's sins. These disasters were the punishment of God upon a people who were unfaithful to the covenant. The disappointment that followed a restoration that did not meet Judah's hopes called for another explanation. As Judah's theologians began reflecting on the tradition they had received and the experience of Judah during the restoration, they began to think of good and evil locked in a conflict that would have to run its course. Jerusalem's oppressors were concrete manifestations of that evil power. The city's suffering was caused not by Judah's sin but by its oppressors' alliance with evil. At the end of that conflict, which will see the triumph of the good, God's righteousness will triumph. The frustrations of the present will make sense when seen against the backdrop of God's eventual victory over every power of evil. One consequence of God's victory over evil will be the rise of a new Jerusalem—a city that transcends the Jerusalem of this age and this world.

---

35. John J. Collins, "Sibylline Oracles," Charlesworth, *Old Testament Pseudepigrapha*, 1:392.

The Liberated City:
The Defense of Jerusalem

The prophetic expectations about Jerusalem's future depended almost entirely on God for fulfillment. What the people of Jerusalem were to do was repent of their sins and follow the Torah—and wait. While the prophets proclaimed that Jerusalem would have a glorious future, that future seemed long in coming. God seemed to postpone the fulfillment of the prophetic word about Zion. In apocalyptic expectations human activity was irrelevant in bringing about the triumph of good. Jerusalem's restoration and glorification were decreed by God and would take place despite what anyone did or did not do. What the people of Jerusalem needed to do was prepare themselves to enjoy the fruits of the victory God has ordained for the city. They were to do this by remaining faithful to the Torah. Still, their fidelity would contribute nothing to the victory that God alone will win over every evil power. There were, however, people in Judah and Jerusalem who were not content to remain passive in the face of threats to their faith, to Zion, and to the Temple. They were determined to do something themselves. While the prophets promised that God would deal with Jerusalem's enemies, some Jews believed that the crisis that they faced following the proscription of their religion by Antiochus IV in the middle of the second century B.C. did not allow them to wait any longer for God's intervention. If they did not act, Judaism and the Jewish people would simply be persecuted out of existence.

Alexander the Great brought the territory of the former Israelite kingdoms under Greek control in 333 B.C. Though Alexander admired the cultures of the ancient Near East, the culture of the Greeks, who controlled the eastern Mediterranean, became dominant. The Jews, however, maintained their ancestral traditions, although some did assimilate. After Alexander's death his empire was divided among his generals. At first the territory of the former Israelite kingdoms was controlled by the Ptolemies, who ruled from Egypt. The Seleucids, who governed Mesopotamia, eventually took possession of Judah and the surrounding region from the Ptolemies. Though Antiochus IV, a Seleucid king, decided that he could take Egypt from the Ptolemies, the Romans, a rising power, prevented this from happening. Antiochus took out his frustration on the Jews.[1] He enacted measures that forced them to abandon their traditions and assimilate. Antiochus' actions provoked an armed rebellion by the Jews. Surprisingly, the Jews prevailed. This victory supported the notion that Jerusalem's future was in the hands of people who were not afraid to take decisive action against its oppressors. Several biblical texts support a militant response to the oppression of the Jews and the subjugation of Jerusalem.

First Maccabees

Jerusalem has a prominent place in First Maccabees. The story of the successful Jewish revolution against the Seleucid Empire focuses its attention on the fate of Jerusalem and its Temple. What happens to the city and Yahweh's shrine serves to symbolize the destiny of the Jewish people. This is clear from Mattathias' lament on Antiochus' desecration of the Temple and prohibition of Jewish religious observance:

> When he saw the sacrileges that were being committed in Judah and in Jerusalem, he said: "Woe is me! Why was I born to see the ruin of my people and the ruin of the holy city, and to sit idle while it is given into the hands of enemies, and the sanctuary into the hands of strangers?" (1 Macc 2:6-7).

Mattathias uses a traditional epithet, "the holy city" to speak of Jerusalem (see Isa 48:2; 52:1; Neh 11:1, 18; Dan 9:24). But the text shows that by the middle of the second century B.C. Jerusalem was much more than a temple city—the place where God chose to dwell. It was much more than a political or administrative center. The fate of the Jewish people became intertwined with that of Jerusalem. To attack Jerusalem, to desecrate its Temple, to transform it into a Greek *polis,* was to threaten the very existence of the Jewish people. The irony was that the people of Jerusalem did not recognize what was happening to them. In fact, many became collaborators in Antiochus' assault on their religion and culture (1 Macc 1:10-

---

1. Lester L. Grabbe, *Judaism from Cyrus to Hadrian* (Minneapolis: Fortress Press, 1991) 1:277.

15). The call to armed resistance came not from the Jewish leadership in Jerusalem but from a priest named Mattathias, who lived in the village of Modein twenty-three miles west of Jerusalem (1 Macc 2:15, 24-35). While the goal of the Maccabean revolution was the liberation of Jerusalem and the cleansing of its Temple from Greek accouterments placed there by Antiochus, the struggle, in fact, was for the very life of the Jewish people.

Mattathias died soon after beginning the revolution, and Judas, one of his sons, succeeded him as the leader of the loyal Jews.[2] Of course, the most important objective of the revolutionaries was the liberation of Jerusalem and the purification of the Temple. Antiochus determined to annihilate the Jews and repopulate Jerusalem with foreigners (1 Macc 3:34-35). Judas proved to be a brilliant military leader, turning a small guerrilla force into an army that was able to defeat the larger, professional forces of Antiochus. The Jewish force was able to capture Jerusalem except for the Akra, a citadel the Greeks continued to control. Upon taking the city Judas and his army went immediately to "Mount Zion"(1 Macc 4:36-37). They lamented the sad state of the Temple and began to restore the structure. When this was completed and a new altar was constructed, Judas had the Temple rededicated three years to the day after Antiochus desecrated it. The celebration lasted for eight days, and Judas decreed that his victory over the Greeks and the rededication of the Temple be celebrated annually (4:59). This is the origin of the feast of Hanukkah,[3] which Jews continue to celebrate.

Judas' initial victories transformed his struggle to save Jerusalem, its people, and its Temple into a war of independence. The rest of First Maccabees tells the story of that war. Judas died in battle (1 Maccabees 9), and his place was taken by his brother Jonathan, who had Jerusalem rebuilt (1 Macc 12:35-37) before his assassination (1 Macc 12:39-53). He was succeeded by his brother, Simon, the last surviving son of Mattathias. After more than twenty years of trying to subdue the Jews without success, the Seleucid Empire recognized the independence of a Jewish state ruled

---

2. See 1 Macc 2:70–3:1. The text states that Judas was "known as Maccabeus." This name likely derives from the Aramaic word *maqqabah,* "hammer." This name is applied to Mattathias' family. They are also known as the "Hasmoneans," that is, the descendants of Hashmon, who was Mattathias' grandfather.

3. The Hebrew word *hanukkah* means "dedication." The Gospel of John places Jesus in Jerusalem for the celebration of this feast (John 10:22-23). Hanukkah is sometimes known as the "feast of Lights," since on each of the eight nights of the feast a light is kindled in memory of a story found in the Talmud that states that when Judas reinstituted worship in the Temple, there was only one day's supply of oil for the lamp that was to be lit in the Temple, but this supply lasted for the entire eight days of the celebration.

by Simon as ethnarch and high priest. The Jews inscribed bronze plaques and placed them in the pillars of the Temple to legitimate Simon's position (1 Macc 14:25-48). Simon, however, was assassinated by his son-in-law Ptolemy in a bid for power (1 Macc 16:11-17). To consolidate his position, Ptolemy sent his supporters to take control of the Temple, but he was unsuccessful. John Hyrcanus, Simon's son, succeeded him (1 Macc 16:18-24). The story of John's accession ends the narrative of First Maccabees.

Though the text of First Maccabees mentions Jerusalem, Zion, and the Temple almost one hundred times, most of these references merely serve to locate the scene of military activity. Still, it is clear that this book accords the highest importance to Jerusalem. It is the first objective of the revolutionaries. When the Jews retake Jerusalem, they set about refurbishing the Temple and have a solemn service of rededication. The city is rebuilt to ensure that it can be defended. The survival of Jerusalem becomes a symbol of the survival of the Jewish people. The victory of Jerusalem is the victory of the Jewish people. First Maccabees testifies to the belief that the destiny of Jerusalem and that of the Jewish people will be forever bound together.

Second Maccabees

Second Maccabees does not continue the story of First Maccabees. It is a separate account of the events described in First Maccabees 1–7. Two letters serve as a preface to the book. The first letter (2 Macc 1:1-9) urges the Jews living in Egypt to celebrate the feast of Hanukkah as a gesture of Jewish solidarity. The second (2 Macc 1:10–2:18) is addressed to Aristobulus, a leading member of the Jewish community in Egypt, and has the same purpose. What is significant about both letters is the prominence each gives to Jerusalem (2 Macc 1:1, 10). The letters are sent from the Jewish community of Jerusalem, which apparently saw itself as arbiter of correct observance and promoter of Jewish unity. The letters, however, do not imply that there were any problems between the Jewish community in Jerusalem and that in Egypt. They are written simply because Hanukkah was not observed in the Diaspora. Its observance, of course, is not mandated in the Torah. It is a Jerusalem-centered festival that celebrated the rededication of the Temple following the victory of the Maccabees. Evidently the Jerusalem community thought it important for the Jews in Egypt to maintain the bonds that tied them to Jerusalem by celebrating this feast.

There were some potential problems between the Jewish community in Jerusalem and that in Egypt. Onias IV, the son of Onias III, the last legitimate high priest, fled to Egypt after his father's murder. The authorities there permitted him to build a temple to Yahweh at Leontopolis. This act was an apparent violation of the Deuteronomic requirement that there be only one temple, in the place that God designates (Deut 12). Of course, Jews agreed that this place was Jerusalem. Still, neither letter alludes to the temple built by Onias. Apparently it was not considered a rival to the one in Jerusalem, nor did the Jerusalem community consider that the Egyptian Jews had separated themselves from their spiritual homeland. The community in Jerusalem suggested the celebration of Hanukkah as a means to strengthen those bonds.

The second letter refers to Jerusalem as the "holy city" (2 Macc 1:12), and one of the book's emphases is the centrality of temple worship. In fact, the book is structured as a series of attacks on the Temple: the first by Heliodorus (2 Maccabees 3), the second by Antiochus (4:1–10:9), and the third by Nicanor (10:10–15:36). Important as the Temple is, however, it is subordinated to the nation: "The LORD, however, had not chosen the people for the sake of the Place, but the Place for the sake of the people" (2 Macc 5:19). The Temple and the city were instruments that made it possible for the Jews to commune with God through ritual and prayer. The fate of the Temple was, then, a barometer of people's relationship with God. If the people proved unfaithful, the Temple would suffer desecration or even destruction. If, however, the people repented, the Temple would be purified and rededicated to reflect the people's standing before God. The Temple would become holy again because the people had become holy again. While Jerusalem is the "holy city," its holiness and its fate derive from those of the people. Thus Jerusalem is holy not because of God's dwelling in the Temple. It is holy because it is the place where people seek God. Here Second Maccabees agrees with the way Jeremiah assesses the nature of Zion's sanctity (see Jer 7:14; 14:13-19; 26). Jerusalem and its Temple are not sacrosanct. It is the holiness of the people that makes the Temple holy.

In its own way Second Maccabees affirms that the fate of Jerusalem and its Temple is intertwined with that of the people, as First Maccabees did. Their fate is determined by the quality of their relationship with God. Second Maccabees saw the real cause of Antiochus' desecration of the Temple to be the infidelity of Jerusalem—the introduction of Hellenism by Jason, who claimed to be the high priest, the sale and purchase of the high priestly office, and the murder of Onias, the legitimate high priest (2 Macc 4:7-38). For Second Maccabees, then, the origin of the crisis that Jerusalem faced because of Antiochus' actions against the city, Temple, and Jewish observance had their roots in the tensions within the Jewish community. These tensions threatened the very existence of the Jewish people, as is clear from the words of Antiochus: "I will make Jerusalem the common graveyard of the Jews" (2 Macc 9:4).

While Second Maccabees gives due credit to Judas Maccabee for the victory of Jerusalem (2 Macc 8:1-7), its goals went beyond praising the deeds of the Maccabees. The book also portrays martyrdom as galvanizing Jewish resistance to Hellenism. The blood of the martyrs was just as significant as the Maccabees' military achievements (2 Macc 6:18–7:42). The attacks on the Temple had temporary success because of the people's sins. The tide turned against those who assailed Jerusalem and the Temple because of the sacrifice made by many faithful Jews. The emphasis on martyrdom points to the intense devotion to the Torah that Second Maccabees wants to promote among the Jews. Death—even suicide (2 Macc 14:37-46)—is preferable to disobedience. The consequence of fidelity is the survival of the Jewish people and their possession of Jerusalem and its Temple.

Baruch

Baruch was Jeremiah's secretary, companion, and friend. The Council of Trent recognized the canonicity of the book that bears his name because of his association with the prophet.[4] Actually, the book of Baruch owes a great debt to Isaianic tradition. In particular, the poem of consolation in 4:5–5:9 is a medley of the most lyrical elements of Second Isaiah. Though the date of the book of Baruch is uncertain, one possibility is that it was assembled following the triumph of the Maccabees over the Seleucid Empire. The book purports to be a reflection on the Babylonian exile, though the exile was likely a symbol of the persecution of the Jews by Antiochus IV. It was the victory of the Jews over Antiochus that led to this reflection on the glorious visions found in Isaiah 40–55 of a restored Jerusalem. The book of Baruch, then, attempted to promote a religious revival following the Maccabean triumph.

The poem that highlights Jerusalem (4:5–5:9) begins with an address to the exiles. They are told that "they grieved Jerusalem," who nursed them (4:5-9a). This insistence that Jerusalem's suffering was due to the sins of its children serves to remind those rejoicing in the victory of the Maccabees that God will respond to the infidelity of the Jewish people. Next, Mother Jerusalem speaks to her "neighbors," that is, the surrounding nations (4:9b-16). She describes the pain of being deprived of her

4. Most of the book was written in Hebrew; however, that version was lost. It is not part of the Hebrew Bible and, therefore, is not among the books of the Old Testament recognized as canonical by Protestant Christians. It has survived in its Greek translation found in the Septuagint.

children but acknowledges that this is God's judgment on their sins—a judgment executed by the Babylonians. Jerusalem, then, speaks to her children in exile (4:17-29). She urges her children to seek God "ten times harder" than their efforts to flee from God by their sins. Jerusalem assures them that God will take them back, giving them "eternal joy." Beginning with 4:30, the poet speaks to both the exiles and Jerusalem. Baruch describes the fall of Babylon (4:30-35) and the return of the exiles (4:36–5:9). Jerusalem can look forward to a new day:

> Jerusalem, take off your robe of mourning and misery;
>> put on the splendor of glory from God forever (Bar 5:1).

While the Jews did succeed in throwing off Antiochus' rule and the religious persecution that prompted their revolution, their victory came at a price. Many Jewish revolutionaries died in battle with the Greeks. Many Jews who remained faithful to their ancestral religious traditions died as martyrs rather than renounce that tradition. Baruch seeks to give meaning to those deaths, so he calls to Mother Jerusalem:

> Up, Jerusalem! stand upon the heights;
>> look to the east and see your children
> Gathered from the east and the west
>> at the word of the Holy One,
> rejoicing that they are remembered by God (5:5).

Those who died for the honor of Jerusalem "are remembered by God." Though this is not an explicit affirmation of belief in resurrection, it assures Jerusalem that God will not forget its children.

Another Isaianic motif used in Baruch in speaking about Jerusalem's future is the giving of a new name to Jerusalem (see Isa 62:4). Jerusalem's new names are to be "Peace through Justice" and "Glory through Devotion" (see Bar 5:4). The revival of Jewish life made possible by the Maccabees should lead to just relationships within Jewish society and authentic and sincere worship. Unfortunately, these hopes were not fulfilled. The descendants of the Maccabees who ruled the Jewish community first as high priests and then as kings and high priests proved to be despots who cared little for their religious heritage. The Pharisees who had supported the Maccabees became the severest critics of their dynastic heirs.

Judith

Ostensibly the book tells the story of a Jewish woman who single-handedly frustrated the plans of the Assyrian king Nebuchadnezzar to conquer Judah (1:1). Actually Nabuchadnezzar was a king of Babylon whose father Nabopolassar destroyed Nineveh, the Assyrian capital, and brought an end to the Assyrian Empire. From the opening verse, the number of historical and geographical blunders is so numerous that it is charitable to say that the book is an imaginative telling of history. In fact, these errors are so egregious that they are likely intentional. They alert the reader to the book's purpose. The book is not simply telling the story of one encounter between Judah and a hostile foreign empire. Judith's story transcends history. It offers a model of how Jews should react to any foreign empire that attempts to conquer their land and proscribe the practice of their religion. The book of Judith, then, emphasizes what Jews are to do for themselves rather than what they can expect God to do for them. While Judith does not ignore God as does Esther, a book with a similar theme,[5] God is not a central actor in the story. In fact, there is only one sentence in Judith in which God is the subject. When the people of Jerusalem heard that the Assyrian army was on the march, they turned to God in prayer. The text comments on the result of their prayer: "The LORD heard their cry and had regard for their distress" (Jdt 4:13). Eventually though, the threat to Judah's existence posed by the Assyrians ended because of the actions of a single woman, who on any power scale is as far removed from God as is possible. Still, she brought victory and ended the threat to Jerusalem.

The book of Judith promotes the practice of Judaism, prayer, the Temple cult, and pious practices such as fasting, so one expects Jerusalem to be the object of concern in this book. When the people of Judah were alerted that the Assyrian army was coming toward their country, they "were in extreme dread of him, and greatly alarmed for Jerusalem and the temple of the LORD, their God" (4:2) because of the Assyrians' reputation for plundering and destroying the temples of countries they conquered. In the book of Judith Jerusalem's Temple is the absolute center of Jewish life. The people react to the threat posed by the Assyrians with prayer and fasting (4:9-15). But the book assumes that the defense of Jerusalem and the Temple require military measures in addition to prayer. During the historical crisis with Assyria in the eighth century, Isaiah had called for quiet trust in God:

> For thus said the Lord GOD,
>   the Holy One of Israel:

5. The Hebrew version of the book of Esther never mentions God. The scribes who translated the book into Greek added several passages that contained prayers addressed to God, correcting what they saw as a deficiency. Similarly, Esther only mentions Jerusalem once—as the place from which the exiles came (2:6). It never mentions the Temple.

> By waiting and by calm you shall be saved,
>   in quiet and in trust your strength lies (Isa 30:15).

Judith, however, opts for a different approach—one akin to that of Nehemiah, who had those who were rebuilding Jerusalem's walls keep their weapons handy (see Neh 4:17).

In the book of Judith the center of resistance to the Assyrian invasion is the fictional village Bethulia. It would seem logical that Jerusalem should have the position of leadership in the revolt as it had during the historical invasion by the Assyrians under Sennacherib at the end of the eighth century B.C. After all, God's miraculous intervention against Sennacherib as described in Isa 37:33-37 appeared to provide a theological precedent for the book of Judith.[6] It may be that presenting Bethulia as the leader of the resistance is a subtle critique of the citizens of Jerusalem, some of whom abandoned their ancestral religion for the economic gains that came with assimilation (see 1 Macc 1:10-17). The collaborators controlled Jerusalem (Jdt 11:14-15). The Maccabean revolt against Antiochus was not led by Jerusalemites but by a priestly family from the village of Modein (see 1 Maccabees 2). This is one of the ironies of the biblical tradition. Though Jerusalem is the place God chose, its people often do not appreciate the significance of this choice and sometimes show themselves indifferent or even neglectful of its value for their lives. Still, even the people of Bethulia recognize that their resistance and Judith's role in it is for Jerusalem's good as they bless Judith: "May the God of our fathers bring you to favor, and make your undertaking a success, for the glory of the Israelites and the exaltation of Jerusalem" (10:8).

Judith planned to seduce Holoferenes, the general of Nabuchadnezzar's army, and then kill him. The first step in implementing her plan was to put aside the widow's garments she wore to mourn the oppression Jerusalem was experiencing. Her change of clothes and demeanor reflected Second Isaiah's charge to Jerusalem:

> Awake, awake!
>   Put on your strength, O Zion;
>   Put on your glorious garments . . .
> Shake off the dust,
>   ascend to the throne, Jerusalem (Isa 52:1-2).

---

6. John Craghan, *Esther, Judith, Tobit, Jonah, Ruth.* OTM 16. (Wilmington, Del.: Michael Glazier, 1982) 71.

Judith is Jerusalem going out to meet and defeat the enemy threatening her. As she summoned the strength needed to implement her plan, she prayed that God may consider her efforts as done for Jerusalem:

> Judith stood by Holofernes' bed and said within herself: "O Lord, God of all might, in this hour look graciously on my undertaking for the exaltation of Jerusalem" (13:4).

In celebrating Judith's heroic deed in saving the city, the people call her "the exaltation of Jerusalem" (Jdt 15:9).

The repetition of the phrase "the exaltation of Jerusalem" (10:8; 13:4; 15:9) reflects the status Jerusalem had in the eyes of the Jewish people— primarily because of the Temple's presence within the city (4:2, 3, 11; 9:1, 13). What is special about this book is Judith's assertion that "the sanctuary, the temple, and the altar *rests with us*" (8:24). The prophets whose ministry took place before the exile had to combat the popular view that it was a matter of divine honor for God to protect Jerusalem from its enemies. After all, the city was the place that God chose and it was the site of God's Temple. Judith turns that thinking inside out. It is the responsibility of the Jews to protect Jerusalem. They cannot allow themselves to remain passive in the struggle to maintain their faith and its practice when threatened—even by a far superior foe. The victory that Judah thought God would bring will come when Judah itself takes action as Judith did.

The book of Judith is a thinly disguised encouragement to resist the Greeks and take up the defense of Jerusalem. The fictional heroine of the story is the female counterpart of the Maccabees, who were the historical leaders of the revolt against the Greeks. In fact, the name Judith is the feminine equivalent of the name Judas, the Maccabee responsible for the liberation of Jerusalem. The story serves to keep the Jews from being cowered by the long odds of a victory over a most powerful army. Judith is a paradigm for action against those who would threaten the existence of Judaism. Of course, her action is taken for "the exaltation of Jerusalem." God is a minor character is Judith's story. The book is not about what God will do for Jerusalem but what the Jews will do for the city.

The *Book of Jubilees*[7]

Though *Jubilees* is a non-canonical text, it is roughly contemporaneous with the biblical texts considered in this chapter and reflects similar

---

7. The text is available in Charlesworth, *Old Testament Pseudepigrapha,* 2:35–142.

ideas. *Jubilees* fills in matters that were passed over in the biblical story of Moses' forty-day stay on Mount Sinai as narrated in the biblical material. While the Exodus story simply mentions this stay without any elaboration (Exod 24:18), *Jubilees* recounts a revelation that Moses received regarding the events of primeval history and the history of Abraham's children until the time of the Exodus. While *Jubilees* follows the outline of the books of Genesis and Exodus, it adapts and expands these stories to underscore the importance of observing the Torah. The first chapter, however, introduces the book by having God tell Moses of the future apostasy and restoration of Israel. It is this chapter that contains a reference to Jerusalem:

> And the Lord will appear in the sight of all. And everyone will know that I am the God of Israel and the father of all the children of Jacob and king upon Mount Zion forever and ever. And Zion and Jerusalem will be holy (*Jub.* 1:28).

Jerusalem is not a primary motif in *Jubilees* because that would be patently anachronistic. Still, this passage does show the status Jerusalem had in Judaism in the second century B.C. Jerusalem is "holy," that is, it is set apart for God. It is also that place from which God will reign forever. It is the place God has chosen to build God's sanctuary (*Jub.* 1:17).

Jubilees represents the perspectives of religious Jews in Palestine, who have just come through the crisis brought on by Antiochus. Because some Jews abandoned their ancestral faith during that crisis, the author of *Jubilees* thought it necessary to reorient his fellow Jews to their most sacred traditions. Among these is the centrality of Jerusalem and the Temple.

Conclusion

A continuing problem in biblical interpretation by people of faith is to extrapolate the perspectives of one strand of the tradition into universally valid theological principles. This is a particular problem with the ideology that stands behind Judith and First Maccabees. Can there be any justification for violence in the name of religion today? Does nationalism contribute to the welfare of the human community or does it threaten it? It is important to remember that not all Jews who experienced the crisis with Hellenism supported the response favored by Judith and First Maccabees. The book of Daniel advises the Jews threatened by Antiochus to remain faithful to the Torah and to await the victory that God will bring them. When Dan 11:34 speaks of the "little help" the pious will receive in the struggle to remain faithful, that "little help" is likely the efforts of the militant nationalists whose ideology is represented by Judith and 1–2 Maccabees.

The religious nationalists did revitalize the Jewish community, whose very existence was threatened in the second century B.C., but their achievement was short-lived. The Hasmonean dynasty, established by the victorious Maccabees, soon became as oppressive as the Greeks their ancestors had fought. The kings of this dynasty even adopted Greek names and titles, and their policies angered the Pharisees. Later generations tried to emulate the example of the Maccabees by revolting against Roman authority several times. The results were disastrous. After the Bar Kochba revolt (A.D. 132–5) the Romans expelled all Jews from Jerusalem, turning it into a Greco-Roman city which they called Aelia Capitolina. While it is important for us to learn the lessons of history, it is also important to remember that the lessons of history are usually ambiguous. Just because the Maccabees succeeded in their revolt against Antiochus, this does not mean their example ought to be followed blindly by people today. Clearly, those who are looking for a peaceful solution to the conflict between the Israelis and the Palestinians have to look elsewhere in the biblical tradition for help. Certainly, religious nationalism will lead both sides in this conflict to catastrophe.

Epilogue: The Fall of Jerusalem According to *Second Baruch*

Events like the fall of Jerusalem at the end of the first Jewish revolt against Rome in A.D. 70 have significance that defies simple explanation. A political historian looking at the triumph of Rome and the destruction of Jerusalem may focus on this event as the end of Jewish independence in Palestine. The theologian reflecting on the same event will try to understand the ways of God, who permitted such a catastrophe to befall the Chosen People. The historian of religion sees these events as effecting a fundamental change in the form of Jewish religion. Students of the New Testament try to understand how Jerusalem's fall affected the Jewish Christian community in Palestine. Archaeologists excavating in Jerusalem try to reconstruct the city's final days by uncovering the material remains of the fallen city. Pious Jews pray at the Western Wall for the restoration of the Temple and the redemption of their people.

Similarly, the people who lived through the fall of Jerusalem had diverse reactions to it. For the Roman legionaries it was the victorious end of the long and difficult siege. For the priests of the Temple it made their temple ministry impossible. The priests in self-imposed exile at Qumran may have believed that the fall of Jerusalem was divine retribution. God punished the city for what they considered the false worship of the Temple. For the Pharisees the fall of the city was a challenge to Judaism's survival to be met by obedience to the Torah. Some Christians interpreted the tragedy as divine judgment and the harbinger of Jesus' second coming. Jews who were captivated by apocalyptic speculations saw the fall of Jerusalem as initiating God's final act of redemption on behalf of Israel.

Some Jews who witnessed the fall of the city and the burning of the Temple left literary records of their reflections on these tragedies. This epilogue deals with one such text: *Second Baruch.*[1] For this book, the fall of the city is not the ultimate calamity. It has the potential of being the first act of an even more unthinkable catastrophe: the very end of the Jewish people.

Second Baruch is also known as the *Syriac Apocalypse of Baruch.* Though it gives the fall of Jerusalem to the Babylonians in 586 B.C. as the occasion for its composition, it was written within fifty years of the fall of Jerusalem to the Romans in A.D. 70. It ponders the significance of that event for the Jewish people. Baruch, the book's purported author, was Jeremiah's companion and secretary (Jeremiah 32; 36; 43; 45). *Second Baruch* is part of an extensive body of literature ascribed to Jeremiah's scribe. None of these texts is part of the Hebrew Bible. The Roman Catholic Bible does include one of the books ascribed to Baruch. St. Jerome placed it after the book of Lamentations in the Vulgate.

Second Baruch is among the books that scholars call the "pseudepigrapha." These Jewish religious texts get this name because later authors, for a variety of reasons, chose to publish their theological reflections under the name of a revered figure from the ancient past. Though *Second Baruch* is not a canonical text, it is important because it shows how some religious Jews in the late first and early second century dealt with what could have been a fatal blow to their religious life.

Among the first words ascribed to God in *Second Baruch* are words of judgment on the people's sins: "Behold, therefore, I shall bring evil upon this city and its inhabitants" (1:4). The evil that came upon the city was its fall and the evil that came upon its citizens was their exile: "I shall scatter this people among the nations" (1:4). Despite the people's sin, Jerusalem was the city of God, which no human army could defeat. The reason the city fell is that God abandoned it. The Romans were able to take the city because angels came from heaven to demolish the walls of the city (7:1). This left the city defenseless before those who besieged it.

The book does not explicitly deal with the destruction of the Temple. It is not until chapter 5 that God alludes to what will happen to the temple: " . . . your haters will come to this place and pollute your sanctuary" (5:1). The book asserts that while the enemy will destroy the Temple of Jerusalem, God's temple will remain inviolate. That temple is in paradise with God. It is not the work of human hands but was prepared from the moment God decided to create the universe. God revealed that temple to Adam, Abraham, and Moses (4:3-6). The Temple the Romans destroyed was not God's temple but only an earthly counterpart. The letter to the

---

1. An English translation of *Second Baruch* is available in Charlesworth, *Old Testament Pseudepigrapha,* v. 1:621-52.

Hebrews uses a similar idea to describe the unique priesthood of Christ (see Hebrews 8–9). Christ exercises his priesthood in the heavenly sanctuary. This makes his priesthood superior to that of the Jewish priests, who minister in an earthly temple.

Second Baruch does not present the destruction of the Temple as the major consequence of the fall of Jerusalem. For early Jewish Christians the cessation of temple service had a momentous symbolic significance. It signaled an end to sacrificial worship. More than this, the destruction of the Temple broke the bonds of their allegiance to their ancestral religion. The loss of the Temple forced Jewish Christians to probe the meaning of their confession of faith in Jesus as the Messiah. This confession led them to recognize that they belonged to a community based not on their ethnic background or their commitment to the Torah. The basis for their community was the acceptance of the gospel and their faith in Jesus as God's final word to the human family.

Second Baruch also tries to probe the significance of Jerusalem's fall for those people who believed the city to be God's dwelling on earth. The intended effect of this work was to reconstitute Jewish identity so it would not fall into ruins with Jerusalem and its Temple. For *Second Baruch,* the primary consequence of Jerusalem's fall was the captivity and dispersion of the people, and the book keeps returning to this theme. We have already cited God's speech at the beginning (1:4). Toward the end of the work the people lament: "We have left our land, and Zion has been taken away from us" (85:3). The devastation of Jerusalem leads to the depopulation of the city.

The reason for this focus on the dispersion of the city's population is the fear that this could be the harbinger of the people's destruction. By the first century A.D. Jerusalem became not merely the religious center of Judea. It was the heart and soul of Judaism. When David captured Jebusite Jerusalem and made it his capital toward the end of the eleventh century B.C. (2 Sam 5:6-10), he set in motion a process that was not complete until Jerusalem became *the* symbol of God's presence in Israel's midst. Solomon made his contribution to this process when he built a temple in the city (1 Kings 8). The book of Deuteronomy states that it was God who chose Jerusalem as *the* place of worship (Deut 12:4). Although the book does not mention Jerusalem by name, it mandates pilgrimage to the chosen city three times a year (Deut 16:1-17). The Former Prophets (Joshua to 2 Kings) evaluate the kings of Judah by their devotion to the worship of Yahweh in Jerusalem. After the return from exile in Babylon, the territory of Judah was reduced to the city of Jerusalem and about twenty square miles surrounding it. The importance of Jerusalem was assured both by virtue and necessity.

After the end of the siege of Jerusalem in A.D. 70, what remained of the city was in the hands of the Romans. Jews had no reason to go there any more. There was no temple where they might offer the sacrifices prescribed by the Torah. The dispersion of the people made it even more unlikely that Jerusalem could continue to be the magnet that drew Jews together in a community of faith. Without this magnet drawing the Jews together, the author of *Second Baruch* saw a new and clear danger that they would be absorbed by the Gentiles among whom they lived.

Second Baruch reminded his readers that they still had two mighty forces that could maintain them in their identity as the people of God: "the Mighty One and (God's) Law" (85:3). During the Babylonian exile some Jews believed that the Torah could function as the religious core of those who still held onto their ancestral faith. With the rebuilding of the Temple following the return, Judaism once again was tied to a geographic center. Focus on the Law freed Judaism from its captivity to geography. The Law accompanied people on their journey into the Diaspora. Living according to the Law made it possible for them to remain firmly bound to their traditional beliefs. *Second Baruch* recaptures the value of the Torah for the survival of the Jews and their religion.

Those who live far from the holy city must never allow themselves to forget Jerusalem and its Temple: "And remember Zion and the Law and the holy land and your brothers and the covenant and your fathers" (84:8). After all, God has delivered Jerusalem into the hands of the enemy only for a time. One day God will restore the city (6:9). In the meantime, what the Jews have is the Torah. Observance of the Torah will mean life despite the destruction and death wrought by the Romans.

For *Second Baruch,* the fall of Jerusalem meant the captivity and dispersion of the Jews. This dispersion had the potential of destroying the faith and the very existence of the people. The book suggests a redefinition of what it means to be a worshiper of ancient Israel's ancestral God. This redefinition places the Torah in the center once occupied by the Temple. *Second Baruch,* then, prepares the way for the rabbis, who were responsible not merely for the survival of Judaism but for its reformulation as a religion based on ethics.

Jewish Christianity had to make a similar redefinition following the fall of the Temple. According to Acts (3:1) the first Christians continued to worship in the Temple. Once that was no longer possible Christians had to explore the meaning of their faith in Jesus as the Messiah—not in some theoretical fashion but because of practical necessity.

The fall of Jerusalem in A.D. 70 caused those who considered themselves children of Abraham to reassess their standing before God. The author of *Second Baruch* believed that fidelity to the ancestral religion of the Jews meant careful observance of the Law. The Torah was the one institution of that tradition that was not affected by the flames that destroyed the Temple. Those same flames moved others in a different way. They saw the revelation of God as not in the Torah alone. Jesus was God's final revelation to Israel and to the nations. By confessing Jesus as Messiah and being faithful to his ideals, the Jewish Christians sought to make sense out of the tragedy that befell Jerusalem.

Neither Jew nor Christian could forget Jerusalem. For both it always remained the "holy city." Still, both Jews and Christians subordinated their reverence for Jerusalem to what was more central to their respective faiths. The study and observance of the Torah became the heart of Judaism. Belief in Jesus and a life according to the gospel became the core of Christianity.

Abbreviations

AB	Anchor Bible
ABD	*Anchor Bible Dictionary*
ANE	*The Ancient Near East,* James B. Pritchard, ed. Princeton, N.J.: Princeton University Press, 1958
ANET	*Ancient Near Eastern Texts Relating to the Old Testament*
ATLA	American Theological Library Association
BZ	*Biblische Zeitscrift*
BZAW	Beihefte Zeitschrift für Alttestamentliche Wissenschaft
CBQ	*Catholic Biblical Quarterly*
CTA	*Corpus des tablettes en cunéiformes alphabétiques découvertes à Ras Shamra-Ugarit,* Andrée Herdner (ed.) Paris: Imprimerie Nationale, 1963. 2 vols.
Fest.	Festschrift
FOTL	The Forms of the Old Testament Literature
HTR	*Harvard Theological Review*
IEJ	*Israel Exploration Journal*
Int	*Interpretation*
JBL	*Journal of Biblical Literature*
JES	*Journal of Ecumenical Studies*
JNES	*Journal of Near Eastern Studies*
JSOT	*Journal for the Study of the Old Testament*
JSOTS	Journal for the Study of the Old Testament Studies
JSP	*Journal for the Study of the Pseudepigrapha*
LA	*Liber Annuus*
M	Mishnah
NAB	*New American Bible*
NCB	*New Century Bible*

NEAEHL	*The New Encyclopedia of Archaeological Excavations in the Holy Land*
NJB	*New Jerusalem Bible*
NJBC	*New Jerome Biblical Commentary*
NRSV	*New Revised Standard Version*
OTL	Old Testament Library
OTM	Old Testament Message
SBLDS	Society of Biblical Literature Dissertation Series
STB	Studies in Biblical Theology
USQR	*Union Seminary Quarterly Review*
VT	*Vetus Testamentum*
VTSupp	*Vetus Testamentum Supplement*
ZAW	*Zeitschrift für Alttestamentliche Wissenschaft*

Bibliography

N.B. A comprehensive bibliography on Jerusalem is available in Purvis, James D., *Jerusalem, the Holy City: A Bibliography.* 2 vols. ATLA Bibliography Series 20. Metuchen, N.J.: Scarecrow, 1988, 1991.

Books

Avi-Yonah, Michael. *The Jews of Palestine.* New York: Schocken Books, 1976.

Blank, Sheldon. *Prophetic Faith in Isaiah.* New York: Harper, 1958.

Charlesworth, James H., ed. *The Old Testament Pseudepigrapha.* 2 vols. Garden City, N.Y.: Doubleday, 1983, 1985.

Chyutin, Michael. *The New Jerusalem Scroll from Qumran: A Comprehensive Reconstruction.* JSP Supplement Series, 25. Sheffield: Sheffield Academic Press, 1997.

Clements, Ronald E. *Isaiah and the Deliverance of Jerusalem.* JSOTS 13. Sheffield: JSOT Press, 1984.

Clifford, Richard. *The Cosmic Mountain in Canaan and the Old Testament.* Cambridge, Mass.: Harvard Univ. Press, 1972.

Davies, W. D. *The Gospel and the Land.* Berkeley: Univ. of California Press, 1974.

Galambush, Julie. *Jerusalem in the Book of Ezekiel: The City as Yahweh's Wife.* SBLDS, 130. Atlanta: Scholars Press, 1992.

Gaudefroy-Demombynes, Maurice. *Mahomet.* 2d ed. Paris: A. Michel, 1969.

Goitein, Shlomo Dov. *Studies in Islamic History and Institutions.* Leiden: Brill, 1966.

Goldziher, I. *Muhammedanische Studien II.* Halle, 1888. Reprint, Heildesheim: George Olms, 1966.

Hayes, John H., and Irvine, Stuart A. *Isaiah, the Eighth Century Prophet: His Times and His Preaching.* Nashville: Abingdon Press, 1987.

Kaiser, Otto. *Isaiah 13–39.* OTL. Philadelphia: Westminster Press, 1974.

Keel, Othmar. *The Symbolism of the Biblical World.* New York: Seabury, 1978.

Le Strange, Guy. *Palestine Under the Moslems.* New York: AMS Press, 1975. Reprint of 1890 ed. by Houghton-Mifflin, Boston.

Murphy-O'Connor, Jerome. *The Holy Land: An Archaeological Guide from the Earliest Times to 1700.* 3d ed. New York: Oxford Univ. Press, 1992.

Ollenburger, Ben C. *Zion, the City of the Great King: A Theological Study of the Jerusalem Cult.* JSOTS, 41. Sheffield: JSOT Press, 1987.

Rad, Gerhard von. *Old Testament Theology.* 1st English ed. Trans. D.M.G. Stalker. Edinburgh: Oliver & Boyd, 1962.

Rohland, Edzard. *Die Bedeutung der Erwählungstraditionene Israels für die Eschatologie der altestamentlichen Propheten.* Diss. Heidelberg, 1956.

Seitz, Christopher. *Zion's Final Destiny: The Development of the Book of Isaiah.* Minneapolis: Fortress Press, 1991.

Sweeney, Marvin. *Isaiah 1–39 with an Introduction to Prophetic Literature.* FOTL. Grand Rapids: Eerdmans, 1996.

Tibawi, Abdul Latif. *Jerusalem: Its Place in Islam and Arab History.* Beirut: The Institute for Palestine Studies, 1969.

Vincent, Hugues. *Jérusalem.* 2 vols. Paris: J. Gabalda, 1954.

Ward, James. *Amos and Isaiah.* Nashville: Abingdon Press, 1969.

Weinfeld, Moshe. *Deuteronomy and the Deuteronomic Tradition.* New York: Oxford, 1972.

Weiser, A. *Psalms.* OTL. Philadelphia: Westminster Press, 1962.

Wilken, Robert. *The Land Called Holy: Palestine in Christian History and Thought.* New Haven, Conn.: Yale Univ. Press, 1992.

Wilkinson, John. *Egeria's Travels to the Holy Land.* Jerusalem: Ariel, 1981.

Yadin, Yigal. *The Temple Scroll.* London: Weidenfeld & Nicolson, 1985.

Articles

Broshi, Magen. "The Expansion of Jerusalem in the Reigns of Hezekiah and Manasseh." *IEJ* 24 (1974) 21–26.

Busse, Heribert. "The Sanctity of Jerusalem in Islam." *Judaism* 17 (1968) 441–68.

Clements, Ronald E. "Zion as Symbol and Political Reality, in *Studies in the Book of Isaiah.*" Fest. Ed. W.A.M. Beuken and others (Leuven: Univ. Press, 1997).

Fiey, J. M. "Le pèlerinage des Nestoriens et Jacobites à Jérusalem." *Cahiers de Civilisation médiéval* 12 (1969) 113–26.

Finkel, Asher. "Jerusalem in Biblical and Theological Tradition: A Jewish Perspective." *Evangelicals and Jews in an Age of Pluralism.* Ed. Marc H. Tanenbaum and others. Grand Rapids: Baker Book House, 1984.

Fitzgerald, Aloysius. "*BTWLT* and *BT* as Titles for Capital Cities." *CBQ* 37 (1975) 167–83.

Follis, Elaine R. "The Holy City as Daughter." *Directions in Biblical Hebrew Poetry.* Ed. Elaine R. Follis, 173–84. JSOTS 44. Sheffield: Sheffield Academic Press, 1987.

_____. "Zion, Daughter of." *ABD* 6:1103.

Goitein, Shlomo Dov. "The Sanctity of Palestine in Moslem Piety." *Bulletin of the Jewish Palestine Exploration Society* 12 (1946) 120–6.

Hamerton-Kelly, R. G. "The Temple and the Origins of Jewish Apocalyptic." *VT* 20 (1970) 1–15.

Hasson, Isaac. "Muslim Literature in Praise of Jerusalem: Fada'il Bayt al-Maqdis." *The Jerusalem Cathedra I.* Ed. Lee I. Levine, 168–89. Jerusalem: Yad Izhak Ben-Zvi Institute, 1981.

Hermisson, Hans-Jurgen. "Die Frau Zion." *Studies in the Book of Isaiah.* Ed. J. van Ruiten and M. Vervenne. 19–39. Fest. Willem A.M. Beuken. Leuven, Univ. Press, 1997.

Hoppe, Leslie J. "The Dome of the Rock: Jerusalem's Hallmark." *Holy Land* 19/2 (Summer 1999) 18–21.

Kapelrud, Arvid S. "Temple Building: A Task for Gods and Kings." *Orientalia* 32 (1963) 56–62.

King, Philip J. "Jerusalem." *ABD* 3:747–66.

Kister, Meir J. "A Comment on the Antiquity of Traditions Praising Jerusalem." *The Jerusalem Cathedra I.* Ed. Lee I. Levine. Jerusalem: Yad Izhak Ben-Zvi Institute, 1981.

_____. "You Shall Only Set Out for Three Mosques," *Le Muséon* 82 (1969) 173–96.

Krinetzki, Leo. "Zur Poetik und Exegese von Ps. 48," *BZ* 4 (1960) 70–97.

Mazar, Benjamin, and others. "Jerusalem." *The New Encyclopedia of Archaeological Excavations in the Holy Land.* Ed. Ephraim Stern. 2:698–800. New York: Simon & Schuster, 1993.

Nestle, E. "Das Deuteronomium und II Könige xxii." *ZAW* 22 (1902) 170–1, 312–3.

Rad, Gerhard von. "Deuteronomy's 'Name' Theology and the Priestly Document's 'Kabod' Theology." *Studies in Deuteronomy.* STB 9. Pp. 37–46. Naperville, Ill.: Allenson, 1953.

Roberts, J.J.M. "The Davidic Origin of the Zion Tradition." *JBL* 92 (1973) 329–44.

_____. "Isaiah 33: An Isaianic Elaboration of the Zion Tradition." *The Word of the Lord Shall Go Forth.* Ed. Carol L. Meyers and M. O'Connor, 15–25. Winona Lake, Ind.: Eisenbrauns, 1983.

_____. "A Note on Isaiah 28:12." *HTR* 73 (1980) 48–51.

_____. "Yahweh's Foundation in Zion (Isa 28:16)." *JBL* 106 (1987) 27–45.

Sawyer, J.F.A. "Daughter of Zion and the Servant of the Lord in Isaiah: A Comparison." *JSOT* 44 (1980) 89–107.

Starcky, Jean. "Jerusalem et les manuscrits de la Mer Morte." *Le Monde de la Bible* 1 (Nov/Dec 1977) 38–40.

Stinespring, W. R. "No Daughter of Zion." *Encounter* 26 (1965) 133–41.

Talmon, Shemaryahu. "The Biblical Concept of Jerusalem," *JES* 8 (1971) 300–16.

Vaux, Roland de. "Le lieu que Yahvé a choisi pour y établir son nom." *Das Ferne und nahe Wort.* 219–28. Fest. L. Rost. BZAW 105. Berlin: Töpelmann, 1967.

Weinfeld, Moshe. "Cult Centralization in Israel in Light of a neo-Babylonian Analogy." *JNES* 23 (1964) 202–12.

_____. "Zion and Jerusalem as Religious and Political Capital." *The Poet and the Historian.* Ed. Richard Elliott Friedmann, 113–5. Chico, Calif.: Scholars Press, 1983.

Wilkinson, John. "Jerusalem Under Rome and Byzantium 63 BC–637 AD." *Jerusalem in History.* Ed. K. J. Asali. Brooklyn: Olive Branch Press, 1990.

Index of Biblical Texts

Index of Ancient Texts

Author Index

Subject Index